REASONED ADMINISTRATION AND DEMOCRATIC LEGITIMACY

Reasoned Administration and Democratic Legitimacy: How Administrative Law Supports Democratic Government explores the fundamental bases for the legitimacy of the modern administrative state. While some have argued that modern administrative states are a threat to liberty and at war with democratic governance, Jerry L. Mashaw demonstrates that in fact reasoned administration is more respectful of rights and equal citizenship and truer to democratic values than lawmaking by either courts or legislatures. His account features the law's demand for reason-giving and reasonableness as the crucial criteria for the legality of administrative action. In an argument combining history, sociology, political theory, and law, this book demonstrates how administrative law's demand for reasoned administration structures administrative decision-making, empowers actors within and outside the government, and supports a complex vision of democratic self-rule.

Jerry L. Mashaw is Sterling Professor of Law Emeritus and Professorial Lecturer at Yale Law School. He is the author of many award-winning books including *Bureaucratic Justice: Managing Disability Claims* (1983), *Greed, Chaos, and Governance: Using Public Choice to Improve Public Law* (1997), and *Creating the Administrative Constitution: The Lost 100 Years of American Administrative Law* (2014). Professor Mashaw has lectured at numerous foreign universities and served as a consultant for United States and foreign government agencies and foundations.

Reasoned Administration and Democratic Legitimacy

HOW ADMINISTRATIVE LAW SUPPORTS DEMOCRATIC GOVERNMENT

JERRY L. MASHAW

Yale University

CAMBRIDGE
UNIVERSITY PRESS

CAMBRIDGE
UNIVERSITY PRESS

University Printing House, Cambridge CB2 8BS, United Kingdom

One Liberty Plaza, 20th Floor, New York, NY 10006, USA

477 Williamstown Road, Port Melbourne, VIC 3207, Australia

314–321, 3rd Floor, Plot 3, Splendor Forum, Jasola District Centre, New Delhi – 110025, India

79 Anson Road, #06-04/06, Singapore 079906

Cambridge University Press is part of the University of Cambridge.

It furthers the University's mission by disseminating knowledge in the pursuit of education, learning, and research at the highest international levels of excellence.

www.cambridge.org
Information on this title: www.cambridge.org/9781108421003
DOI: 10.1017/9781108355827

First published 2018

Printed in the United States of America by Sheridan Books, Inc.

A catalogue record for this publication is available from the British Library.

Library of Congress Cataloging-in-Publication Data
NAMES: Mashaw, Jerry L., author.
TITLE: Reasoned administration and democratic legitimacy: how administrative law supports democratic government / Jerry L. Mashaw.
DESCRIPTION: Cambrdige [UK]; New York, NY: Cambridge University Press, 2018.
IDENTIFIERS: LCCN 2018031528| ISBN 9781108421003 (hardback) | ISBN 9781108413114 (paperback)
SUBJECTS: LCSH: Administrative agencies—United States. | Administrative law—United States. | Administrative procedure—United States. | Legitimacy of governments—United States. | Rule of law—United States. | Democracy—United States.
CLASSIFICATION: LCC KF5407 .M38 2018 | DDC 342.73/06—DC23
LC record available at https://lccn.loc.gov/2018031528

ISBN 978-1-108-42100-3 Hardback
ISBN 978-1-108-41311-4 Paperback

Contents

Preface and Acknowledgments

Critiques of administrative governance go back at least to the Jeffersonian Republicans' objections to the creation of the First Bank of the United States. And, like those early "partisan" laments, critical commentary is often focused on a presumed democratic deficit.[1] For many, countering the pernicious effects of "big government," and re-establishing democracy and the rule of law, entails returning lawmaking to Congress and the judiciary.[2]

These complaints continue unabated in the academic literature, judicial decisions, and popular political discourse.[3] For example, conservative legalists have embraced Philip Hamburger's book, *Is Administrative Law Unlawful?*[4] (answer: "yes"), notwithstanding Hamburger's thoroughgoing misunderstanding of both modern American administrative law,[5] and the functioning of seventeenth-century royal prerogative to which Hamburger compared our modern administrative jurisprudence.[6] No less than the Chief Justice of the US Supreme Court has weighed in with his own concerns that Americans now live in a gigantic and all-powerful

---

[1] *See generally*, Jud Mathews, Minimally Democratic Administrative Law 68 *Admin. L. Rev.* 605 (2016).
[2] *See, e.g.*, David Schoenbrod, *Power without Responsibility: How Congress Abuses the People through Delegation* (1993).
[3] For a thorough exploration of these matters and their resonance with the anti-administrative state attacks on the New Deal *see* Gillian E. Metzger, Forward: 1930s Redux: The Administrative State Under Siege, 131 *Harv. L. Rev.* 1 (2017).
[4] Philip Hamburger, *Is Administrative Law Unlawful?* (2014).
[5] Adrian Vermeule, No, 93 *Texas L. Rev.* 1547 (2015).
[6] Paul P. Craig, *The Legitimacy of U.S. Administrative Law and the Foundations of English Administrative Law: Setting the Historical Record Straight*, Oxford Legal Studies Research Paper No. 44(2016). Justice Thomas cited Hamburger's book numerous times in his concurrence in *Dep't of Transp.* v. *Ass'n of Am. R. R. S. Railroads*, 135 S. Ct. 1225, 1242-4 (2015) (Thomas, J., concurring).

administrative state.[7] As these words are written, multiple bills are before Congress that would, among other things, make all significant agency regulations ineffective unless specifically approved by Congress and instruct reviewing courts to give agency interpretations of their organic statutes no deference upon judicial review.

There is, of course, an equally long tradition of defense of administrative government based on efficacy, efficiency, expertise, legality, energy, flexibility, institutional balance, and in Gillian Metzger's recent defense, necessity for the protection of the constitutional separation of powers under modern conditions of social complexity and institutional overload.[8] The argument of this book is in that latter, apologist tradition, but with a somewhat different focus. My claim is straightforward: to the extent that critiques of administrative government and proposals to reform it or reduce its scope are based on a concern that administrative governance is "undemocratic," they are profoundly misguided. They operate both on a misunderstanding of how the American administrative state operates and on naïve or incomplete visions of democracy.

In these pages I will not seek to critique the critiques in any detail. I will instead attempt to explain how the American administrative state is structured, how its modern mode of legitimation – what I call in these pages "reasoned administration" – emerged and how its contemporary functioning fits within a realistic appraisal of democratic governance. The emphasis here is on the many ways in which American administrative law demands administrative action based on reason. The multiple dimensions of that legal requirement affect agency processes and internal structures, create participatory and responsive processes for agency action, and erect protections against unreasonable or arbitrary government action. Describing how American administrative law operates in practice sets the stage for a normative argument concerning what democracy might mean and how administrative governance responds to democracy's normative demands. On this account, administrative governance is no enemy of democracy, but instead its friend – indeed, perhaps its most prominent instantiation.

The Trump administration's first year in office suggests that the preservation of "reasoned administration" is of critical importance. We seem to be witnessing an administration that, at least implicitly, conceptualizes democracy in plebiscitary terms and interprets its electoral mandate as a mandate to engage in quasi-authoritarian rule. I will not attempt to detail here the many insults to conventional

---

[7] *See* Justice Roberts' dissent in *City of Arlington v. Federal Communications Commission*, 569 U.S. 313 (2013) (Roberts, C. J., dissenting).

[8] Metzger, "Forward." *See also*, Adrian Vermeule, Bureaucracy and Distrust: Landis, Jaffe, and Kagan on the Administrative State, 130 *Harv. L. Rev.* 2463 (2017) (brilliantly explicating the thinking of James Landis, Louis Jaffe, and Elena Kagan on the structure and justifications for administrative governance).

governmental practices of fact-finding, deliberation, and reasoned government action evidenced in the Trump administration's brand of governance. How far this administration intends to go in rejecting scientific inquiry, broad participation in administrative decision-making and respect for the rule of law is unclear. What I hope will be clear from the pages that follow is that the resources required to check this, or any, administration's excesses, and resist its blinkered understanding of democratic governance, lie in the model of reasoned administration that is at the heart of modern American administrative law.

This book has been long in the making and my debts to students and colleagues both at Yale and in other universities, domestic and foreign, is profound. Indeed, the process has gone on for so long that I could not possibly remember or recount the contributions of the many students, scholars, and institutions that have enriched my understanding of what this project was really about. Three people must nevertheless be singled out for thanks. David Berke, my former student and sometime coauthor, provided truly extraordinary research and editorial assistance. My long-suffering administrative assistant, Patricia Page, once again wrestled dictation tapes, hand-written drafts, and multitudinous revisions into a final manuscript. And, my wife, Anne, who attempted to purge the manuscript of all lapses into the passive voice, had the good grace not to ask whether this project was ever going to be completed, and provided the love and support that makes my life worth living and, therefore, my scholarship worth doing.

1

Why Reasons?

"Why" is a multipurpose word. It is the language of curiosity, evidence of intellectual engagement. We revel in our children's and our students' whys; reward their curiosity with attention and serious responses; turn their whys back on them – "Why do *you* think?" – to stimulate independent thought and reflection.

On Charles Tilly's account, "why" is the ubiquitous language of all human relationships.[1] Reasons, according to Tilly, are given to negotiate, establish, repair, affirm, or deny relationships. The type of relationship determines the type of reasons that are appropriate and, therefore, potentially persuasive or acceptable. As articulate social animals, reason-giving is the lifeblood of our sociability.

"Why" is also a language of attention getting, even harassment. One of my favorite cartoons (which I can no longer locate) shows a small child leaning forward from the back seat close to his driving father's ear. The conversation must have been the familiar one with a bored four-year-old on a car trip: "Why aren't we there yet?" "Why are you going so slow?" "Why does Grandma live so far away?" "Are we lost?" and so on. The caption at the bottom gives the harassed father's response: "'Shut up,' he explained."[2]

"Why" is also the language of disappointment, even despair. It articulates a demand for comfort and for justice; a quest for understanding that often reaches beyond the facts of the matter. Indeed, "why" may signal the collapse of a worldview, an anxious, even desperate, attempt to reimagine ourselves and our world in a way that makes sense, that permits our lives to go on as an understandable narrative.

These most excruciating whys, the ones that reveal our souls' confusion and torment, may be simultaneously irrepressible and hopeless. Job repeatedly asked God "why," but the answers were of little use to him. In Carl Jung's famous interpretation

---

[1] Charles Tilly, *Why?: What Happens When People Give Reasons... and Why*, (Princeton University Press, Princeton, NJ, 2006).

[2] For what appears to be the original version of this exchange, *see* Ring W. Lardner Jr., *The Young Immigrunts*, 78 (Bobbs-Merrill Co., Indianapolis, IN, 1920).

1

of the Book of Job, Job's quest is for an answer that he could not possibly accept.[3] Job's "why" sounds in morality and justice. God's answer is articulated in the will-fulness of the Old Testament, a will beyond human understanding. For Jung, Job's quest for understanding demonstrates his moral superiority to the God he interrogates. His is a human quest for justice in the face of a force for whom justification seems synonymous with power.

It is another coercive discourse of "whyness" – the dialogue between public officials and those affected by their authoritative decisions – that I want to explore in this book. Reason has become the modern language of law in a liberal state. The anguished why of the contemporary Job confronting contemporary secular authority often carries with it an enforceable demand for justification. But why does the law demand reasons? Why do reasons matter? What reasons count? When do reasons satisfy our longing for justice? When do they fail? And, of course, why?

These are deep and abiding questions about which legal and political philosophers have had much to say over hundreds of years. I will not attempt to plumb the philosophic depths of these issues, but will instead creep up on them from the vantage point of my own particular field, administrative law. I do not believe that this limitation trivializes the subject. Indeed, I want to convince you that the discourse of whyness and of reason-giving is more important here than anywhere else in American law. Administrative law's struggle with the uses of reason and reason-giving as the foundation of legal legitimacy provides insights of a special sort into the relationship of law and reason, and into the work that remains to be done to better realize our aspirations not only for government under law, but also for democratic self-rule.

THE ROLE OF REASON IN ADMINISTRATIVE LAW

One might object that the substitution of reason for myth, tradition, culture, or inherited power, as the basis for law and political legitimacy, describes the whole political project of modernity. As self-actualizing agents in the Cartesian sense – we think, therefore we are – we are also self-governing moral agents. We can understand ourselves only to the extent that we can give ourselves reasons for actions that correspond to a life plan that we recognize as our own. And we can understand ourselves as members of an acceptable system for collective governance, bound together by authoritative rules and principles, only to the extent that we can explain why those rules and principles ought to be viewed as binding. The authority of all law relies on a set of complex reasons for believing that it should be authoritative. Unjustifiable law demands reform. Unjustifiable legal systems demand revolution.

---

[3] C. G. Jung, *Answer to Job* (R. F. C. Hull trans., Princeton University Press, Princeton, NJ, 2010) (1960).

But the reign of reason plays itself out in different ways in different domains of authoritative legal decision-making. American law has in crucial ways given up on the project of rationality as applied to legislative action. As a constitutional matter, we do not require that the legislature have a "rational basis" for its actions, only that we could imagine one.[4] And, while it is virtually impossible to avoid purposive interpretation of statutory pronouncements, that is, to attempt to apply the statute consistently with the "reasons" underlying its enactment, we know that those reasons are post-hoc constructions ascribed to a metaphorical "it" that is really a "they." Save in special constitutional contexts where the legislature must adduce pressing state needs to override certain fundamental human interests, the legislature need not have investigated the facts of the matter, analyzed them cogently, or been motivated by whatever reasons can be constructed as justifications for its action.[5]

The difference between reason as a legitimating basis for legislative and administrative action was candidly acknowledged some years ago by Judge Malcolm Wilkey of the District of Columbia Circuit Court of Appeals. The case – *National Tire Dealers & Retreaders Association* v. *Brinegar* – involved the validity of tire labeling standards adopted by the National Highway Traffic Safety Administration.[6] The court struck down portions of the agency's regulation because they lacked adequate rationalization. However, the court felt constrained to uphold two exactly parallel parts of the agency's rule that Congress had expressly mandated by statute. Recognizing that his discussion of the apparent irrationality of the rule applied equally to all its parts (both administrative and congressional), Judge Wilkey remarked simply, "No administrative procedure test applies to an act of Congress."[7]

Nor has reason colonized judicial decision-making as an exclusive ground for legitimacy in the way that it inhabits administrative law. At first blush, this claim may seem odd. Law talk as it is carried on in the profession, as well as in the academy, is almost maniacally fixated on the reasons that appellate judges give as justifications for their decisions. Yet the law treats the necessity and the importance of reason-giving in judicial dispute resolution very differently than it treats the force of reason in administrative law. The bulk of all private adjudication is settled prior to

---

[4] See *Williamson* v. *Lee Optical of Oklahoma Inc.*, 348 U.S. 483, 488 (1955) ("It is enough that there is an evil at hand for correction, and that it might be thought that the particular legislative measure was a rational way to correct it."); *United States* v. *Carolene Products Co.*, 304 U.S. 144, 152 (1938) ("[T]he existence of facts supporting the legislative judgment is to be presumed, for regulatory legislation affecting ordinary commercial transactions is not to be pronounced unconstitutional unless in the light of the facts made known or generally assumed it is of such a character as to preclude the assumption that it rests upon some rational basis within the knowledge and experience of the legislators.").

[5] Struggles concerning which human interests are "fundamental," and what level of rationality must be demonstrated to override those interests, nevertheless generate much litigation and massive scholarly analysis. For a selection, *see*, for example, Geoffrey R. Stone et al., *Constitutional Law*, 721–1026 (7th edn., Aspen Publishers, New York, NY, 2013).

[6] *Nat'l Tire Dealers & Retreaders Ass'n* v. *Brinegar*, 491 F.2d 31 (D.C. Cir. 1974).

[7] Id., at 37.

judgment.[8] The judge need give no reason for failing to render a decision other than that the parties themselves decided to forgo judicial intervention. For anyone committed to adjudication as the preeminent rational discourse for the development of law, the prevalence of settlement is deeply disturbing.[9]

Moreover, many civil cases, and most criminal ones, that go to trial are decided by jury verdicts. We have self-consciously made the jury a black box. Its results are known, but its reasons are both mysterious and irrelevant to the path of the law. A jury verdict is illegitimate only in those exceedingly rare cases where no rational argument can be constructed to justify the result.[10] Like the legislature's duty to satisfy the "rational basis" test, the jury's verdict is subject only to the constraint of hypothetical reason, and its conclusions reversible only if no reasonable person could have found as it did.

Even in the realm of appellate court judgment, numerous legal rules suppress the importance of the judicial rationale. That a lower court gave the wrong reasons for a correct decision is not by itself a justification for reversal or remand. By contrast, perhaps the most common contemporary ground for reversal of an American administrative institution's order is a court's judgment that it has failed to rationalize its decision adequately. Moreover, when analyzing the authoritativeness of prior judicial determinations, it is commonplace for lawyers, judges, and commentators to strip away all judicial rationalization that is not found, on post-hoc analysis, to be absolutely essential to the decision. Most of what courts say in justification for their decision-making is cast by common convention into the outer darkness of *obiter dictum*.[11]

I am not claiming, of course, that reason plays no role in legitimating both legislative and judicial action. My claim is only that the legitimacy of legislative or judge-made law draws on sources other than rationality and reason-giving. We speak unselfconsciously of legislative will rather than of legislative reason. In its legislative form, law is the aggregation of preferences legitimated by periodic elections. It is at best a clunky system and a deep disappointment to those who believe that democracy should be deliberative and expressive – that is, rational rather than willful.[12] Indeed, in an earlier era in which parliaments struggled to wrest power from

---

[8] *See, e.g.*, Marc Galanter and Angela Frozena, The Continuing Decline of Civil Trials in American Courts, *Pound Civ. Justice Inst.* 3–5 (2011), www.poundinstitute.org/sites/default/files/docs/2011%20judges%20 forum/2011%20Forum%20Galanter-Frozena%20Paper.pdf (Last accessed May 25, 2018).

[9] Owen M. Fiss, Against Settlement, 93 *Yale L. J.* 1073 (1984).

[10] *Jackson* v. *Virginia*, 443 U.S. 307, 319 (1979) ("[T]he relevant question is whether, after viewing the evidence in the light most favorable to the prosecution, *any* rational trier of fact could have found the essential elements of the crime beyond a reasonable doubt.").

[11] Michael Abramowicz and Maxwell Stearns, Defining Dicta, 57 *Stan. L. Rev.* 953, 961 (2005) ("A holding consists of those propositions along the chosen decisional path or paths of reasoning that [1] are actually decided, [2] are based upon the facts of the case, and [3] lead to the judgment. If not a holding, a proposition stated in a case counts as dicta.").

[12] For an attempt to square administrative governance with civic republican aspirations and for citation of some of the extensive civic republicanism literature, *see* Mark Seidenfeld, A Civic Republican Justification for the Bureaucratic State, 105 *Harv. L. Rev.* 1512 (1992).

monarchs, the legislature's image was that of a deliberatively rational institution juxtaposed against the willfulness of the executive embodied in the crown. But that was then. Today, statutes are often described as bargains among powerful economic interests,[13] and courts and commentators despair of knowing legislative purposes save from rigorous attention to the ordinary meaning of the text.[14] "Purposivism" as an interpretive technique has its adherents, but "textualism" – divorced from a search for the legislature's underlying intentions or reasons beyond the plain text – is a leading competitor. Why the legislature acted may be obscure; what it said lies on the face of the statute.

Adjudicative legitimacy flows as much from judges' capacities to settle disputes authoritatively as from their capacity to create well-justified legal norms. There is no common law obligation to give reasons,[15] and the vast majority of American judicial decisions are issued without opinion. Trial courts are required to state findings of fact and conclusions of law, but not the reasons that connect the two. Appellate courts often rule in unpublished opinions that have no precedential value and thus make no contribution to a reasoned dialogue about the shape of the law.[16] The vast majority of Supreme Court decisions – decisions about whether to take a case – are made with no disclosure of reasons.

By contrast, a retreat to political will or an unexplained decision is almost always unavailable to modern American administrative decision makers. Administrators, of course, have two possible connections to the electorate: the president's appointment and the Senate's approval of all high-level administrative personnel, and the ultimate derivation of virtually all administrative authority from the legislature. But it is a rare case in which an administrator called upon to justify a decision can respond simply, "The president, or Congress, made me do it."

Indeed, claims to an electoral mandate sometimes delegitimate administrative actions rather than support them. Pressure from the people's representatives in congressional hearings may cause invalidation of an agency's adjudicatory determinations, or cause the testifying administrator to be disqualified as an administrative adjudicator.[17] Even managerial actions, such as an administrator's decision about where to build a road segment, may be invalidated based on congressional

---

[13] *See, e.g.*, Michael T. Hayes, *Lobbyists and Legislators: A Theory of Political Markets* (1981).

[14] *See, e.g.*, John F. Manning, Textualism as a Nondelegation Doctrine, 97 *Colum. L. Rev.* 673 (1997).

[15] *See generally*, David Dyzenhaus and Michael Taggart, "Reasoned Decisions and Legal Theory", in *Common Law Theory* (Douglas E. Edlin ed. Cambridge University Press, Cambridge, 2007).

[16] According to one count, 80 to 90 percent of federal appellate court decisions for the years 2000–8 were unpublished. Aaron S. Bayer, Unpublished Appellate Decisions Are Still Commonplace, *Nat'l L. J.*, August 24, 2009, at 14. In 2014, over 81 percent of opinions and orders in the U.S. Courts of Appeals were unpublished, totaling almost 30,000 unpublished decisions. *The Judicial Business of the United States Courts: 2014 Annual Report of the Director*, Admin. Off. U.S. Cts. Tbl. B-12 (2014), www.uscourts.gov/file/19025/download (Last accessed May 25, 2018).

[17] *Pillsbury Co. v. FTC*, 354 F.2d 952, 963-65 (5th Cir. 1966).

pressure.[18] In "quasi-legislative" rulemaking proceedings, administrative law doctrine counsels administrators against communication with elected officials unless those communications are memorialized and described in the rulemaking record.[19]

Directives from the president often fare no better, as Harry S. Truman learned in the famous *Steel Seizure* case during the Korean conflict.[20] More recently, the almost equally famous *State Farm* case emphasized that a change of administrative ideology consequent upon a new political party winning the White House does not alone provide sufficient basis for rescinding an administrative rule.[21] The rescission of a rule, like its adoption, must be rationalized in terms of relevant statutory criteria, with supporting social, economic, or scientific facts spread upon the rulemaking record.

More recently yet, President Bill Clinton announced that he was "authorizing" the Food and Drug Administration (FDA) to regulate tobacco as a drug.[22] This presidential "authorization" was unable to protect the FDA's tobacco regulations from invalidation. The FDA did not even attempt to invoke the political legitimacy of presidential power as a basis for its exercise of jurisdiction. Rather, the FDA's legal argument emphasized technocratic rationality – new knowledge concerning the way in which cigarettes were manufactured and marketed.[23]

To some extent, these failures of presidential political justification illustrate a judicial solicitude for a different connection between administration and electoral politics – an attempt to ensure an agency's fidelity to the statute that elected representatives enacted (and that an elected president likely signed). But while the democratic legitimacy inherent in statutory authority is a necessary condition for legitimate administrative action, it is far from sufficient. Authority must be combined with reasons, which usually means accurate fact-finding and sound policy or legal analysis. Otherwise, an administrator's rule or order will be declared "arbitrary," "capricious," or "an abuse of discretion."[24] Moreover, as those who decry the toothlessness of the

---

[18] *D.C. Fed. of Civic Ass'ns v. Volpe*, 459 F.2d 1231, 1248 (D.C. Cir. 1971); *see Aera Energy LLC v. Salazar*, 642 F.3d 212, 224 (D.C. Cir. 2011) ("[W]e have never questioned the authority of congressional representatives to *exert* pressure, and we have held that congressional actions not targeted directly at [agency] decision makers – such as contemporaneous hearings – do not invalidate an agency decision. But sometimes political pressure crosses the line and prevents an agency from performing its statutorily prescribed duties." [citations and internal quotation marks omitted]). Some commentators critique the judicial posture in *Volpe* and *Aera Energy*. *See* Jamelle C. Sharpe, Judging Congressional Oversight, 65 *Admin. L. Rev.* 183, 216 (2013) (arguing that courts should "lift the specter of judicial invalidation where agencies cite congressional post-delegation policy preferences as a factor in the policy choices they make.").

[19] *Sierra Club v. Costle*, 657 F.2d 298, 400–8 (D.C. Cir. 1981).

[20] *Youngstown Sheet & Tube Co. v. Sawyer*, 343 U.S. 579 (1952).

[21] *Motor Vehicle Mfrs. Ass'n. of the United States v. State Farm Mut. Auto. Ins. Co.*, 463 U.S. 29 (1983).

[22] President Bill Clinton, Press Conference at the White House (August 10, 1995), 1995 WL 472181.

[23] *FDA v. Brown & Williamson Tobacco Corp.*, 529 U.S. 120, 170–1 (2000) (discussing the FDA's legal justifications for its tobacco regulations).

[24] *See* Administrative Procedure Act, Pub. L. No. 79-404, § 10(e), 60 Stat. 237, 243–4 (1946) (codified as amended at 5 U.S.C. § 706(2)(A) (2012)) (stating that a "reviewing court shall ... hold unlawful

nondelegation doctrine constantly remind us, the common vagueness and vacuity of statutory directives stretches the thread that binds administrative action to electoral preferences virtually to the breaking point.[25] When Congress tells the National Highway Traffic Safety Administration in the Motor Vehicle Safety Act of 1966 to "meet the need for motor vehicle safety,"[26] it has done little more than to tell the agency to go forth and do good.

Nor can agencies borrow much legitimacy from simple conflict resolution or jury-like allocation of decisional competence to ordinary citizens. The insinuation of stakeholder negotiation into administrative procedures is often viewed as a potential corruption of the administrative process. Agency use of advisory committees or "regulatory negotiation" is strictly constrained to ensure that the agency remains firmly in control of the ultimate regulatory product.[27] Moreover, none of these devices reduces the agency's obligation to explain its decision in instrumentally rational terms.

Even settlements, while hardly unknown in agency enforcement, may nevertheless be subject to demands for rationalization backed by judicial review. And many encounters between government agencies and private parties cannot, in any meaningful sense, be "settled." Whether a citizen is entitled to Social Security disability benefits, or to a commercial aviation license, has to be decided. The reasons given for these decisions are then subject to judicial review to ensure that an adequately reasoned explanation was provided. Where an agency's mission demands actions that outrun cogent articulation of reasons we have usually stumbled into an arena in which lotteries or market solutions are more appropriate means of decision-making. Reform then proceeds in the direction of deregulation. The alternative economic rationality of the market, or the probabilistic equality of a fair drawing,[28] is substituted as a legitimating device for the reasonableness of administrative law. An auction mechanism, for example, has mercifully replaced the Federal Communications Commission's exquisite and often baffling attempts to explain why one or another

---

and set aside agency action, findings, and conclusions found to be ... arbitrary, capricious, an abuse of discretion, or otherwise not in accordance with law").

[25] *See generally* Symposium, The Phoenix Rises Again: The Nondelegation Doctrine from Constitutional and Policy Perspectives, 20 *Cardozo L. Rev.* 731 (1999) (reviewing the jurisprudence and literature concerning the non-delegation doctrine).

[26] National Traffic and Motor Vehicle Safety Act of 1966, Pub. L. No. 89–563, §103(a), 80 Stat. 718, 719 (1966) (repealed 1994).

[27] *E.g.*, Negotiated Rulemaking Act of 1990, Pub. L. No. 101-648, 104 Stat. 4969 (1990) (codified as amended at 5 U.S.C. §§ 561–70 (2012)); Administrative Dispute Resolution Act, Pub. L No. 101-552, 104 Stat. 2736 (1990) (codified as amended at 5 U.S.C. §§ 571–84 (2012)); Federal Advisory Committee Act, Pub. L. No. 92–463, 86 Stat. 770 (1972), *amended by* Pub. L No. 94-409, 90 Stat. 1241 (1976) (codified at 5 U.S.C. app. 2 §§ 1–15 (2012)).

[28] *See, e.g.*, The Vietnam Lotteries, Selective Serv. Sys., www.sss.gov/About/History-And-Records/lotter1 (Last accessed May 25, 2018).

otherwise qualified applicant for a broadcast license would better serve the "public interest."[29]

This connection between administration and reason is a familiar theme in the social and political theory of modernity. Max Weber famously explained the legitimacy of bureaucratic activity as its promise to exercise power on the basis of knowledge.[30] The American Progressive movement extolled the virtues of administration in terms both of substantive expertise and the creation of "rational democracy."[31] But administrative decision-making in the United States was not always so focused on rationality and reason-giving as the touchstones of legal legitimacy. Indeed, pre-New Deal administrative law had relatively thin rationality requirements.

An apt illustration is Justice Louis Brandeis' decision in a 1935 case involving agricultural regulation in Oregon.[32] The Oregon agricultural authorities, operating under a statute dictating that they "'promote ... the horticulture interests' of the State,"[33] adopted a regulation on the marketing of berries. The regulation required that commercial berry sellers use one particular style of box to hold their for-sale berries – a box that just happened to be manufactured in Oregon.[34] The reasons for the state agricultural authority's choice of fruit box were nowhere revealed in its regulatory issuances. But confronted with a due-process challenge that asserted the substantive irrationality of the regulation, Justice Brandeis simply analogized administrative regulation to legislation. The constitutional question, he said, was simply whether some state of affairs might be imagined under which the Oregon regulation would be a rational means for carrying out the legislative mandate.[35] Because few more imaginative justices ever graced the bench, Justice Brandeis found himself easily equal to the task. As a constitutional matter, administrative rationality, at least in the domain of rulemaking, was to be subjected to no stronger test than the hypothetical rationality applied to legislation.

But the burgeoning of the administrative state during the New Deal and the Second World War produced a strong reaction against what Roscoe Pound, among

---

[29] For information on FCC auctions consult the FCC website at http://wireless.FCC.gov/auctions/default.htm?job=auctions_home. For a critique of the auction process *see* Gregory F. Rose and Mark Lloyd, *The Failure of FCC Spectrum Auctions*, Center for American Progress (May 2006) available at https://cdn.Americanprogress.org/wp-content/uploads/kf/SPECTRUM_AUCTIONS_may06.pdf.

[30] Max Weber, 3 *Economy and Society* 956–1003 (Guenther Roth and Claus Wittich eds., Ephraim Fischoff et al. trans., 1968) (University of California Press, Berkeley, CA, 1922).

[31] For classical discussions of the progressive view of good government, *see* Woodrow Wilson, The Study of Administration, 2 *Political Science Quarterly* 197 (1887); Herbert Croly, *Progressive Democracy* (Macmillan, New York, NY; 1914); John Dewey, *The Public and Its Problems* (Holt, New York, NY, 1927). For a comprehensive review of progressive thought *see* Eldon Eisenach, *The Lost Promise of Progressivism* (University of Kansas Press, Lawrence Kansas, 1994).

[32] *Pac. States Box & Basket Co.* v. *White*, 296 U.S. 176 (1935).

[33] Id., at 178.

[34] Id., at 180-2.

[35] Ibid.

others, described as "administrative absolutism."[36] The statutory embodiment of this reaction is the 1946 Administrative Procedure Act (APA).[37] While the APA seemed at the time to make modest demands for agency articulation of reasons, developments since that time – both in the interpretation of the APA and the more far-reaching rationality prescriptions of other statutes – make contemporary requirements for administrative reason-giving ubiquitous.

The modest suggestion in Section 553 of the APA that agencies must file a "concise statement of the basis and purpose"[38] of a regulation has developed into a requirement for a comprehensive articulation of the factual bases, methodological presuppositions, and statutory authority that justifies any exercise of rulemaking. To make certain that this exercise in instrumental rationality is real, rather than hypothetical, courts routinely reject "'post-hoc' rationalizations,"[39] the agency's use of untested facts outside the rulemaking record,[40] and attempts to rely on unarticulated reservoirs of agency "expertise."[41] Courts demand, in addition, persuasive responses to cogent objections from outside parties.[42]

Specific regulatory statutes have gone far beyond the APA. They have added a host of analytic requirements to particular regulatory functions. A plethora of more general framework statutes have made agency rulemaking into what some have characterized as an exercise in "synoptic" rationality.[43] In addition to rationalizing action in terms of their principal missions, agencies must routinely consider the environmental consequences of their actions, provide cost–benefit analyses of regulatory alternatives, consider impacts on particular clienteles, and assure objectors that they have chosen the least burdensome method to accomplish their statutorily specified ends.[44]

Abstractly considered, these requirements can be seen as an attempt to ensure that agency action is not only *reasoned* but *reasonable*. Mission-oriented administrators pursuing public policies within particular domains are cautioned – by the

---

[36] Roscoe Pound, Administrative Law: Its Growth, Procedure, and Significance, 7 *U. Pitt. L. Rev.* 269, 280 (1941).

[37] Administrative Procedure Act, Pub. L. No. 79-404, 60 Stat. 237 (1946) (codified as amended at 5 U.S.C. §§ 551–706 (2012)).

[38] 5 U.S.C. § 553(c).

[39] *See, e.g., Citizens to Preserve Overton Park, Inc.* v. *Volpe*, 401 U.S. 402, 419 (1971).

[40] *See, e.g., United States* v. *Nova Scotia Food Prods. Corp.*, 568 F.2d 240 (2d Cir. 1977) (requiring release during notice and comment period of scientific data used as basis for rule).

[41] *See, e.g., Portland Cement Ass'n* v. *Ruckelshaus*, 486 F.2d 375, 398 (D.C. Cir. 1973).

[42] For a compendium of materials on the requirements of administrative rulemaking, *see* Jeffrey S. Lubbers, *A Guide to Federal Agency Rulemaking* (5th edn., American Bar Association, Chicago, IL, 2012).

[43] *See generally* Thomas O. McGarity, *Reinventing Rationality: The Role of Regulatory Analysis in the Federal Bureaucracy* (Cambridge University Press, Cambridge, 1991).

[44] A compendium of these statutes, along with related executive orders, can be found in the *Federal Administrative Procedure Sourcebook* (William F. Funk et al. eds., 4th edn., American Bar Association, Chicago, IL, 2008). The Sourcebook now runs to a mere 1,172 pages.

demand that they consider environmental, economic, and distributional values –
that implementing the goals of their special-purpose statutes does not exhaust citizens' demands for sensible and effective government. In a massive administrative
state with hundreds of specialized agencies, this anti-tunnel-vision effort is praise-
worthy. Moreover, the requirement that agencies analyze their actions based on
competing values is broadly consistent with the basic notion that administrative
legitimacy flows from transparent revelation of the agencies' reasoning process.

But demands for reason-giving are not costless. In some arenas of agency rulemaking observers claim that these multiple requirements for synoptic or comprehensive
rationality have brought policy making to a virtual standstill. Others suspect that the
demand for rationality has moved from a concern for justification and legitimacy
into the realm of harassment.[45] Many agencies would certainly relish the opportunity to follow the practice of the disgruntled father, who had at least some chance of
getting away with an utterance like, "Shut up." Rationality as the touchstone of legitimacy in the liberal, administrative state has been enthroned as a sometime tyrant.

A similar story can be told about other domains of administrative action. The due
process revolution, along with congressional attentiveness in modern statutes to the
provision of formal adjudicatory process, has dramatically increased the demand
for transparently rational administrative adjudication. With only modest recent
retrenchments, the multi-decade judicial project of eliminating domains of inarticulate administrative discretion has brought reason-giving to administrative inaction,
enforcement, and agenda setting – areas long thought to be protected from judicial
supervision and its incessant demand for transparent rationality.[46]

To be sure, the triumph of reason has not been complete in administrative law.
I have painted with a broad brush here, leaving aside many qualifications and counter-
currents. Much executive action concerning military and foreign affairs is exempt
from the procedural and reason-giving requirements of the federal APA. Indeed, the
recent expansion of the national security state brings more and more legal terrain
within its ambit, and secrecy routinely undermines reason-giving in these national
security cases.[47] Reasons for inaction may never see the light of day. Affected parties
may doubt that the reasons given reveal the true motivation for decisions. These and
other limitations on the model of reasoned administration developed in these pages
will be addressed to a greater or lesser degree in the chapters that follow.

---

[45] My own intemperate remarks on this matter can be found in Jerry L. Mashaw, Reinventing
Government and Regulatory Reform: Studies in the Neglect and Abuse of Administrative Law, 57
U. Pitt. L. Rev. 405 (1996).

[46] Notwithstanding the broad dicta in *Heckler* v. *Chaney*, 470 U.S. 821 (1985), the courts have found a
multitude of devices for submitting administrative enforcement and regulatory discretion to review,
thereby requiring that agencies justify their failure either to enforce or to regulate. *See generally* Jerry
L. Mashaw et al., *Administrative Law: The American Public Law System* 1177–218 (7th edn., West
Publishing, St. Paul, MN, 2014).

[47] *See, e.g., Mokdad* v. *Lynch*, 804 F.3d 807, 808–11 (6th Cir. 2015).

Nevertheless, I believe that my central point is undeniable. The path of American administrative law has been the path of the progressive submission of power to reason. The promise of the administrative state was to bring competence to politics. It is the institutional embodiment of the enlightenment project to substitute reason for the dark forces of culture, tradition, and myth. Administrators must not only give reasons; they must give complete ones. We attempt to ensure that they are authentic by demanding that they be both transparent and contemporaneous.[48] "Expertise" is no longer a protective shield to be worn like a sacred vestment. It is a competence to be demonstrated by cogent reason-giving.

From this perspective, the development of American administrative law represents the triumph of the idea of reason in public life. For a host of reasons, this triumph is to be celebrated. We do not want environmental regulation based on myth, or an individual's deservedness for public benefits decided on the basis of inarticulate cultural premises. We are deeply divided over appeals to the sacred in public life, and whatever the sociological fact of the matter, reliance on hereditary status as a basis for exercising power has always seemed un-American. We treasure an independent judiciary, but only as long as we are convinced that we keep most of public policy making out of its hands. We do not wish to be governed by the "artificial reason" of the law in courts. While we prize elections, we seldom believe that politicians have received a mandate for relentless and unchecked pursuit of their particular vision of the good. We do not view ourselves as in the business of electing dictators who can rule by decree while hiding behind "the will of the people."

Indeed, as will be further developed in Chapter 7, contemporary political philosophy has long been dominated by a "public reason" school of thought. This school attempts to harmonize state coercion with individual freedom, under conditions of value pluralism, precisely through the demand that exercises of state power be justified by reasons that all might reasonably accept. That attempt is, at the philosophical level, only partially successful. But for now, it is the most successful family of normative political theories on offer. And, strange as it may seem, administrative governance that conforms to a model of what I am calling "reasoned administration," may provide the most democratic form of governance available to us in a modern, complex, and deeply compromised political world.

My claim, then, is that American administrative government is not just a story of the triumph of reason. It is a story of the triumph of legitimate, liberal democratic governance in a world full of dangerous alternatives. Yet the demand for "reasoned administration" raises a host of questions or puzzles. Let me suggest a few of them.

---

[48] The iconic statement of this position is *Citizens to Preserve Overton Park, Inc. v. Volpe*, 401 U.S. 402 (1971).

SOME PUZZLES

One puzzle is historical. Until well into the twentieth century, while federal officials may often have given reasons for their actions, there were seldom any legal
requirements for them to do so. Moreover, federal officials were not immunized
from liability in damage actions if, in the course of their administrative duties, they
made an error of fact or law. These officials were legally unprotected even when
they had exercised reasonable judgment under the circumstances. In these damage
suits legality was tested solely by authority or jurisdiction. Courts would not inquire
into whether the discretion exercised was reasonable, or indeed reasoned. Yet by the
late twentieth century, failure to adequately explain a decision was the most common ground on which United States judges overturned administrative actions. And
virtually any administrative act, and at least some failures to act, could be challenged
for failure to provide adequate reasons. How are we to explain reason's move from
irrelevance to prominence? That is the historical puzzle. Indeed, it turns out to be
something of a mystery.

From a more contemporary perspective, how should we understand the demand
for reasoned administration? If reasons are required, what precisely does it mean
to give an adequate reason or to make a reasoned or reasonable decision? What
reasons "count" as relevant and legitimating? Is the demand for reasons largely a
procedural or substantive demand? Do administrators merely need to demonstrate a
reasoning process? Or must they convince reviewing courts that their ultimate substantive decisions were reasonable ones? And, if "reasonableness" is required, how is
reasonableness to be given content?

What are the effects of a legal requirement that administrative decisions be both
reasoned and reasonable? Are administrative decisions improved? Does reason-
giving enhance or detract from the effectiveness and timeliness of administrative
actions? How do reason-giving requirements affect the locus of policy making power
within government? To what extent do they empower nongovernmental parties to
influence governmental or administrative decision-making? To put that question
more pointedly: is the demand for reasons a critical support for other public law
values, such as transparency and participation, or is it a gateway for capture by well-
resourced interest groups or for harassment and obstruction by opponents of governmental actions?

Looking inside bureaucracies, what are the organizational dynamics of reasoning
in administrative institutions? For the practice of reason-giving to play the legitimating role that it seems to have in the legal system, what must the requirement
of reason-giving presume about the organization of administrative bureaucracies?
If reason-giving and reasonableness are legal requirements, what actors within a
bureaucracy are empowered by those demands?

Finally, what are the underlying legal and political justifications for demanding
reasons? Is reason-giving instrumental to other legal and political rights? Or is it more

fundamental, a practice that is necessary to harmonize the exercise of public coercive authority with individual autonomy and democratic self-rule?

To be sure, these are not the only questions and puzzles surrounding our contemporary demand for reasoned administration. If my story of the ascendency of reason is correct, another question is why the ubiquitous complaint that bureaucracies are opaque and unresponsive coexists with extensive requirements for administrative explanation. What is missing from reasoned administrative decision-making that leaves many citizens with the sense that the reasons administrators give for their actions do not speak to them?

THE PLAN OF THE BOOK

This book struggles with these questions over its next seven chapters. To briefly chart the book's course, Chapter 2 explores "The Rise of Reason-Giving." It traces the evolution of requirements for reason-giving as a basis for administrative legality from irrelevance in the nineteenth century to dominance in the twenty-first century. At the doctrinal level, this early twentieth-century shift is a somewhat bizarre story of inadvertence, doctrinal confusion, and the conflation of statutory substantive reasonableness criteria with procedural demands for reason-giving. Other causal elements include the unintended consequences of congressional compromise in regulatory reform legislation, and the proceduralization of rationality review by courts seeking to solve a problem of the legitimacy of judicial review of administrative action in the late twentieth-century administrative state.

Chapter 3, "Reasons, Reasonableness, and Accountability in American Administrative Law," summarizes the many sources of (and varying demands for) reason-giving and reasonableness in contemporary American administrative law. This chapter is necessary background for understanding the more evaluative and theoretical discussion that follows. It develops the model of "reasoned administration" that dominates current approaches to administrative legality, the implications of which are explored in the remainder of the book.

Chapter 4, "Reasonableness, Accountability, and the Control of Administrative Policy," addresses three questions: (1) How do legal requirements for reasoned administration affect the internal organization and processes of agencies that are subject to their demands? (2) How do these demands, and agency responses to them, empower different internal and external actors in an agency's legal environment? And, (3) what can be said about how reasoned administration as a legal requirement affects agency outputs and the quality or character of agency decision-making?

Chapter 5, "Reason, Reasonableness, and Judicial Review," addresses the perennial issue of how to judge the ultimate reasonableness or nonarbitrariness of agency action after various procedural and evidentiary approaches have been exhausted. The crucial argument of this chapter is twofold: first it argues that determining whether adequate reasons have been provided for agency action or inaction presupposes a judgment about the appropriate range of reasons that are required and the weight that particular considerations should have in a final administrative determination. Reviewing courts' attempts to avoid substantive judgments are ultimately futile and may lead to intervention in the name of deference. Second, the focus of what I term "proceduralized rationality review" mischaracterizes administrative decision-making in narrowly instrumental terms that conceal its normative and democracy reinforcing nature. The American approach to reasonableness review is compared and contrasted with the more direct substantive approach of many European systems that employ judicial review for "proportionality."

Chapter 6, "Reasons, Administration, and Politics," explores the legitimacy or illegitimacy of invoking "political" considerations as reasons for administrative action. "Political" here includes both: (a) reasons based in political ideology or partisan political advantage, and (b) reasons that can be described simply as policy considerations that are not a part of the criteria for action provided in a particular agency's organic statute. This discussion highlights the tension between democratic political accountability and accountability based on the model of instrumental rationality developed in Chapter 3. The chapter argues for broader acceptance of policy and value-based reasoning by administrative agencies which necessarily serve as discoverers, not just as implementers, of legislative purposes.

Chapter 7, "Reasoned Administration and Democratic Legitimacy," explores two models of democratic accountability – aggregative and deliberative – and the way in which the legal structure of "reasoned administration" responds (or not) to both. American democracy is, in general, a compromise or blending of these two competitive visions of democratic governance. Administrative law's approach to administrative legality can thus be understood as a vehicle for the political legitimation of the administrative state in the American constitutional system. Rather than detaching governance from sources of democratic legitimation, reasoned administration completes and enhances an attractive vision of democratic government – or so Chapter 7 argues.

Chapter 8, "Reason and Regret," asks why, given the strong reasons to celebrate the legitimacy and efficacy of the administrative state, American legal and political culture constantly questions the democratic credentials of contemporary administrative governance. Is this skepticism just a stubborn unwillingness to give up on an idealized vision of democratic governance that never was? A hostility to virtually all government? A postmodern consciousness that is suspicious of reason as justificatory? Or is there some gap or lapse in our current model of reasoned administration that provides an opportunity for meaningful reform?

2

The Rise of Reason-Giving

For twenty-first century-citizens of modern, liberal, democratic states, the association of reason and reason-giving with administrative governance may seem relatively nonproblematic. Administrative governance is part and parcel of the rise of modernity, the substitution of reason for myth, custom, and heredity; the march from charismatic to bureaucratic authority. And respect for the rights of free and equal citizens would be difficult to square with rule by administrative fiat. But the making of the modern world and modern nation states has hardly been a linear historical development. Max Weber's early nineteenth-century pronouncement that the promise of bureaucratic authority was to exercise power on the basis of knowledge was, when made, as much a prediction as a statement of the social fact of the matter.[1] The rise of reason and reason-giving as a requirement for the legality of administrative action has a similarly complicated history. As Justice Holmes also famously remarked, "The life of the law has not been logic. It has been experience."[2] To grasp the vast change from nineteenth- to twenty-first-century American visions of the connection between reason-giving and administrative legality, we must explore that experience, beginning in the early Republic.

REASONABLENESS AND REASON-GIVING IN
NINETEENTH-CENTURY AMERICA

Administrative law was not talked about as a separate field of law in the United States until the very late nineteenth or early twentieth century. But this hardly meant that there were no administrative offices or agencies, or that administrators did not make

---

[1] Weber, 3 *Economy and Society*, 956–1003.
[2] Oliver Wendell Holmes, *The Common Law* 9 (Harvard University Press, Cambridge, MA, 2009) (1881).

thousands of decisions with legal effect.[3] Many of these functions were carried on within the context of published substantive and procedural rules. Official decisions were often subject to appeal within the administration to appeals boards or supervisory personnel. The decisions of those boards had precedential force and supplemented the explanatory material contained in agency manuals, opinion letters, and guidelines.[4]

In short, reasons were often given for decisions, and policies were explained to those whom they affected. Then, as now, this explanation of why given policies were adopted greatly facilitated the public's voluntary compliance and acceptance of administrative action. However, virtually none of this reason-giving was required by statute or by the common law of judicial review. As characterized by Bruce Wyman's path-breaking treatise on American administrative law, these rules, precedent decisions, and explanatory guidelines were a part of the "internal law" of administration.[5]

By contrast, Wyman's "external law" was essentially the common law as it applied to the actions of administrative officers. That common law was of generally two types: damage actions against an officer based on some standard form of common law action (trespass, trover, assumpsit, or the like), or an action premised on a prerogative writ, basically mandamus or injunction. The reasonableness of an administrator's actions played no role in either form of action. In short, in this "bipolar model"[6] of a judicial review, review was all or nothing. Either the court decided all the questions for itself, giving no deference to reasonable administrative action, or it declined to review because the administrative action was discretionary.

Suits for mandamus or injunction – suits to compel or prohibit official action – provide the simplest cases. The federal courts took a straightforward position on when these writs would lie: if the officer had jurisdiction to act and acted within that jurisdiction, the court would not inquire into the grounds for, or reasonableness of, the officer's acts. Indeed, in the iconic case of *Marbury* v. *Madison*, Chief Justice Marshall described the proposition that a suit in mandamus could be brought to control the discretion of an officer as "[a]n extravagance, so absurd and excessive ... [that it] could not have been entertained for a moment."[7] On the other hand, if the officer's duty was nondiscretionary – a purely ministerial act, such as the delivery of the certificates of appointment at issue in *Marbury* – the officer's failure to act as mandated was not excused because the officer had good reasons for his failure.

[3] *See generally* Jerry L. Mashaw, *Creating the Administrative Constitution: The Lost 100 Years of American Administrative Law* (Yale University Press, New Haven, CT, 2012) (describing American administrative processes during the late eighteenth and nineteenth centuries).

[4] *See id.*, at 251–84.

[5] *See generally* Bruce Wyman, *The Principles of the Administrative Law Governing the Relations of Public Officers* (Keefe-Davidson, St. Paul, MN, 1903) (describing and distinguishing between the "internal" policies and procedures of administrative law and the "external" law of proto-judicial review of administrative action).

[6] Mashaw, *Creating the Administrative Constitution*, at 301–8.

[7] 5 U.S. (1 Cranch) 137, 170 (1803).

In mandamus actions, the question before the court was a question of jurisdiction or authority, not reasonableness.[8]

The same was true in actions for injunction. In *Gaines* v. *Thompson*, the Supreme Court described its mandamus jurisprudence as part of a "general doctrine:"[9] "an officer to whom public duties are confided by law, is not subject to the control of the courts in the exercise of the judgment and discretion which the law reposes in him as a part of his official functions."[10] This general principle was based on an even more general idea – separation of powers. Nineteenth-century federal courts took very seriously the position – often associated with French administrative juris-prudence – that to judge administration is to engage in administration.[11] Indeed, it was not until late in the nineteenth century that the Supreme Court admitted that Congress could by statute provide federal courts with appellate jurisdiction over administrative action.[12]

Damage actions against officers excluded reasonableness considerations for a quite different reason: reasonableness was not a defense in most common law suits for damages. When a customs officer seized a ship or its cargo for nonpayment of customs duties, the owner could test the legality of the officer's action by an action in trespass. Trespass was, of course, an intentional tort. The only question was whether the officer had wrongfully seized the property. If the officer had made an error of either law or fact, the seizure was wrongful. The purity of the officer's motives and the reasonableness of his beliefs were simply beside the point. To be sure, the officer's defense that he was acting in his official capacity and according to the law put the legality of the officer's acts at issue. But legality was judged by cor-rectness, not reasonableness.[13] In a few cases, Congress recognized that officials bore unreasonable risks of damages liability and provided a reasonableness defense.[14] But such statutory provisions were rare.

Courts also avoided attempts to insinuate reasonableness or reason-giving into a plaintiff's statement of his cause of action against a federal official. *Crowell* v.

---

[8] *See* id., at 171.

[9] 74 U.S. (7 Wall.) 347, 352 (1868).

[10] Ibid.

[11] Henrion de Pansey, *De L'Autorité Judici are en France* (1818) ("juger l'administration, c'èst encore administrer").

[12] *See generally* Thomas W. Merrill, The Origins of the American-Style Judicial Review, in *Comparative Administrative Law* 389 (Peter Lindseth and Susan Rose-Ackerman eds., Edward Elgar, Northampton, MA, 2011) (describing the rise of appellate judicial review of administrative action in the United States).

[13] *Little* v. *Barreme*, 6 U.S. (2 Cranch) 170 (1804).

[14] *See, e.g.*, An Act to Regulate the Collection of the Duties Opposed by Law Upon the Tonnage of Ships or Vessels, and on Goods, Wares and Merchandises imported into the United States, Ch. 5, Sec. 36, 1 Stat. 29, 47–48 (1789) ("[W]hen any prosecution shall be commenced on account of the seizure ... and judgment shall be given for the claimant ... if it shall appear to the court ... that there was a reasonable cause of seizure ... the claimant shall not be entitled to costs, nor shall the person who made the seizure, or the prosecutor be liable").

M'Fadon,[15] for example, involved seizure of a vessel under a statute authorizing seizure whenever, in the collector's opinion, the vessel intended to violate the embargo statutes. The plaintiff argued that the Collector of Customs who seized the vessel could rely on his opinion only if he could demonstrate a reasonable basis for forming it. The Supreme Court rejected this rather plausible argument on the grounds that the statute simply required that the collector have an opinion, not that he have a reasonable one.

Otis v. *Watkins*,[16] another embargo case, sharpened the point. The plaintiff there tried to import reasonableness ideas from negligence law. He argued that a collector must exercise reasonable care in seeking information to form his opinion of a vessel's intentions. Reversing the lower court opinion for the plaintiff because of a faulty jury instruction, the Supreme Court said:

> The jury are told that it was the collector's duty to have used reasonable care in ascertaining the facts on which to form an opinion ... [B]ut the law exposes his conduct to no such scrutiny. If it did, no public officer would be hardy enough to act under it. If the jury believed that he honestly entertained the opinion under which he acted, although they might think it incorrect and formed hastily or without sufficient grounds, he would be entitled to their protection.[17]

Chief Justice Marshall was disturbed by the majority's position. In his separate opinion, he noted that the statute under which the collector had acted required that the Collector detain the vessel and hold it "until the decision of the president of the United States be had thereon."[18] In Marshall's view, "It follow[ed] necessarily from the duties of forming an opinion, and of communicating that opinion to the president for his decision in the case, that reasonable care ought to be used in collecting the facts to be stated to the president and that the statement ought to be made."[19] For that reason, Marshall thought that the jury instruction that the collector should be required to use reasonable care in ascertaining the facts was not erroneous. But, he apparently could convince none of his colleagues that the reasonableness of the collector's actions should be insinuated into a cause of action for damages.

Customs enforcement obviously entailed thousands of informal administrative adjudications each year. And, under the prevailing jurisprudence, none of these decisions needed to be justified by providing adequate reasons. Perhaps the second largest case load for administrative adjudication in the early Republic was the determination of rights to public lands. Upon the adoption of the US Constitution in 1787, the original thirteen colonies ceded virtually all their claims to lands west

---

[15]　12 U.S. (8 Cranch) 94 (1814).
[16]　13 U.S. (9 Cranch) 339 (1815).
[17]　Id., at 355–56.
[18]　Id., at 356 (Marshall, C. J., dissenting).
[19]　Id., at 358.

of the Allegheny Mountains to the federal government. These grants, combined with the purchase of the Louisiana Territory in 1803, doubled the size of the United States before the Union was even two decades old. The central government sought to sell off these lands, both as a money raising measure and in an attempt to populate its western territory as a buffer against hostile Native American tribes and the territorial ambitions of the British, French, and Spanish governments. But, settlors had not waited for the United States to survey its public lands and put them up for sale before moving West. These early westerners held titles from the former American colonies, and from British, French, and Spanish grants. Selling the public lands required determining what parts of these territories were in fact "public." Because federal territorial courts were not up to the task, administrative commissions were set up to determine the validity of tens of thousands of putative title holder's land claims.[20]

Judicial review with respect to land claims was both substantively and procedurally different from review of federal functions, such as tax collection or embargo enforcement. A claim that a land commission had made an erroneous decision with respect to a land title did not sound in tort. Damages were unavailable. Mandamus was similarly unavailing. Not only were these adjudicatory decisions "discretionary" in the mandamus sense of that word, the land commissioners did not hold title to the property in dispute. They could not be ordered to convey it to a claimant contending to be its rightful owner. Issues concerning whether a land patent was valid tended, therefore, to arise collaterally in actions for ejectment between private parties.

In the early nineteenth century, these collateral attacks on land commission decisions were nevertheless resolved in a fashion reminiscent of mandamus actions. If the land commission was determined to have had jurisdiction over the parcel involved, the courts treated the commission determination as res judicata.[21] If jurisdiction were lacking, the commission's actions were invalid, and the court then tried the action as an original proceeding in equity. Over time, the judiciary began to broaden review by expanding the idea of "jurisdictional error"[22] and by allowing appeal to the court's equitable powers to remedy "mistakes, injustice, and wrong."[23] But even when exercising this broader jurisdiction, the courts addressed issues of legal error, not issues of the reasonableness of the land commission's determination.

The land cases of the nineteenth century were nevertheless important stepping stones toward judicial review for reasonableness. For, by the end of the nineteenth century, land claims were probably the most common judicial proceedings in the

---

[20] For description of this administrative process, *see* Mashaw, *Creating the Administrative Constitution*, at 119–46.

[21] Ann Woolhandler, Judicial Deference to Administrative Action – A Revisionist History, 43 *Admin. L. Rev.* 197, 216–21 (1991).

[22] Id., at 219.

[23] *Johnson v. Towsley*, 80 U.S. (13 Wol.) 72, 84 (1871).

federal courts.[24] What courts of equity did in these cases was likely to have influence in other equitable proceedings. Second, the idea that courts could intervene as a matter of equity to correct errors of law began to cement the law–fact distinction that has loomed so large in the subsequent course of judicial review of administrative action. Recall that, in the early Republic, judges not only abjured investigation of the reasonableness of agency decisions, they did not "review" questions of law. Mandamus was an original action in which the only question was whether the officer had jurisdiction to act. And, similarly, in damage actions the cause of action went to court as a de novo proceeding. The court was not reviewing the officers' actions; it was deciding cases. The legality of an officer's actions might be put at issue in the case by way of defense, but the officer was before the court as an ordinary litigant. The plaintiff was not appealing the officer's decision, but prosecuting a tort claim or perhaps a common law action sounding in property or contract. For, remember, until late in the nineteenth century, the Supreme Court's position was that an appeal to the judiciary from an administrative determination would be unconstitutional.

But the law began to change. According to Professor Louis Jaffe's standard account,[25] the federal courts' equitable powers to correct errors and injustice morphed into something like a general presumption of the reviewability of administrative action for legal error. This development was greatly facilitated by the creation of general federal question jurisdiction in 1875.[26] By 1902, the Supreme Court seemed willing to reject virtually the whole of the deferential mandamus and injunction jurisprudence of the nineteenth century. In ringing tones heralding the federal courts as the guardians of the rule of law, the Court said, "The acts of all ... officers must be justified by some law, and in case an official violates the law to the injury of an individual the courts generally have jurisdiction to grant relief."[27] Barriers to direct judicial review did not fall all at once,[28] but the seeds of that collapse were sown in the late nineteenth-century land office cases.

The connection to the land office cases is just this: the broad statement just quoted from *American School of Magnetic Healing* v. *McAnnulty* occurred in a case seeking direct judicial review of a Post Office fraud order stopping delivery of the plaintiff's advertising. But, the only cases cited for the general proposition that errors

[24] *See* Antonin Scalia, Sovereign Immunity and Non-Statutory Review of Federal Administrative Action: Some Conclusions from the Public-Lands Cases, 68 *Mich. L. Rev.* 867, 884–85 (1970) (describing the "considerable volume of public-lands litigation").

[25] Louis L. Jaffe, *Judicial Control of Administrative Action* 327–53 (Harvard University Press, Cambridge, MA, 1965).

[26] The Jurisdiction and Removal Act of 1875, ch. 137, 18 Stat. 470, 470 ("[T]he circuit courts of the United States shall have original cognizance, concurrent with the courts of the several States, of all suits of a civil nature at common law or in equity, where the matter in dispute exceeds ... five hundred dollars, and arising under the Constitution or laws of the United States ...").

[27] *Am. Sch. of Magnetic Healing* v. *McAnnulty*, 187 U.S. 94, 108 (1902).

[28] *See*, Jaffe, Judicial Control of Administrative Action, at 337–9.

of law were generally reviewable were public land cases.[29] And Justice Peckham, the author of the *McAnnulty* opinion, did not mention that, unlike the case before the Court, all the cited precedents concerned contests *between private parties* litigating title to public lands. Federal officials were not before the courts in the land cases that his opinion cited. The notion that federal courts could directly review administrative action for errors of law in suits for injunctive relief seems to have slipped into the jurisprudence by selective myopia. The Court (consciously or not) failed to notice that the authorities upon which it relied were from quite dissimilar proceedings that therefore did not raise the same separation of powers issue.

Once appellate review was established, a familiar dynamic could emerge. In this now common scenario, administrative agencies make initial adjudicative decisions, and courts review those decisions for errors of law. But because agencies, like courts, must apply law to fact, their ultimate judgments are neither purely factual nor purely legal decisions. Courts claiming to review errors of law must somehow draw a line between law and fact while reviewing decisions that are not pure forms of either.[30] The stage was thus set for courts to address the more fundamental questions of the appropriate relations or roles of courts and agencies when they inhabit the same jurisdictional space – a space composed of mixed questions of law, fact, and policy. The nineteenth century's neat division of labor between courts and agencies had broken down. But, what that meant for judicial review, and in particular for review for reasonableness (or for the adequacy of agency reason-giving), remains to be seen. Here things become somewhat mysterious.

REASONABLENESS REVIEW AND THE APPELLATE MODEL

As long as the bipolar model of judicial review persisted, review for reasonableness (or of the reasoning of administrative agencies) was irrelevant. Courts either decided cases de novo or merely ruled on whether the officer had jurisdiction to act. In mandamus, courts might require officers to carry out a nondiscretionary duty, but the reasonableness of their refusal to act was not part of the case.

Reasonableness review was also unnecessary in the following sense: the bipolar model kept judges from invading the space of administrative discretion. Hence, as Professor Thomas Merrill has emphasized, the nineteenth century judiciary's concern that the judicial process not be "contaminat[ed]" by taking on aspects of administration was easily satisfied.[31] But, when courts began to review administrative

---

[29] *Am. Sch.*, 187 U.S. at 108–09.

[30] Notably, precursors to the law–fact distinction also emerged in Land Office cases. *See* Jerry L. Mashaw, Rethinking Judicial Review of Administrative Action: A Nineteenth Century Perspective, 32 *Cardozo L. Rev.* 2241, 2246 n.19 (2011).

[31] Thomas Merrill, Article III, Agency Adjudication, and the Origins of the Appellate Review Model of Administrative Law, 111 *Colum. L. Rev.* 939, 980 (2011) ("During the earlier era, the primary concern was that Article III courts would be drawn into matters of 'administration' that were not properly

actions in something like the way they reviewed lower-court decisions, some means of distinguishing the judicial function from that of administration was urgently required. This separation of powers concern provides clues for answering two additional questions. First, how did the appellate review model – a model so familiar that twenty-first-century administrative lawyers take it for granted – come to dominate judicial review of administrative action? Second, why has reasonableness, or the adequacy of agency reasons, come to play such an essential role in mediating the court-agency "partnership"?[32]

Professor Merrill has given us the most comprehensive account of the emergence of the appellate model of judicial review in American administrative law.[33] According to his analysis, the critical period lies in the early twentieth century. And the crucial developments involved the Interstate Commerce Commission (ICC).

Under the original Interstate Commerce Act of 1887, the ICC's orders were not self-executing.[34] The Commission had to go to court to seek enforcement, and the courts treated this action as a de novo action in the district court. The district courts took evidence, re-weighed the facts and revisited the Commission's legal conclusions.[35] Viewing these regulatory decisions as a judicial question, the federal courts routinely overturned ICC determinations.[36] The Supreme Court seemed to have a particular lack of respect for the Commission's findings, and its decisions rendered the Commission virtually toothless.[37] Populist outrage at the Court's treatment of the Commission prompted a reconsideration of the respective roles of the Commission and the reviewing courts.[38]

In the congressional debates leading up to the passage of the Hepburn Act of 1906, the role of judicial review was perhaps the most hotly contested issue.[39] Moreover, the question of how the courts were to review the reasonableness of ICC orders was front and center. Everyone apparently agreed that the courts could review for constitutional reasonableness – that is, whether the rates were "confiscatory" (and

---

judicial. In other words, the concern was not dilution of the judicial power but contamination of that power."). I agree with Merrill's account, although the analysis that follows does not exactly track his argument.

[32] *Greater Bos. Television Corp.* v. *FCC*, 444 F.2d 841, 851 (D.C. Cir. 1970) ("[A]gencies and courts together constitute a 'partnership' in furtherance of the public interest ...").

[33] Merrill, Article III, Agency Adjudication.

[34] Ch. 104, § 16, 24 stat. 3769, 384–5

[35] *See e.g., ICC* v. *Cincinnati, New Orleans and Tex. Pac. Ry. Co.*, 167 U.S. 479, 500–1 (1897); *Cincinnati, New Orleans and Tex. Pac. Ry. Co.* v. *ICC*, 162 U.S. 184, 187 (1896); *see also* Stephen Skowronek, *Building a New American State: The Expansion of National Administrative Capacities 1877–1920*, 154–5 (Cambridge University Press, Cambridge, 1982); Merrill, Article III, Agency Adjudication *supra* note 31, at 953–4.

[36] Merrill, Article III, Agency Adjudication *supra* note 31, at 953 (noting "aggressive judicial review of decisions of the ICC").

[37] *See* Robert L. Rabin, Federal Regulation in Historical Perspective, 38 *Stan. L. Rev.* 1189, 1212–15 (1986).

[38] *See* Merrill, The Origins of the American-Style Judicial Review, *supra* note 12, at 394.

[39] Id., at 394–7.

therefore took private property without just compensation as prohibited by the Fifth Amendment to the Constitution).[40] Others wanted to go further to prescribe a judicial review standard that went beyond constitutional minima.[41] For example, Senator Bailey of Texas offered an amendment to the statute that would have provided explicitly both for constitutional review and for an inquiry into whether "the regulation or practices are unjust and unreasonable."[42] Indeed, the final text of the Hepburn Act is replete with variations on the word "reasonable."[43] All of these uses of the word, however, appear in substantive provisions that establish criteria for ICC determinations. Reasonableness does not appear in the final version of the Hepburn Act's judicial review provisions because the statute's final version contains no standard for judicial review at all.[44] Deep disagreements among congressman and senators led to a compromise provision merely providing that ICC orders, "except orders for the payment of money," take effect in not less than thirty days unless they were "suspended or set aside by a court of competent jurisdiction."[45] As Senator Dolliver put the matter, "[N]obody knows exactly what the courts of the United States will do with an order of the Commission ... [A]side from providing the venue of the suits and distinctly providing that the orders of Commission may be set aside or suspended by a court of competent jurisdiction, we said nothing."[46] Nevertheless, the Hepburn Act revision – making ICC orders self-executing unless challenged and overturned – was a major change from prior practice in which courts tried ICC cases de novo.[47]

The Supreme Court got the message that its earlier practice had been much too aggressive. A first harbinger of change was the Supreme Court's decision in *Texas & Pacific Railway Co.* v. *Abilene Cotton Oil Co.*[48] Although that case did not involve the scope of review of ICC determinations, the Supreme Court held that the Interstate Commerce Act preempted all common law actions concerning whether railroad rates were unreasonable or discriminatory. The opinion emphasized that Congress had intended to give the question of the reasonableness of rates to the ICC, not to the courts.[49]

The second shoe dropped in a pair of cases involving the Illinois Central Railroad. *Illinois Central I*[50] is crucial for its treatment of the distinction between questions of

---

[40] Id., at 396.
[41] Ibid.
[42] 40 Cong. Rec. 7025 (statement of Sen. Dolliver) (describing an amendment offered by Senator Bailey) (1906).
[43] E.g., Pub. L. No. 59-337, §§ 1, 2, 4, 34 Stat. 584–5, 588–90 (1906).
[44] Merrill, The Origins of the American-Style Judicial Review, *supra* note 12, at 397.
[45] 34 Stat. at 589.
[46] 40 Cong. Rec. 6778 (1906).
[47] See Merrill, The Origins of the American-Style Judicial Review, *supra* note 12, at 395.
[48] 204 U.S. 426 (1907).
[49] Id., at 441, 448.
[50] *Ill. Cent. R.R. Co.* v. *ICC*, 206 U.S. 441 (1907).

fact and law. Distinguishing away most of its prior jurisprudence on review of ICC determinations, the Court declared that the question of the reasonableness of an ICC-established rate was a question of *fact* not reviewable by the court. In summing up its ruling, the Court said:

> The question submitted to the Commission, as we have said, with tiresome repetition, perhaps, was one which turned on matters of fact. In that question, of course, there were elements of law, but we cannot see that any one of these or any circumstances probative of the conclusion was overlooked or disregarded. The testimony was voluminous. It is not denied that it was conflicting, and, by concession of counsel, it included a large amount of testimony taken on behalf of appellants in support of the propositions contended for by them. Whether the Commission gave too much weight to some parts of it and too little weight to other parts of it is a question of fact, and not of law. It seems from the findings, report, and conclusions of the Commission that it considered every circumstance pertinent to the problem before it.[51]

Two aspects of the *Illinois Central I* opinion were critical for subsequent developments. First, by assigning the question of reasonableness to the facts side of the law-fact distinction, the Court gave up de novo review of the reasonableness of ICC rate orders. Here, the Court beat a strategic retreat from its prior jurisprudence that had created a political firestorm. Second, and equally important, the Court reviewed the ICC determination on the basis of the record before it and perused that record to see whether the ICC had overlooked or disregarded any "circumstance pertinent to the problem before it."[52] Here lie the seeds of reasonableness review in a modern "proceduralized" form. The Court declined to determine the substantive issue or the weight of the evidence. It contented itself with seeing that the ICC had given the issue the consideration necessary to make a reasoned decision.

The emergence of reasonableness review in a proceeding involving the substantive reasonableness of a rate might not appear to be of great significance. But reasonableness as a standard migrated quickly to other areas of ICC action and beyond. Three years after *Illinois Central I*, the Court decided *Illinois Central II*.[53] The latter case involved the ICC's authority under the Hepburn Act to allocate railcars in periods of car shortages. When reviewing the Commission's self-executing order, the Supreme Court described its reviewing power as embracing: (1) "all relevant questions of constitutional power or right," (2) "all pertinent questions as to whether the administrative order is within the scope of the delegated authority," and (3) whether the exercise of authority "has been manifested in such an unreasonable manner

---

51 Id., at 466.
52 Ibid.
53 ICC v. *Ill. Cent. R.R. Co.*, 215 U.S. 452 (1910).

as to cause it" to exceed the scope of delegated authority.[54] The question of legal authority here morphs into a question of that authority's reasonable exercise.

Two years later, in *ICC v. Union Pacific Railroad Co.*,[55] the Court added yet another formulation of reasonableness review – the famous and much-debated "substantial evidence" test. Moreover, in *Union Pacific*, the question for the Court was not so obviously a question of fact. The complaining parties argued that the ICC's application of law to fact was so defective as to amount to reversible error. These "mixed questions of law and fact," the Court said, were "subject to review, but when supported by evidence ... [t]he courts would not examine the facts further than to determine whether there was substantial evidence to sustain the order."[56] Although *Union Pacific* is the first opinion to use the substantial evidence standard in the administrative law context,[57] it was a well-established standard for the review of jury verdicts on appeal from trial courts.[58]

The appellate model of judicial review – entailing: (1) the development of the record in the administrative forum; (2) the scope of judicial review varying with the comparative competencies of the reviewing court or the trier of fact; and (3) the law–fact distinction as the crucial determinate of comparative competence – was well on its way. Various formulations of reasonableness review traveled with it. As Professor Merrill details,[59] although the initial cases all involved the ICC, Congress deployed similar standards when establishing judicial review of decisions by the Federal Trade Commission (FTC), the National Labor Relations Board (NLRB), and other alphabet agencies.[60]

Note, however, that this legislative expansion of the appellate model based on the law–fact distinction said nothing about how that distinction was to be applied. Nor did the statutes contain any particular formulation of the reasonableness standard. Hence, while the appellate model, post-Hepburn, was deployed deferentially with respect to the ICC, it provided the basis for aggressive judicial intervention with respect to FTC determinations of "unfair business practices."

---

[54] Id., at 470.

[55] 222 U.S. 541 (1912).

[56] Id., at 547–8.

[57] E. Blythe Stason, "Substantial Evidence" in Administrative Law, 89 *U. Pa. L. Rev.* 1026, 1040–1 (1941).

[58] Id., at 1042; Robert L. Stern, Review of Findings of Administrators, Judges and Juries: A Comparative Analysis, 58 *Harv. L. Rev.* 70, 73–4 (1944).

[59] *See* Merrill, The Origins of the American-Style Judicial Review *supra* note 12, at 403–8.

[60] Federal Trade Commission Act of 1914, Pub. L. No. 63-203, § 5, 38 Stat. 717, 720 (1914) (establishing that the "findings of the commission as to the facts, if supported by testimony, shall ... be conclusive."); National Labor Relations Act, Pub. L. No. 74-198, § 10(e), 49 Stat. 449, 454 (1935) (establishing the same standard for the NLRB). For other examples, *see* Federal Radio Commission Act, Pub. L. No. 71-494, § 16(d), 46 Stat. 844, 845 (1930); Tariff Act of 1930, Pub. L. No. 71-361, § 337(c), 46 Stat. 590, 704; the Communications Act of 1934, Pub. L. No. 74-416, § 402(e), 48 Stat. 1064, 1094; and the Public Utility Act of 1935, Pub. L. No. 74-333, § 313(b), 49 Stat. 803, 860.

Like the question of whether a rate was "unreasonable," the question under Section 5 of the Federal Trade Commission Act (FTCA) of whether a particular business practice was "an unfair method of competition"[61] involved the application of law to fact. But in its first encounter with the FTCA, the Supreme Court made clear that, in this context, what practices could be described as "unfair methods of competition" was a question of law.[62] The law–fact distinction formally structured review, but it apparently failed to determine its substantive intensity when applied to legal conclusions that were, in reality, mixed questions of law and fact. Everything hinged on how the reviewing court labeled the administrative finding. And here political context was critical. Unfair competition was actionable at common law, but had a narrow scope. The FTCA both "federalized" and broadened this concept where interstate commerce was involved, and put enforcement in a federal agency. But the FTCA did not necessarily reflect congressional unhappiness with judicial application of common law doctrine, as had been the case with judicial treatment of ICC decisions prior to the passage of the Hepburn Act.[63] Hence the courts did not respond by downshifting the intensity of their involvement in determining which practices were "unfair."

The judiciary's approach to review of NLRB determinations reveals a similar contextual dynamic in which a Court–Congress dialogue shapes the intensity of review under a nominally unchanged doctrinal standard. The Supreme Court's initial approach to review under the National Labor Relations Act (NLRA) of 1935 mirrored its post-Hepburn Act approach to ICC orders. In the famous *Hearst* case,[64] the Court confronted the question of whether the NLRB's classification of so called "newsboys" as "employees," rather than as independent contractors, was consistent with the NLRA. Once the Court determined that Congress did not intend to adopt the common law distinction between employees and independent contractors in the NLRA, the Court concluded that the question was one of whether, all things considered, the parties were within the purposes of the Act and required its

---

[61] 38 Stat. at 719.

[62] *FTC v. Gratz*, 253 U.S. 421, 427 (1920) ("The words 'unfair method of competition' are not defined by the statute and their exact meaning is in dispute. It is for the courts, not the commission, ultimately to determine as matter of law what they include."); *see* discussion in Merrill, Article III, Agency Adjudication *supra* note 31, at 970–1; *but see Gratz*, 253 U.S. at 437 (Brandeis, J., dissenting) ("Recognizing that the question whether a method of competitive practice was unfair would ordinarily depend upon special facts, Congress imposed upon the commission the duty of finding the facts, and it declared that findings of fact so made (if duly supported by evidence) were to be taken as final. The question whether the method of competition pursued could, on those facts, reasonably be held by the commission to constitute an unfair method of competition, being a question of law, was necessarily left open to review by the court.").

[63] It did reflect unhappiness with the scope of the Sherman Antitrust Act and, to some degree, the Supreme Court's "Rule of Reason" approach under that statute. *See* Neil W. Averitt, The Meaning of "Unfair Methods of Competition" in Section 5 of the Federal Trade Commission Act, 21 *B.C. L. Rev.* 227, 230 (1980).

[64] *NLRB v. Hearst Publ'ns*, 322 U.S. 111 (1944).

protection.[65] In the majority's view, the everyday experience of the Board in administering the statute gave it special insight into these questions. This was, the Court opined, a case-by-case determination that "belongs to the usual administrative routine" of the Board.[66] Hence, the only question for a court reviewing the Board's employee-status determination was whether that conclusion had "'warrant in the record' and a reasonable basis in law."[67] Indeed, in this articulation of the judicial role, the reasonableness standard seemed to apply to Board determinations of legal questions, including statutory interpretation, as well as to questions of fact.

Hearst almost certainly responded to the widespread unhappiness with pre-NLRA judicial practice that was viewed as anti-union.[68] Congress displaced judicial regulation of labor matters through common and criminal law actions with administrative regulation, and the courts got the message. But by the early 1940s, attitudes toward administrative governance, and New Deal administrative governance in particular, were shifting from support to concern. In a reversal of its ICC experience, this time the Supreme Court's lenient attitude toward the NLRB got it into political difficulties. The Court's approach to substantial evidence in NLRB cases was that the Board should be upheld if there was substantial evidence anywhere in the record for its determination, notwithstanding strong contrary record evidence. This judicial posture was the source of biting criticism and, ultimately, legislative reform.[69]

---

[65] Id., at 129.

[66] Id., at 130.

[67] Id., at 131.

[68] One can see this unhappiness manifested in the 1932 Labor Disputes Act (more commonly known as the Norris-LaGuardia Act), Pub. L. No. 72-65, 47 Stat. 90 (1932) (codified as amended at 29 U.S.C. §§ 101-15 (2012)) The act forbid federal courts from engaging in their prior, pro-employer practice of issuing injunctions against lawful union organizing on the theory that it constituted restraint of trade. *See* ibid., at § 5 ("No court of the United States shall have jurisdiction to issue a restraining order or temporary or permanent injunction upon the ground that any of the persons participating or interested in a labor dispute constitute or are engaged in an unlawful combination or conspiracy because of the doing in concert of the acts enumerated in section 4 of this Act [which describes ordinary-course organizing activity]."); Philip Dray, *There Is Power in a Union: The Epic Story of Labor in America* 417 (Doubleday, New York, NY, 2010).

[69] *See, e.g., Wilson & Co. v. NLRB*, 126 F.2d 114, 117 (7th Cir. 1942) ("We have recognized (or tried to) that [NLRB] findings must be sustained, even when they are contrary to the great weight of the evidence, and we have ignored, or at least endeavored to ignore, the shocking injustices which such findings, opposed to the overwhelming weight of the evidence, produce."); *NLRB v. Standard Oil Co.*, 138 F.2d 885, 887 (2d Cir. 1943) (characterizing NLRB substantial evidence review as, according to Judge Hand, "an abdication of any power of review"); *see also Hearings Before a Subcommittee of the S. Comm. on the Judiciary on S. 674, S. 675, and S. 918, Part 3,* 77th Cong. 1355-56 (1941) (statement of E. Blythe Stason, Dean, University of Michigan Law School) (characterizing the Supreme Court's interpretation of the substantial evidence rule as, in some circumstances, meaning little more than a sort of modified scintilla rule – the rule formerly regarded as sufficient to block a motion for directed jury verdicts). A recent political science account of this period is Joanna Grisinger, *The Unwieldy American State: Administrative Politics since the New Deal* (Cambridge University Press, Cambridge, 2014). An intellectual history of liberal opposition to administrative discretion in the wake of the New Deal is Anne Kornhauser, *Debating the American State: Liberal Anxieties in the New Leviathan: 1930–1970* (University of Pennsylvania Press, 2015).

In both the Administrative Procedure Act (APA) adopted in 1946 and in the 1947 amendments to the NLRA, Congress made clear that substantial evidence was to be determined on the basis of the record as a whole. And once again, the Supreme Court recognized that this legislation was not effecting a mere technical change, but expressed dissatisfaction with the appellate courts' and the Supreme Court's excessive deference to Board determinations.[70] Although the statutory language only spoke to how much of the record a court was to take into account in determining substantial evidence, in the Supreme Court's view, "We should fail in our duty to effectuate the will of Congress if we denied recognition to expressed [c]ongressional disapproval of the finality accorded to Labor Board findings by some decisions of this and lower courts or even of the atmosphere which may have favored those decisions."[71] Whether the weight of the evidence favored the Board's determinations was now said to be a question "which Congress has placed in the keeping of the Courts of Appeals."[72]

Section 706 of the APA – providing the scope of judicial review applicable to all federal agencies – adopted both: (1) the fact–law distinction at the heart of the appellate model of judicial review, and (2) the "arbitrary and capricious" and "substantial evidence" standards by which reasonableness was to be determined.[73] But, given the mushiness and malleability of both the law–fact distinction and the concepts of arbitrariness or substantial evidence, one wonders why this approach was attractive to drafters of a statute that would later take on quasi-constitutional status in the administrative state. One answer may be that the drafters largely were in the business of codifying what they considered to be the existing best practices of both courts and agencies.

Perhaps. But the Attorney General's Committee that oversaw the APA's formulation was hardly blind to the scope of review problems that the contemporary form of the appellate model posed. The Attorney General's Report on Administrative Procedure noted that court decisions suggested a sharp differentiation between questions of law and fact.[74] But it also understood that the distinction was extremely malleable. Indeed the Report here reads like a legal realist treatise. It suggests that different judges were easily capable of conceptualizing the same question as one either of law or fact. The reporters quoted John Dickinson's famous conclusion that the classification of a question as law or fact was simply a means to a judge's

---

[70] *Universal Camera Corp. v. NLRB*, 340 U.S. 474, 477–91 (1951) (describing criticism of substantial evidence review in relation to the legislative history of the relevant statutes).

[71] Id., at 490.

[72] Id., at 491.

[73] 5 U.S.C. § 706(2)(A), (E) (2012); *see* Richard J. Pierce, Jr., *Administrative Law Treatise* §§ 11.2, 11.4 (4th edn., Wolters Kluwer, Austin, TX, 2002).

[74] Att'y Gen's Comm. on Admin. Proc., Final Report of Attorney General's Committee on Administrative Procedure 87–88 (1941) [hereinafter AG Report].

sought-after result.[75] Echoing the *Hearst* case's formulation of the NLRB review standard, the reporters suggested that review for reasonableness applied to questions of law as well as to questions of fact and mixed questions of law and fact. In the Report's words:

> The question of statutory interpretation might be approached by the court de novo and given the answer which the court thinks to be the "right interpretation." Or the court might approach it, somewhat as a question of fact, to ascertain, not the "right interpretation," but only whether the administrative interpretation has substantial support. Certain standards of interpretation guide in that direction. Thus, where the statute is reasonably susceptible of more than one interpretation, the court may accept that of the administrative body. Again, the administrative interpretation is to be given weight – not merely as the opinion of some ... lower tribunal, but as the opinion of the body especially familiar with the problems dealt with by the statute and burdened with the duty of enforcing it.[76]

These words, written in 1941, seem to foreshadow the so-called *Chevron* Doctrine, articulated four decades later, that courts should defer to reasonable agency interpretations of ambiguous statutes.[77] To be sure, with some ingenuity, the *Chevron* approach can be squared with the APA's injunction that courts decide all questions of law, including questions of statutory interpretation.[78] The court need only interpret the statute as delegating the authority to interpret to the administrative agency,[79] subject to review for clear error or arbitrariness.[80]

Chevron has generated its own cottage industry, one might almost say industrial sector, of academic commentary.[81] This scholarship debates wonderfully arcane issues, but we need not pursue those debates further at this stage. The point is merely that by the time of *Chevron* in 1984 – and perhaps even by the time of the APA in 1946 – reasonableness review had not only infiltrated judicial review of findings of

[75] Id., at 88 (quoting John Dickinson, *Administrative Justice and the Supremacy of Law in the United States* 55 (Harvard University Press, Cambridge, MA, 1927)).

[76] Id., at 90–1.

[77] *Chevron U.S.A., Inc. v. Natural Res. Def. Council*, 467 U.S. 837 (1984).

[78] 5 U.S.C. § 706 ("[T]he reviewing court shall decide all relevant questions of law [and] ... interpret ... statutory provisions."). See generally, John Duffy, Administrative Common Law in Judicial Review, 77, 113, *Tex. L. Rev.* (1998).

[79] *Smiley* v. *Citibank (S.D.), N.A.*, 517 U.S. 735, 740–1 (1996) (describing *Chevron* deference as based on "a presumption that Congress, when it left ambiguity in a statute meant for implementation by an agency, understood that the ambiguity would be resolved, first and foremost, by the agency ...")

[80] *But see Perez* v. *Mortgage Bankers Ass'n*, 135 S. Ct. 1199, 1211 (2015) (Scalia, J., concurring in judgment) ("Heedless of the original design of the APA, we have developed an elaborate law of deference to agencies' interpretations of statutes and regulations. Never mentioning § 706's directive that the 'reviewing court ... interpret ... statutory provisions,' we have held that *agencies* may authoritatively resolve ambiguities in statutes.").

[81] *See, e.g.*, Thomas W. Merrill and Kristin E. Hickman, Chevron's Domain, 89 *Geo. L. J.* 833, 834 nn.6–8 (2001); Orin S. Kerr, Shedding Light on Chevron: An Empirical Study of the Chevron Doctrine in the U.S. Courts of Appeals, 15 *Yale J. on Reg.* 1, 3 nn.5–7 (1998).

fact and mixed questions of law and fact, but also questions of law, including questions of statutory interpretation.

Given its well-known vagueness and malleability, why has the appellate review model, with its mushy standards of reasonableness, survived? Professor Merrill suggests that the doctrine's staying power derives precisely from its malleability. In large part, it is a judge-made doctrine, and it leaves judges in the driver's seat.[82] As Dickinson and the Attorney General's Committee recognized, within that model, the judges can speak the language of deference to congressional and administrative policies while overturning decisions with which they seriously disagree.[83] Moreover, it gives the judges cover when the political mood or "atmosphere" changes. As the ICC and NLRB experiences illustrate, it allows the judiciary to remain politically responsive while maintaining its stance as the neutral guardian of the rule of law.[84]

Whatever the true explanation, the appellate model of review and the general triumph of reasonableness standards for exercising that review are surely fellow travelers, even if not linked by some tight conceptual bond. The appellate review model and the fact–law distinction provided a space for reasonableness review that was unavailable in the bipolar model of the nineteenth century. And deployment of some sort of reasonableness standard may have been necessary to bridge the gap between law and fact that inhabits every decision. Whether this law applies to these facts is a question that simply cannot be cabined within the law–fact dichotomy. It is neither, or both, and perhaps the best a court can do is to decide whether the ultimate conclusion is reasonable.

But that raises additional questions. What is built into that judicial determination other than intuition? What are the criteria by which a court decides whether an agency's decision or ultimate conclusion is arbitrary, capricious, without warrant in the record, or lacking in substantial evidence? Without answering that question in some way, courts are hard-pressed to explain how they are not taking over the policy functions of the legislature or the executive when declaring an administrative decision unreasonable or arbitrary. The answer that inhabits much of contemporary American administrative law revolves around a proceduralization of reasonableness review. The basic technique is to translate the question of reasonableness into a question of adequate reason-giving. And, as we shall see, a key change in the prevailing forms of administrative decision-making and the timing of judicial review precipitated this proceduralizing move.

---

[82] Merrill, Article III, Agency Adjudication *supra* note 31, at 997.

[83] AG Report, Final Report of Attorney General's Committee on Administrative Procedure *supra* note 74, at 88.

[84] *See* Merrill, Article III, Agency Adjudication *supra* note 31, at 997–1000.

RULEMAKING AND REASON-GIVING

The special role of reasons and reason-giving in legitimating agency action emerged in the 1970s. It was seemingly prompted by the convergence of several loosely connected developments. One was a general concern that federal administrative agencies were not functioning well. Various causes were offered as grounds for agency dysfunction, ranging from capture by private interests,[85] to the structure of agency legislation, to the lethargy of aging bureaucratic institutions. The federal courts responded both by increasing their vigilance concerning the justifications offered for agency action or inaction[86] and by empowering plaintiffs to seek review through a revision of standing, ripeness, and reviewability doctrines.[87]

These judicial developments coincided with a strategic agency shift of regulatory action from individualized adjudications to generalized rulemaking.[88] To be sure, federal agencies had historically possessed rulemaking authority. But these rules had been adopted largely for the purpose of facilitating the exercise of the agencies' other statutory powers, such as licensing or enforcement, or had been confined to procedural and evidentiary matters.[89] Statutes tended to be self-executing – that is, the implementing agency was not required to make rules before the statute could be enforced. The FTCA, for example prohibited "unfair methods of competition in commerce."[90] The FTC could enforce this prohibition simply by bringing charges against alleged offenders. When it adopted rules, the FTC tended simply to provide advice on how it would exercise its prosecutorial functions.[91] These rules did not demand anything of regulated parties beyond the statutory requirement. They were, instead, "safe harbor rules," advising participants in particular industries that operation in accordance with the rules would insure that their activities did not violate the statute.

---

[85] Louis L. Jaffe, The Administrative Agency and Environmental Control, 20 *Buff. L. Rev.* 231, 235 (1970) (bemoaning that agencies are "unduly responsive to special interests").

[86] *See generally* Sidney A. Shapiro and Richard E. Levy, Heightened Scrutiny of the Fourth Branch: Separation of Powers and the Requirement of Adequate Reasons for Agency Decisions, *Duke L. J.* 387, 1987 (describing the rise of the "rationalist" model in appellate agency view, with its focus on adequate reason giving).

[87] *See* Richard B. Stewart, The Reformation of American Administrative Law, 88 *Harv. L. Rev.* 1667, 1716 (1975) (noting "the expansion of standing to seek judicial review of agency action and the extension of non-constitutional rights to participate in agency proceedings").

[88] *See, e.g., Nat'l Petroleum Refiners Ass'n v. FTC,* 482 F.2d 672 (D.C. Cir. 1973).

[89] *E.g.,* id., at 685.

[90] Federal Trade Commission Act of 1914, Pub. L. No. 63-203, § 5, 38 Stat. 717, 719 (1914). The current codified version of the statutory provision prohibits "[u]nfair methods of competition in or affecting commerce, and unfair or deceptive acts or practices in or affecting commerce." 15 U.S.C. § 45 (2012).

[91] *See* Bernie R. Burrus and Harry Teter, Antitrust: Rulemaking v. Adjudication in the FTC, 54 *Geo. L.J.* 1106, 1121 (1966).

Ratemaking agencies like the ICC or the Federal Power Commission issued accounting rules and rules of procedure,[92] but exercised their coercive powers through licensing and ratemaking – both hybrid forms of adjudication. This was true also of licensing agencies like the FDA.[93] FDA regulations specified what evidence was relevant to a determination that a drug preparation was safe and therefore entitled to be marketed, but the operative standard for obtaining a license was the statutory criterion of the safety of the drug for its intended use.

Under this regime, judicial review of administrative action continued to look much like judicial review of a lower court. Review was of agency adjudication, and the question was whether there was substantial evidence for the agency's findings. The issue before the court usually was not the validity of the agency rules, but whether the agency had properly interpreted and applied the statute. Indeed, some high-volume adjudicatory agencies, like the NLRB, adopted no rules whatsoever.

In the 1960s, this picture began to change. First, some agencies began to adopt rules that had rather clear substantive effects. The FCC, for example, adopted a rule limiting the number of broadcast outlets that a single firm could own. If an applicant revealed that it owned more than the specified number, its request for an additional license would be denied on that ground alone. And the applicant's request for a hearing on the matter, which was a right the Communications Act itself provided, could be denied on the straightforward ground that there were no facts in dispute that the hearing process might illuminate. As was the case in civil litigation, an administrative adjudicator need not hold a hearing if the pleadings and other submissions revealed that there were no contested issues of fact between the parties. Hence, if a disappointed applicant wanted judicial review of the FCC's determination, it was not asking the court to review an adjudicatory record. Rather, it was asking the court to determine whether the FCC had the authority to adopt the rule.[94] The Federal Power Commission,[95] the FTC,[96] and the FDA[97] adopted similar "legislative" rules.

Numerous factors provoked this move from procedural, evidentiary, and safe-harbor rules to legislative rules. Agencies faced criticism of their lackluster regulatory performance, and resource constraints motivated the agencies to attempt to

---

[92] E.g., Uniform System of Accounts Prescribed for Class A and Class B Public Utilities and Licensees, 25 Fed. Reg. 5014 (June 7, 1960) (codified as amended at 18 C.F.R. pt. 101); Interstate Commerce Comm'n, Revised and Amended Rules of Practice in Cases and Proceedings before the Commission (1889).

[93] Thomas W. Merrill and Kathryn Tongue Watts, Agency Rules with the Force of Law: The Original Convention, 116 *Harv. L. Rev.* 467, 558 (2002) ("[F]or thirty years after the adoption of the FDCA the agency made no effort to ... promulgate legislative rules.").

[94] See *U.S. v. Storer Broadcasting Co.*, 351 U.S. 192 (1956) (upholding the FCC's rule limiting the number of FM radio stations and television outlets that a single person or firm could own).

[95] *FPC v. Texaco, Inc.*, 377 U.S. 33 (1964).

[96] *Nat'l Petroleum Refiners Ass'n v. FTC*, 482 F.2d 672 (1973).

[97] *Weinberger v. Hynson, Westcott & Dunning, Inc.*, 412 U.S. 609 (1973).

avoid resource-intensive formal hearings. These critiques of the Progressive and New Deal alphabet agencies' performance had profound effects on the form of new, regulation-enabling legislation as well.

The 1960s and early 1970s saw a massive outpouring of new regulatory legislation. This legislation was strikingly different in form from Progressive and New Deal models. Rather than establishing a broad standard of conduct for an independent commission to police, these statutes tended to create single-headed executive agencies whose primary task was to adopt regulations specifying the conduct that the regulatory legislation required or prohibited.[98] While these statutes had some self-executing provisions, their principle thrust was to empower new agencies to adopt legislative rules. Until those rules were adopted, the legislation had little effect.

Moreover, Congress recognized that it was conferring broad new powers on agencies like the Environmental Protection Agency, the National Highway Traffic Safety Administration, the Consumer Product Safety Commission, and the Occupational Safety and Health Administration. While some agencies, like the Securities and Exchange Commission, had long had legislative rulemaking authority with respect to particular topics, these new agencies were given general rulemaking power under broad legislative standards.[99] Those rules would affect large and important industries and, in some cases, virtually all economic activity. As a consequence, the congressional drafters built numerous accountability mechanisms into these new regulatory regimes. The most important for purposes of this discussion was a common provision that an agency's legislative rules could be tested by judicial review immediately upon their promulgation.[100] In these proceedings courts would not be asked to determine whether an agency had properly applied its statute to the facts of an individual case. Instead, courts would be asked to determine whether the agency's policy choice was one: (1) that the legislation authorized, and (2) that the agency's supplied rationale adequately supported.

---

[98] This was particularly true of the new health and safety regulatory statutes, such as the Clean Water Act, Pub. L. No. 95-217, 91 Stat. 1566 (1977); Consumer Products Safety Act, Pub. L. No. 92-573, § 7(a), 86 Stat. 1207, 1212-13 (1972) (codified as amended at 15 U.S.C. § 2056); Occupational and Safety Health Act of 1970, Pub. L. No. 91-596, § 6(b), 84 Stat. 1590, 1953 (codified as amended at 29 U.S.C. § 655); Clean Air Act, Pub. L. No. 91-604, §§ 108-09 84 Stat. 1676, 1678-79 (1970) (codified as amended at 42 U.S.C. §§ 7408-09); and National Traffic and Motor Vehicle Safety Act, Pub. L. No. 89-563, § 103(a), 80 Stat. 718, 719 (1966) (codified as amended at 49 U.S.C. § 30111). For an extended case study of the development and operation of one such statute, the Motor Vehicle Safety Act, *see* Jerry L. Mashaw and David L. Harfst, *The Struggle for Auto Safety* (Harvard University Press, Cambridge, MA, 1990).

[99] *See, e.g.*, Consumer Products Safety Act, 86 Stat. at 1212 ("The Commission may by rule ... promulgate consumer product safety standards."); Occupational Safety and Health Act of 1970, 84 Stat. at 1953 ("The [Labor] Secretary may by rule promulgate, modify, or revoke any occupational safety or health standard ...").

[100] *E.g.*, National Traffic and Motor Vehicle Safety Act, § 105(a)(1), 80 Stat. at 720 ("[A]ny person who will be adversely affected by such order when it is effective may at any time prior to the sixtieth day after such order is issued file a petition with the United States court of appeals ...").

This new form of proceeding created something of a crisis for the judiciary. Federal courts had managed to preserve the appearance, and often the reality, of keeping their constitutionally required distance from administrative policymaking by manipulation of the law—fact distinction when reviewing agency adjudications. They were now thrust into an entirely new role. The courts were not reviewing an agency adjudication that was similar to a trial court decision. The exercise of agency discretion under review was transparently a question of policy choice. How could the courts determine the reasonableness of agency policies while maintaining their position as simply the monitors of the *lawfulness* of agency actions?

To understand the judiciary's response, we need to remember another aspect of separation of powers in the American legal culture. The constitutional myth is that Congress legislates; agencies merely implement. But broad delegations of authority, like those contained in the 1960s and 1970s health and safety statutes, seemed to demand agency legislation. This delegation was in some sense a reluctant necessity.[101] It was justified by the complexity of the regulatory tasks involved but, nevertheless, adopted against the background of a constitutional culture skeptical of administrative lawmaking. Faced with the requirement that they review these new and powerful forms of agency rulemaking in the abstract, the courts took their legislatively mandated reviewing role seriously. But they encountered some problems.

The first was that in rulemaking there is no record of the type that courts are accustomed to reviewing from trial courts or agency adjudications.[102] All the APA seemed to require of agencies adopting legislative rules was that they provide a "concise general statement of the basis and purpose" of the rules.[103] To review within the standard appellate model, the courts needed more. Judge Carl McGowan articulated — and, in effect, created a solution for — this need in one of the first cases to review a legislative rule under these new statutes.[104] The case involved a National Highway Traffic Administration's rule concerning the provision of head restraints in new automobiles. Judge McGowan said:

> [O]n the occasion of this first challenge to the implementation of the new statute it is appropriate for us to remind the Administrator of the ever present possibility of judicial review, and to caution against an overly literal reading of statutory terms "concise" and "general." These adjectives must be accommodated to the realities of judicial scrutiny, which do not contemplate that the court itself will, by a laborious examination of the record, formulate in the first instance the significant issues faced by the agency and articulate the rationale for their resolution. We do not expect the

---

[101] And for some, a constitutionally problematic one. E.g., *Indus. Union Dep't, AFL-CIO v. Am. Petroleum Inst. (The Benzene case)*, 448 U.S. 607, 685–7 (1980) (Rehnquist, J., concurring in judgment) (arguing rulemaking authority under the OSHA is an unconstitutionally broad delegation of authority).

[102] For general discussion of the problems created by the absence of well-understood record for review, *see* William F. Pedersen, Jr., Formal Records and Informal Rulemaking, 85 *Yale L. J.* 38 (1975).

[103] 5 U.S.C. § 553(c).

[104] *Auto. Parts & Accessories Ass'n v. Boyd*, 407 F.2d 330 (D.C. Cir. 1968).

agency to discuss every item [raised] ... in informal rulemaking. We do expect that, if the judicial review which Congress has thought it important to provide is to be meaningful, the "concise general statement of ... basis and purpose" mandated by [the APA] will enable us to see what major issues of policy were ventilated by the informal proceedings and why the agency reacted to them as it did.[105]

As Judge McGowan's opinion further reveals, the issues of policy "ventilated" in the rulemaking proceeding included objections made by participants in that process.[106] And, if the agency was to demonstrate to the court "why ... it reacted to them as it did,"[107] the rulemaking record must reveal the agency's responses to those issues. In short, the court is not reviewing the agency's policies; it is reviewing the agency's reasons for those policies. The APA requirement that agency action not be "arbitrary" is thus transformed into a requirement that the agency demonstrate an adequate reasoning process. But this does not quite answer the question of why the court is translating a presumably substantive issue of reasonableness or nonarbitrariness into a proceduralized issue of whether the agency has sufficiently revealed the reasons for acting as it did. Why not simply decide whether the court thinks the policy adopted is a reasonable exercise of the agency's regulatory authority?

The answer seems to be that pre-enforcement review compelled reviewing courts to address general policy questions in a context that makes it difficult for the judiciary, or anyone else for that matter, to describe judicial review as merely deciding cases according to law. In a suit to enforce a rule, the claim that the rule was invalid had always been a defense. Thus, when these new statutes moved judicial review from the enforcement stage to review immediately after a rule's adoption, they superficially changed only the usual timing of review. But the consequences of a shift to pre-enforcement review are profound. Affected parties are allowed to go to court without attempting to comply. Hence, review addresses not the particular circumstances of a rule's application, but the abstract legality of its commands. There are no specific facts concerning the effects of the regulation on regulated parties or on the accomplishment of the statutory goals of the regulatory scheme against which to judge the new regulation's reasonableness.

Indeed, put in this way, pre-enforcement review implicates the constitutional justiciability of the issues put before the reviewing court. From *Marbury* v. *Madison*[108] forward, the American legal culture has maintained that courts do not decide abstract issues of law. They declare the law only as a by-product of the adjudication of concrete controversies. To remain in the Motor Vehicle Safety Act context, an enforcement action against a manufacturer for violating a National Highway Traffic Safety Administration (NHTSA) rule is a conventional, concrete case or controversy

[105] Id., at 338.
[106] Ibid.
[107] Ibid.
[108] 5 U.S. (1 Cranch) 137 (1803).

within the meaning of Article III of the Constitution. Adjudication is about individual rights and responsibilities on the basis of particular facts. That a court might need to address the validity of the NHTSA rule would be a mere by-product of the need to determine those individual rights. A manufacturer's suit to invalidate that rule before its effective date on any of multiple grounds – including that the policy chosen was unreasonable – is not a concrete case cast in the same mold.

Without pursuing the dense thicket of federal jurisprudence on justiciability, it is perhaps enough to say that judicial review of this sort of abstract controversy is constitutionally problematic. In order to square the command to decide cases in the abstract with the conventional judicial role of deciding "cases and controversies," courts have been forced to develop a process of review seemingly analogous to the review of adjudications. This translation of rulemaking review into something approximating the appellate model is rhetorically simple, but nevertheless transformative. By analogy to adjudicatory decision-making, rules could be said to be arbitrary in two situations: (1) if they have no adequate factual predicate, i.e., an evidentiary interpretation of the arbitrariness standard, or (2) if they violate existing legal norms, in particular the statute delegating authority to the agency, i.e., a jurisdictional or ultra vires interpretation of arbitrariness. Simple enough, but in the context of rulemaking review, serious problems arise, particularly given the broad language of the statute involved.

For example, the MVSA requires that the NHTSA's rules "meet the need for motor vehicle safety," protect against "unreasonable risks," be "practicable" and "appropriate," and be stated in "objective" terms.[109] All these quoted terms demand policy choices.

Take for example the question of whether a standard adopted by the agency in fact guards against an "unreasonable risk."[110] Presumably the court has to answer this question in order to ensure that the agency is not violating its statute. But how is "unreasonableness" to be judged? On the basis of common law standards of reasonableness?[111] On the basis of some analysis of the magnitude of public health consequences should the agency not act? On the basis of a consideration of the ratio of costs to benefits in providing a new protection to motorists or pedestrians? On the basis of some understanding of current social perceptions of the acceptability of particular risks? Other interpretations are also possible.

The language of the statute does not answer this question. Choosing among possible approaches, however, will have a profound consequence for the policies chosen. If a court chooses a particular construction of "unreasonable risk," it has in a substantial sense chosen the agency's regulatory program. On the other hand, if it

---

[109] National Traffic and Motor Vehicle Safety Act, Pub. L. No. 89-563, § 103(a), 80 Stat. 718, 719 (1966) (codified as amended at 49 U.S.C. § 30111).

[110] 49 U.S.C. § 30102(a)(8).

[111] *E.g.*, Restatement (Second) of Torts § 283 (1965) ("[T]he standard of conduct to which [an actor] must conform to avoid being negligent is that of a reasonable man under like circumstances.")

decides that the agency can choose any interpretation it pleases, judicial review has become a skimpy fig leaf over the naked reality that these statutes make a constitutionally controversial (but almost always permitted) delegation of legislative policy choice to an administrative agency.

To be sure, courts have had difficulty persuading everyone that they are operating in a legal, and not a policy, space when reviewing agency adjudications. In manipulating the law–fact distinction when reviewing adjudicatory actions, however, courts have mostly managed to conceal the difficulty. They are not addressing broad policy issues in the abstract, but an agency application of law to fact in adjudicating some party's rights. If determining those rights demands inquiry into the scope of the agency's statutory authority, that just raises an issue of law. If, on review, the court discovers that the agency is acting outside its powers, the plaintiff wins, but the congressional policy embodied in the statute (as judicially interpreted) remains in place. Alternatively, if the court finds the question falls into the category of "findings of fact," it is simply recognizing that such issues, like the definition of "employee" in the *Hearst* case,[112] are routinely decided in agency adjudicatory proceedings.

In *pre-enforcement* rulemaking review, deft deployment of the law–fact distinction will not so neatly solve the problem. When answering whether an agency rule conforms to its statutory mandate, the statutory norms put at issue are not even remotely like the "ultimate facts" (e.g., these parties are or are not "employees") routinely involved in agency adjudications. Moreover, these statutory norms are not rules of conduct but criteria for agency rulemaking *designed precisely to confer policy discretion on the administrator.* A claim that the court is merely interpreting the law is as superficially implausible as the claim that the question is merely an issue of fact.

These difficulties pushed courts in the direction of developing the "evidentiary" interpretation of arbitrariness, that is, that rules are arbitrary to the extent that they have no adequate factual predicate. Yet, here again, the courts encounter an awkward gap between their traditional reviewing function and their role in the pre-enforcement review of rules. Judicial review of agency adjudications focuses on whether the trial record contains appropriate proof to sustain the findings of fact. But in a rulemaking process there are no obvious boundaries on the rulemaking record, no accepted standards of "proof" for policy judgments, and no procedural vehicles that sharply delineate the "issues" in a rulemaking proceeding. As Judge McGowan noted, the agency is engaged essentially in a legislative activity[113] – an activity that, if carried out by Congress itself, could operate on no evidence at all.[114]

---

[112] *NLRB* v. *Hearst Publ'ns*, 322 U.S. 111 (1944).

[113] Auto. Parts & Accessories Ass'n v. *Boyd*, 407 F.2d 330, 338 (D.C. Cir. 1968) ("The paramount objective is to see whether the agency, given an essentially legislative task to perform, has carried it out in a manner calculated to negate the dangers of arbitrariness and irrationality in the formulation of rules for general application in the future.").

[114] *Nat'l Tire Dealers & Retreaders Ass'n, Inc.* v. *Brinegar*, 491 F.2d 31, 37 (D.C. Cir. 1974).

However, agencies are not legislatures. In many instances, they are substituted for legislatures precisely because a given policy needs to be based on a more expert understanding of the problems addressed than the legislature can muster on its own. Agencies are supposed to get the facts right, and in Judge McGowan's view, provide the reviewing court with a record upon which the court can determine whether the agency has dealt adequately with the issues. His decision creatively transformed the APA informal rulemaking requirement of a "concise statement of ... basis and purpose"[115] into a demand for the presentation of a rule's factual support and policy rationale, including the agency's responses to issues raised by rulemaking participants. These materials can then constitute a "record" from which the court can judge means-end rationality.[116] In this posture, the court seems to be policing for "arbitrariness" in its traditional form, that is, the adequacy of the record to support the agency's conclusions.

So structured, judicial review necessarily transforms the image of rulemaking from a legislative-political endeavor into an analytic-policymaking enterprise. The judicial role is not to remake political choices, but to examine agency reasons for agency choices in the light of an appropriate factual record. This is presumably only a familiar role in a new context. It may not fool the sophisticated regulatory players, but a focus on agency reasons and reason-giving has managed to paper over, or more generously put, harmonize, the competing demands of the constitutional legal culture. Agency rules must be subject to judicial review in order to maintain the rule of law, but courts must stay out of policymaking in order to maintain an appropriate separation of governmental powers. The tension between these competing demands is a problem that can only be managed, not solved. The important point for this analysis is the prominence that managing that problem gives to a judicial focus on agency reasoning.

To be sure, the rise of substantive rulemaking by American administrative agencies in the 1960s and 1970s is hardly a complete explanation for the emphasis in contemporary American administrative law on agency reason-giving. The seeds of reason-giving requirements were planted elsewhere as well. For example, agencies often have only contingent authority to act and their decisions can be reversed for failing to make findings demonstrating that the relevant contingency has occurred.[117] And Kevin Stack has argued that the foundational *Chenery*[118] opinion holding that judicial review must be predicated on the reasons the agency gave for the

---

[115] 5 U.S.C. § 553(c).

[116] It is worth emphasizing just how substantial this transformation is relative to the APA as originally interpreted. Early interpretation explicitly disavowed that the "concise statement" requirement demanded some form of an exclusive record. Dep't of Justice, Attorney General's Manual on the Administrative Procedure Act 31 (1947) ("It is entirely clear, however, that [the APA's informal rulemaking procedures] do[] not require the formulation of rules upon the exclusive basis of any 'record' made in informal rule making proceedings.")

[117] *See Mahler v. Eby*, 264 U.S. 32, 43–5(1924).

[118] *SEC v. Chenery Corp.*, 332 U.S. 194 (1947).

decision, not on any the court might supply, grew out of the constitutional necessity to demonstrate that delegated power was in fact being exercised.[119] Legislative and Executive Branch demands for various forms of analysis prior to agency action have also been a factor. As subsequent chapters will demonstrate, reason-giving as a crucial element of agency legitimacy and accountability is not simply an artifact of pre-enforcement judicial review of agency rules. And the judicial understanding of what constitutes reasoned administration is only one among many perspectives on what reasons and processes of reasoning legitimate administrative actions. But the rise of adequate reason-giving as the modern touchstone of an administrative action's legality owes much to evolving notions of the role of federal courts, which were thrust, somewhat against their will, into pre-enforcement review of federal administrative rulemaking.

The awkward position of federal courts when reviewing agency rules is, of course, only one aspect of the more general problem of administrative legitimacy in a system of government that seems to presume that policy questions will be decided by the political branches, but in which policy choice has steadily migrated toward bureaucratic institutions that are, by design, insulated in various degrees from political control and influence. The proper role of "politics" in administrative decision-making, the democratic pedigree of the American administrative state and continuing anxieties about administrative government are the subjects of the last three chapters of this book. These chapters will argue that the model of reasoned administration that has been worked out over the past five or six decades is more the completion of an attractive model of democratic governance than a normatively problematic betrayal of American democratic aspirations. But to lay the groundwork for that argument we must spend some time looking more closely at what that model of reasoned administration entails, how it is institutionalized, and how the demand for administrative reasons and reasonableness is monitored by both legal and political institutions.

---

[119] Kevin Stack, The Constitutional Foundation of Chenery, 116 *Yale L. J.* 952, 983–5 (2007).

3

Reasons, Reasonableness, and Accountability in American Administrative Law

The Basic Legal Framework

INTRODUCTION

Chapter 2 portrays the historical development of the reasonableness and reason-giving requirements in American administrative law as primarily a function of judicial review and of the changes in reviewing courts' procedural posture as the nature of agency actions shifted over time. In particular, that analysis emphasizes changes from the largely informal administrative decision-making of the nineteenth century, first to the formal adjudicatory functions of many Progressive and New Deal regulatory agencies, and then to the emphasis on rulemaking that inhabits many Great Society regulatory statutes as well as much contemporary legislation. A striking feature of some of Congress' recent and controversial legislation, such as the Dodd-Frank Act[1] and the Affordable Care Act,[2] is the remarkable number of rules[3] that are required to be adopted to make that legislation operational.

But the interaction of agency rulemaking with the appellate model of judicial review – and the associated separation of powers concerns that are the hallmark of those developments – hardly provide the whole story of the legal demands for both reasonableness and reason-giving in American administrative law. Legal demands for administrative reasonableness and reason-giving form a crucial, perhaps *the* crucial, mechanism for making administrators legally and politically accountable.

---

[1] Dodd-Frank Wall Street Reform and Consumer Protection Act, Pub. L. No. 111-203, 124 Stat 1376 (2010).

[2] Patient Protection and Affordable Care Act, Pub. L. No. 111-148, 124 Stat. 119 (2010).

[3] The Dodd-Frank legislation specifically requires the adoption of at least 243 rules. Davis Polk & Wardwell LLP, *Summary of the Dodd-Frank Wall Street Reform and Consumer Protection Act* ii (July 21, 2010), www.davispolk.com/sites/default/files/files/Publication/7084f9fe-6580-413b-b870-b7c025ed2ecf/Preview/PublicationAttachment/1d4495c7-0be0-4e9a-ba77f786fb90464a/070910_Financial_ Reform_Summary.pdf (Last accessed May 25, 2018). On rulemaking requirements under the Affordable Care Act, see Curtis W. Copeland, Cong. Research Serv., R41180, Regulations Pursuant to the Patient Protection and Affordable Care Act (P.L. 111-148) (Apr. 13, 2010), www.ncsl.org/documents/health/Regulations.pdf (Last accessed May 25, 2018).

Accountability here has a broader scope than simple accountability to law enforced through judicial review of administrative action. As I have argued elsewhere,[4] administrators operate within a host of overlapping accountability regimes – regimes that may be characterized or described by asking a series of straightforward questions: who is accountable to whom; about what; when; through what processes; judged by what standards; and with what effects? Demands for substantive reasonableness and appropriate reason-giving are constructed differently in different accountability regimes, but as we shall see, these demands are ubiquitous in American administrative law.

Reason-giving and reasonableness requirements come from multiple sources – the Constitution, congressional statutes, executive orders, and administrative regulations, in addition to the case law of judicial review of administrative action. The content of those requirements are wonderfully heterogeneous. Different agencies, activities, processes, and subject matters impose differing requirements and constraints – both concerning the types of reasons that are acceptable and the level of persuasiveness that those reasons must achieve. The occasions upon which reasons are required and reasonableness can be demanded are many, but not universal. Administrators are humans, and we can hardly be expected to give reasons for everything that we do (or do not do). The question then is for what types of actions, and under which circumstances, must administrators give reasons that will withstand some form of reasonableness test.

This question of which occasions or types of actions give rise to demands for reasons or reasonableness is closely related to the question of when those reasons must be provided and when reasonableness must be demonstrated. As we shall see, the timing of when reasons are given, or are required to be given, may influence our view of their authenticity, our understanding of why reasons are required, and, indeed, the level of persuasiveness that reasons must have in order to pass a reasonableness test. Finally, to understand the law's demands for administrative reasonableness and reason-giving, we must look at the ways in which these demands are enforced. What audiences are targeted by reason-giving requirements? Who may demand that agency action be both reasoned and reasonable? Through what processes are reasons to be tested or reviewed? And what are the effects of the failure to give adequate reasons or to behave reasonably?

These questions about sources, content, occasions, timing, and enforcement are interconnected. We cannot hope to examine exhaustively all the variations on these themes that would fully describe the accountability regimes within which American administrators operate. This chapter will highlight critical questions and significant variations in the legal requirements for reasoned administration. The discussion that

---

[4]   Jerry L. Mashaw, Structuring a "Dense Complexity": Accountability and the Project of Administrative Law, 6 *Issues in Legal Scholarship*, Article 4 (Mar. 2005).

follows attempts only to provide an understanding of the basic architecture of the administrative state's accountability regime and the role of reason-giving and reasonableness in that structure.

SOURCES OF LAW

The sources of legal requirements for reasonableness or reason-giving are as various as all sources of law in the United States. These requirements may emanate from the Constitution, statutes, executive orders, administrative regulation, and, of course, from case law. These sources have been listed essentially in their hierarchical order, in what we might call "the great legal chain of being."[5] Statutes must be in conformity with the Constitution; executive orders and agency rules must conform to both the Constitution and statutory requirements; and so on. Moreover, because there is no federal general common law in the American legal system, the case law's demands for reason-giving and reasonableness are, in a formal (and often a real) sense, interpretations of the requirements of one of these other sources of law.

The courts' strategic position as interpreters of that other law gives them a peculiar importance in determining what the law is – and therefore what "reasoned administration" means in the American administrative system. This chapter will, therefore, focus primarily on important judicial opinions that flesh out administrators' reason-giving responsibilities. However, it is important to remember that many statutory, regulatory, and executive order requirements for reasons or reasonableness are not enforceable in court. In this discussion, I am not equating "legal requirement" or "law" with "judicially enforceable." Accountability for meeting legal requirements of reasonableness or reason-giving can be monitored by other actors – Congress, the Executive Office of the President, the affected public, and other public institutions. I will look more carefully at the influence of these other audiences and monitors of agency performance in Chapter 4 when I take up the question of the effects of various legal requirements on agency structures, processes, and outputs.

This chapter looks briefly at each source of reason-giving requirements to illustrate the variety of reason-based accountability regimes within which American administrators function. It then turns to a more detailed discussion of some significant issues concerning the content, occasions, timing, and enforcement of requirements for reasoned administration.

The Constitution

Article II of the US Constitution specifies the roles of the president and Congress in appointing federal officers; charges the president with seeing that the laws are

---

[5]   *See* Arthur O. Lovejoy, *The Great Chain of Being: A Study of the History of an Idea* (Transaction Press, Piscataway, NJ, 2009) (1936).

"faithfully executed"; and empowers the president to demand reports in writing from department heads. The Constitution is otherwise silent concerning administration other than the provision in Article I[6] giving Congress the authority to provide the necessary legislation and resources to enable other branches to carry out their functions. Federal administrative institutions are created by statute, and only occasionally by executive order in circumstances where the president has independent constitutional, or statutorily delegated, authority to do so.[7] Nevertheless, the Fifth Amendment's Due Process Clause imposes both substantive reasonableness and procedural reason-giving requirements on federal administrative agencies.

On the substantive side, both statutes and administrative acts are – as a constitutional matter – subject to at least a weak form of reasonableness or "non-arbitrariness" constraint. In short, both must bear some reasonable relationship to the pursuit of a public purpose authorized by the Constitution or by statute. To successfully assert that this constitutional requirement has been violated, the claimant is required to demonstrate that no state of affairs can be imagined that would justify the legislature's or the agency's action.[8] Few statutory or administrative acts will fail to satisfy this test.

This weak constitutional constraint on substance – that agency action must bear some relationship to an authorized purpose – is rarely invoked in judicial review of federal administrative agencies.[9] Most agencies are subject to the stronger non-arbitrariness constraints of the Administrative Procedure Act (APA).[10] Moreover, because this sort of claim can often be recharacterized as a claim that the agency has acted in excess of its jurisdiction or has otherwise acted ultra vires, it is seldom necessary to reach the constitutional question.[11] The claim of constitutional arbitrariness,

---

[6] U.S. Const. Art. I, sec. 8.

[7] For instance, presidents have effectively created new administrative agencies pursuant to congressional grants of executive reorganization authority. *See, e.g.*, Barry D. Karl, Executive Reorganization and Presidential Power, 1977 *Sup. Ct. Rev.* 1, 6 (describing President Dwight D. Eisenhower's creation of the Department of Health, Education, and Welfare). President Richard Nixon created the Environmental Protection Agency (EPA) by executive order, pursuant to this reorganizational authority. 5 U.S.C. app., Reorganization Plan No. 3 of 1970 (2012). As decided years later, the legislative veto provisions common in these reorganization acts are unconstitutional. *EEOC v. CBS, Inc.*, 743 F.2d 969, 971 (2d Cir. 1984) (citing *I.N.S. v. Chadha*, 462 U.S. 919 [1983]). Congress has since declined to renew the president's reorganization authority.

[8] *Pac. State Box & Basket Co. v. White*, 296 U.S. 176 (1935).

[9] Indeed, some courts – conflating the constitutional and APA-based review standards somewhat – have concluded that the APA review standard has superseded the more deferential constitutional standard. *Sierra Club v. Peterson*, 185 F.3d 349, 368 (5th Cir. 1999) ("Overton Park ... vastly expanded the range of arbitrary and capricious review under § 706(2)(A). Prior to Overton Park ... arbitrary and capricious review was essentially a carte blanche for agency action. *See, e.g.*, *Pacific States Box & Basket Co. v. White*, 296 U.S. 176, 182 (1935).").

[10] *See* 5 U.S.C. § 706(2)(A).

[11] The Court has recognized this artificial line between jurisdictional and non-jurisdictional claims in its *Chevron* jurisprudence. *City of Arlington v. F.C.C.*, 133 S. Ct. 1863, 1870 (2013). ("[E]very new application of a broad statutory term can be reframed as a questionable extension of the agency's jurisdiction.")

however, can be deployed to obtain a federal court review of state administrative action.[12]

To be sure, there are stronger constitutional reasonableness requirements for administrative actions that impinge on specific constitutional guarantees of individual liberty. Where regulation affects free speech or the free exercise of religion, for example, agencies may be required to demonstrate that they have chosen the least restrictive means for carrying out their statutory responsibilities.[13] The one mention of reasonableness in the US Constitution – the Fourth Amendment's guarantee that persons will be free from unreasonable searches and seizures – has generated its own, somewhat arcane jurisprudence.[14] But these special reasonableness requirements are more properly thought of as a part of American constitutional law, applicable to all public exercises of authority, rather than as specific requirements of American administrative law.

Reason-giving requirements also have been imposed on administrators as an aspect of procedural due process.[15] That constitutional requirement applies, however, only to administrative adjudicatory action where life, liberty, or property interests are determined on the basis of facts relating to particular individuals or firms.[16] In these circumstances, persons adversely affected by administrative action have the right to a hearing that includes certain procedural and evidentiary elements, including that the decision maker provides reasons for its ultimate determination. Quasi-legislative rules of general applicability are not constitutionally required to be adopted after an opportunity for a hearing, nor does the Constitution subject them to any reason-giving requirements.[17]

Statutory Requirements

American administrative agencies are awash in statutory requirements for reason-giving, analysis, and explanation. For purposes of providing a broad view of the landscape, I will divide these statutes into three categories: (i) the requirements of the Federal APA which applies to most agency actions that have legal effects; (ii) framework statutes that require agencies to analyze the particular effects of their actions

---

[12] *See* 28 U.S.C. § 1331 (2012), providing federal court jurisdiction over "federal questions".

[13] *See, e.g.*, Alan O. Sykes, The Least Restrictive Means, 70 *U. Chi. L. Rev.* 403 (2003).

[14] On the jurisprudence of administrative searches see, Jerry L. Mashaw et al., *Administrative Law: The American Public Law System* 839–68 (7th edn. 2014).

[15] Basic requirements for administrative due process are elaborated in *Goldberg* v. *Kelly*, 397 U.S. 254 (1970).

[16] *See, e.g.*, *United States* v. *Fla. E. Coast Ry. Co.*, 410 U.S. 224, 244–6 (1973) (noting constitutional due process distinction between generalized rulemaking and particularized adjudication); *Bd. of Regents of State Colls.* v. *Roth*, 408 U.S. 564 (1972) (denying due process claim because no liberty or property interest was at stake); *Perry* v. *Sindermann*, 408 U.S. 593 (1972) (allowing due process claim to proceed because a constitutionally cognizable property interest may be at issue).

[17] *Compare Londoner* v. *City and Cty. of Denver*, 210 U.S. 373 (1908) *with Bi-Metallic Inv. Co.* v. *State Bd. of Equalization*, 239 U.S. 441 (1915).

that are incidental to carrying out their statutory functions; and (iii) a wide range of specific procedural, substantive, and evidentiary requirements in agencies' organic acts – that is, the statutes that establish them and provide their jurisdictions, powers, and specific procedures.

Provisions of the Federal APA[18] apply to any "authority" of the United States other than Congress and the courts[19] – and by judicial construction, the president.[20] In broad terms, reasons must be provided for any decision made in accordance with the formal adjudicatory processes established by APA Sections 554–7[21] and for rules subject to Section 553.[22] Formal adjudicatory process is required any time a statute specifies that an agency adjudicatory decision be made "on the record after opportunity for an agency hearing."[23] Section 553's rulemaking provisions apply to substantive agency rules of conduct, but not to agency rules of procedure or evidence, or to policy statements or interpretations that do not have the force of law.[24] In addition, the APA's Section 555(e) requires that agencies provide a response to any petition filed in connection with "any agency proceeding."[25] That term is defined to include any agency action that would be characterized as adjudication, rulemaking, licensing, or rate-making.[26] The scope of these provisions is obviously not self-interpreting. Distinguishing, for example, substantive and legislative rules (that are required to be adopted in accordance with Section 553) from policy statements, interpretative rules, and evidentiary (or procedural) rules has given rise to a substantial – and often confusing – jurisprudence.[27]

While the APA's demands for both reason-giving and substantive reasonableness are significant we should be clear that large gaps remain. The exceptions in Section 553 for rules relating to military and foreign affairs,[28] public grants, benefits, and contracts[29] are quite broad. The interpretive rule and policy statement categories

---

[18] 5 U.S.C. §§ 551 et seq.
[19] 5 U.S.C. § 701(b)(1).
[20] *See Franklin v. Massachusetts,* 505 U.S. 788, 800–1 (1992).
[21] 5 U.S.C. §§ 554–7.
[22] Ibid., § 553.
[23] *See* ibid., § 554(a); *United States v. Fla. E. Coast Ry. Co.,* 410 U.S. 224, 234–8 (1973).
[24] 5 U.S.C. § 553(b)(A).
[25] Ibid., § 555(e).
[26] Ibid., § 551(12).
[27] *See, e.g.,* David L. Franklin, *Legislative Rules, Non-Legislative Rules, and the Perils of the Short Cut,* 120 *Yale L. J.* 276, 287–8 (2010).

> [C]ourts have been left to struggle with the task of distinguishing legislative from nonlegislative rules. The most difficult cases … arise when a party asserts that a document promulgated without notice and comment is really a legislative rule and is therefore procedurally invalid. Courts have described the tests that govern these cases as "fuzzy," "tenuous," "blurred," "baffling," and "enshrouded in considerable smog."

> (citations omitted).

[28] 5 U.S.C. § 553(a)(1).
[29] Ibid., § 553(a)(2).

cover a huge range of "guidance" documents that may deal with matters of great national importance. The Department of Homeland Security's (DHS) enforcement guidelines concerning the legal status of certain undocumented immigrants for example, may determine the eligibility of millions of persons to remain in the United States and effectively decide issues of significant policy controversy.[30]

Where Section 553 does not apply, the requirements that outside parties be permitted to participate in rulemaking processes, and that reasons are given for promulgated rules, are inapplicable unless another statute or agency regulation demands them. In addition, agencies invoke the "good cause" exception to Section 553 thousands of times each year for substantive or legislative rules.[31] However, when invoking this exception, agencies must provide reasons why use of the APA rulemaking process is "impracticable, unnecessary, or contrary to the public interest."[32] On judicial review, these excepted rules: (i) must be substantively justified by reasons, assuming the plaintiff challenges these rules as substantively unreasonable under the APA;[33] and (ii) can be attacked on the basis that the "good cause" exception was improperly invoked.[34]

In the APA, substantive reasonableness is treated as an aspect of the scope of judicial review of agency action. As noted in Chapter 2, courts may overturn agency action under the APA because the action is found to be "arbitrary and capricious," not supported by "substantial evidence," and, for good measure, for "abuse of discretion."[35] Inaction may be reviewed for "unreasonabl[e]" delay.[36] Giving content to these standards has been the work of countless judicial decisions and is the focus

---

[30] In 2014, DHS published enforcement guidelines that provided temporary lawful presence for certain undocumented immigrants with lawfully present children – the so-called DAPA program. Memorandum from Jeh Johnson, Sec'y, Dep't of Homeland Sec., to León Rodriguez, Dir., USCIS, et al. (Nov. 20, 2014), www.dhs.gov/sites/default/files/publications/14_1120_memo_deferred_action.pdf (Last accessed May 25, 2018). DHS argued that the DAPA memorandum – though a rule under the APA's capacious definition – constituted a policy statement exempt from the APA's notice-and-comment requirements. For now, DHS has lost that argument. The Fifth Circuit found, at least preliminarily, that the DAPA memorandum is a legislative rule that was improperly excluded from § 553 notice and comment. A shorthanded Supreme Court could not muster a majority on the issue. *See Texas v. United States*, 809 F.3d 134, 171–6 (5th Cir. 2015), *aff'd by an equally divided court*, 136 Sup. Ct. 906 (2016). This technical APA question effectively determines the legal status for as many as 4.3 million undocumented immigrants. Ibid., at 148.

[31] *See* Connor Raso, Agency Avoidance of Rulemaking Procedures, 67 *Admin. L. Rev.* 65, 91–2 (2015) ("Agencies avoided the notice-and-comment process on almost 52% of rules on which final action was taken from 1995 to 2012 ... Good cause was the primary exemption cited by agencies for both major and non-major rules." (citations omitted)).

[32] 5 U.S.C. § 553(b)(B).

[33] *E.g., Haw. Helicopter Operators Ass'n v. FAA*, 51 F.3d 212, 214–16 (9th Cir. 1995); *Buschmann v. Schweiker*, 676 F.2d 352, 355 (9th Cir. 1982).

[34] A litigant can choose to only make this process claim, rather than both the substantive and process claims. *E.g., Nat. Res. Def. Council, Inc. v. Evans*, 316 F.3d 904, 910–12 (9th Cir. 2003).

[35] 5 U.S.C. § 706(2).

[36] Ibid., § 706(1).

of voluminous academic debate. We will have more to say about the content of reasonableness under the APA, and the vexing problem of Section 555(e)'s application to agency inaction.

A second category of statutory legal requirements for reason-giving involves framework statutes that apply, like the APA, to all or most federal administrative agencies. As outlined in Chapter 1, the purpose of these statutes might be described generally as preventing agencies from forgetting that their core missions are not the only values that are of concern to Congress and the public at large. Put slightly differently, these framework statutes are largely what might be described as "anti-tunnelvision" statutes. The National Environmental Policy Act,[37] for example, requires agencies engaged in any major federal action affecting the "quality of the human environment" to analyze those effects in an environmental impact statement.[38] The Regulatory Flexibility Act (RFA)[39] requires agencies issuing regulations that have significant economic effects to analyze the particular effects that their regulations will have on small entities, both public and private. In a somewhat similar vein, the Paperwork Reduction Act[40] requires agencies to analyze the burdens that might attend their proposed recordkeeping and/or reporting requirements, or, indeed, any demand for information.

Finally, virtually every agency operates under organic legislation that imposes specific procedural, substantive, and evidentiary requirements on that agency. This legislation either explicitly or implicitly demands reason-giving. The Securities and Exchange Commission (SEC), for example, must make specific findings concerning the effect of certain of its rules on competition and capital formation.[41] Failure to provide adequate analysis is grounds for invalidation.[42] The Federal Trade Commission is required to make rules under amendments to its original statute that demand evidentiary findings beyond the usual requirements for establishing the factual predicate for general rules.[43] Indeed, because reviewing courts require that agencies explain how they resolve contested issues in either adjudicatory or rulemaking proceedings, virtually any substantive requirement or criterion for agency action provides a basis for requiring explanation. In short, proceduralized rationality review (see Chapter 2) can plug the gaps in the APA's rulemaking requirements so long as judicial review is available.

---

[37] Pub. L. No. 91-190, 83 Stat. 852 (1970) (codified at 42 U.S.C. §§ 4321 et seq.).

[38] Ibid., § 4332(C).

[39] Pub. L. No. 96-354, 94 Stat. 1164 (1980) (codified as amended at 5 U.S.C. §§ 601–12).

[40] Pub. L. No. 96-511, 94 Stat. 2812 (1980) (codified as amended at 44 U.S.C. §§ 3501 et seq.).

[41] 15 U.S.C. §§ 78c(f), 78w(a)(2), 80a–2(c).

[42] *Bus. Roundtable* v. *SEC*, 647 F.3d 1144 (D.C. Cir. 2011).

[43] *E.g.*, Federal Trade Commission Improvements Act of 1980, Pub. L. No. 96-252, § 15, 94 Stat. 374, 388–9 (1980) (codified at 15 U.S.C. § 57b-3[b]); Magnuson-Moss Warranty-Federal Trade Commission Improvement Act, Pub. L. No. 93-637, § 109(A), 88 Stat. 2183, 2189 (1975) (codified at 15 U.S.C. §§ 2309[a]).

For example, the National Traffic and Motor Vehicle Safety Act of 1966[44] requires that the National Highway Traffic Safety Administration make rules that "meet the need for motor vehicle safety,"[45] are stated in "objective terms,"[46] protect against unreasonable risks to vehicle safety, and are "practicable and appropriate" for the types of vehicles to which the rules apply.[47] Contestation about any of these matters will require that the agency explain why it resolved those substantive issues as it did. Statutory criteria for agency action thus become a checklist of the topics about which an agency is expected to make a reasoned decision and provide a reasoned explanation.

Executive Orders

The Constitution charges the president with the responsibility to see "that the Laws be faithfully executed."[48] To the extent not inconsistent with governing statutes, presidents have a longstanding practice of issuing instructions to all members of the Executive Branch concerning various aspects of their implementing functions. Presidential executive orders, proclamations, and memoranda are used for a host of purposes ranging from the trivial (e.g., giving federal employees a half-day off on Christmas Eve)[49] to the momentous (e.g., Abraham Lincoln's Emancipation Proclamation).[50] The ones most pertinent to the current discussion are a series of executive orders dating back to the Jimmy Carter administration that require agencies issuing regulations with major economic significance to provide a regulatory impact analysis of their proposed rules.[51] Over the years, these executive orders on regulatory process have become more and more demanding. The order – in effect as these words are written – requires that agencies whose regulations are likely to impose costs of $100 million per year or more on the national economy investigate: (i) the costs and benefits of the proposed regulation, (ii) the regulation's cost effectiveness by comparison with other potential regulatory actions, (iii) the distributional effects of the costs and benefits to be imposed, and (iv) a series of other factors. These requirements are further explicated by guidance issued by the Office of Information and Regulatory Affairs in the Office of Management and Budget

---

44   Pub. L. No. 89-563, 80 Stat. 718.
45   49 U.S.C. § 30111(a).
46   Ibid.
47   Ibid., § 30111(b)(3).
48   U.S. Const. Art. 2, § 3.
49   Exec. Order No. 13,713, 80 Fed. Reg. 78,117 (Dec. 11, 2015).
50   Proclamation No. 17 (Emancipation Proclamation), 12 Stat. 1268–9 (Jan. 1, 1863).
51   Exec. Order No. 12,866, 58 Fed. Reg. 51,735 (Oct. 4, 1993). President George W. Bush amended that executive order twice. Exec. Order No. 13,422, 72 Fed. Reg. 2763 (Jan. 18, 2007); Exec. Order No. 13,258, 67 Fed. Reg. 9385 (Feb. 26, 2002). President Barack Obama restored the order to its original, Bill Clinton-era text. Exec. Order No. 13,497, 74 Fed. Reg. 6113 (Jan. 30, 2009). The Donald Trump Administration has added some additional deregulatory requirements, but left the basic analytic structure intact. See Exec. Order No. 13,771, 82 Fed. Reg. 9339 (Feb. 3, 2017).

(OMB).[52] Regulatory impact analysis has generated vast literature, much of it elaborating and critiquing the methodology of cost–benefit analysis.[53]

Agency Regulations

Agencies exempt from reason-giving requirements with respect to all (or parts) of their functions may nevertheless impose requirements on themselves by rule. For example, because its rules relate almost exclusively to public benefits matters, the Social Security Administration (SSA) is generally exempt from the rulemaking requirements of APA Section 553, including the requirement that it provide a statement of a rule's basis and purpose. Nevertheless, by rule, the SSA has bound itself to follow Section 553's procedures when adopting substantive rules.[54]

To use a different example, general prosecutors and administrative agencies engaged in enforcement need not explain an exercise of prosecutorial discretion to withhold enforcement,[55] save in those rare instances where statutes demand an explanation for failures to prosecute or engage in some other type of enforcement action. Some agencies, however, have established internal procedures by which complaining parties can contest a failure to act on complaints and, as a by-product of that right to contest, receive reasons for the agency's inaction. The National Labor Relations Board (NLRB), for example, has a formalized appeal procedure within the NLRB General Counsel's office. Complaining parties can seek internal review of the agency's failure to act on a complaint.[56]

Case Law

The case law surrounding reason-giving is not formally an independent source of requirements for reasoned administration.[57] Courts explicate and interpret the

---

[52] Office of Mgmt. & Budget, *Circular* A-4 (Sept. 17, 2003), www.whitehouse.gov/sites/default/files/omb/assets/regulatory_matters_pdf/a-4.pdf (Last accessed May 25, 2018).

[53] *See, e.g.,* Matthew D. Adler and Eric A. Posner, *New Foundations of Cost-Benefit Analysis* (2006); John C. Coates IV, Cost-Benefit Analysis of Financial Regulation: Case Studies and Implications, 124 *Yale L.J.* 882 (2015).

[54] *See,* Administrative Practices and Procedures, 47 Fed. Reg. 26,860 (June 22, 1982); Public Participation in Rulemaking, 36 Fed. Reg. 2532 (Jan. 28, 1971). A number of other agencies have followed suit, as recommended by the Administrative Conference of the United States, a subpart of the Executive Office of the President. ACUS Recommendation No. 16, Recommendations and Reports 29–30 (1970). For a partial list see Mashaw et al., *Administrative Law,* 684–5.

[55] *Heckler* v. *Chaney,* 470 U.S. 821 (1985).

[56] *See* 29 C.F.R. § 102.19 (2016). This internal appeals process has a long history. *See generally* Jonathan B. Rosenblum, A New Look at the General Counsel's Unreviewable Discretion Not to Issue a Complaint under the NLRA, 86 *Yale L.J.* 1349 (1977) (describing and evaluating the history of the General Counsel's role).

[57] *Vt. Yankee Nuclear Power Corp.* v. *Nat. Res. Def. Council, Inc.,* 435 U.S. 519, 541 (1978) ("[A]bsent extraordinary circumstances it is improper for a reviewing court to prescribe the procedural format an agency must follow.").

demands of other sources of those requirements, at least to the extent that particular requirements are subject judicial review. This hardly detracts from the importance of the case law and judicial doctrine elucidating reasonableness, both as a substantive and as a procedural matter. Most statutory and other requirements for reason-giving or reasonableness are vague, often verging on vacuous. The APA tells us nothing about what is required in a rule's "concise general statement of basis and purpose."[58] Similarly, the requirements that agency actions are nonarbitrary, or are sustained by substantial evidence, provide little information concerning either the necessary formal or substantive content of reason-giving and reasonableness.[59] And, the simple availability of judicial review may leverage a demand for reasons in order that judicial review can be both effective and faithful to the limited constitutional role of the judiciary in a system of separated powers. Hence, like the OMB's guidelines on cost–benefit analysis, case law determines much of the scope and content of reason-giving and reasonableness in American administrative law. Here statutory interpretation is difficult to distinguish from federal common law.[60]

THE OCCASIONS FOR REASON-GIVING

The sources of legal requirements for nonarbitrariness and the provision of reasons reveal the legal underpinning for reasonableness requirements. In a formal sense, of course, the necessity for reasons might be said to be that the Constitution, a statute, an executive order, or an agency regulation requires them. But why require reasons? First, a number of requirements for reason-giving and nonarbitrariness are justified as instrumental to the protection of other legal rights – usually the right to a hearing or the right to a judicial review.[61] Often, these two instrumental grounds for reason-giving are combined. Providing reasons for an adjudicatory decision both: (i) establishes a basis for a reviewing court to determine whether the decision is, in fact, based on the hearing record and accords with statutory criteria; and (ii) gives affected parties information necessary to pursue (or decline to pursue) further administrative or judicial processes. The same thing can be said about the rulemaking process. When courts demand more or better reasons for rules, they generally emphasize the necessity for systematic reason-giving as a facilitator of judicial review. However, reasons also inform participants concerning both the agency's understanding of the

---

[58]   5 U.S.C. § 553(c) (2012).

[59]   5 U.S.C. § 706(2)(A), (E).

[60]   *See*, Gillian E. Metzger, Ordinary Administrative Law as Constitutional Common Law, 110 *Colum. L. Rev.* 479, 485 (2010). "Although some administrative law requirements are plainly constitutionally required and others clearly rooted only in statutory or regulatory enactments, a number of basic doctrines occupy a middle ground."

[61]   The United States is not alone in this instrumental approach to reasons requirements. *See* Jerry L. Mashaw, Reasoned Administration: The European Union, the United States, and the Project of Democratic Governance, 76 *Geo. Wash. L. Rev.* 99, 105–12 (2007).

material issues in the rulemaking proceeding and the potential for success of a petition for agency reconsideration or a lawsuit seeking judicial review.

We might generalize by saying that whenever agencies have the authority to make law by substantive rule, or to adjudicate the legal rights of particular parties, they are bound both to act reasonably and to provide reasons. Although this statement is correct, it is insufficiently inclusive. Statutes, executive orders, and agency rules demand reasons in circumstances in which agency decisions do not, in any conventional sense, decide anyone's legal rights or make binding rules of conduct. Judicial review of administrative action is also broader than these two categories of agency decision-making. One of the Supreme Court's most important twentieth-century decisions on the availability of judicial review, *Citizens to Preserve Overton Park* v. *Volpe*,[62] involved a routing decision for interstate highway I-40 in Memphis. Specifically, America's highest court was reviewing whether I-40 could, consistent with federal statutory criteria for roadbuilding, cut through a local park. That routing decision made no law, nor did it determine any legal rights of the plaintiffs. The Court nevertheless rejected the Department of Transportation's (DOT) argument that this sort of managerial decision concerning road building was not subject to judicial review. In the Court's view, judicial review was presumptively available for any agency's final decision, unless there was some reason to believe that Congress had intended to provide the agency with unreviewable discretion.[63] Finding no such intention in the Federal Highway Acts (and finding that the plaintiffs were sufficiently affected to have standing to complain), the Court proceeded to provide judicial review of the decision.

Moreover, the secretary's decision was invalidated essentially on the sole ground that the agency had not provided a contemporaneous explanation of its finding that, in the statute's words, there was no "feasible and prudent alternative" to use of the parkland.[64] The Court was thus not only insistent that these sorts of decisions be reasoned, it rejected the agency's litigation affidavits in an opinion that characterized those documents as "post-hoc rationalizations"[65] that were an insufficient basis for judicial review. The demand was for reasoned administration, not just the ability to produce reasons after the fact.

The case went back to the trial court, where the Administrator of the Federal Aid Highway Program was required to attempt to demonstrate, in a lengthy proceeding, both what the contemporaneous reasoning process was for the contested location decision and why those reasons were sufficient to satisfy the statutory requirements.[66]

[62] 401 U.S. 402 (1971).
[63] Ibid., at 410.
[64] 23 U.S.C. § 138(a).
[65] *Overton Park*, 401 U.S. at 419.
[66] The DOT lost the case on remand. When the DOT cried mercy and decided against the route through the park, the state of Tennessee sued on similar administrative grounds and won. The Sixth Circuit reversed and sided with the beleaguered DOT. *Citizens to Pres. Overton Park, Inc. v. Volpe*, 335 F. Supp. 873 (W.D. Tenn. 1972), *supplemented*, 357 F. Supp. 846 (W.D. Tenn. 1973), *rev'd sub nom. Citizens to Pres. Overton Park, Inc. v. Brinegar*, 494 F.2d 1212 (6th Cir. 1974).

The practical effect of the case, of course, was to instruct the Administrator that if he and other DOT officials did not want to spend long days in trial courts trying to reconstruct the agency's decision process, he would be well advised to document and provide contemporaneous reasons when making these sorts of location decisions.

One might doubt whether any set of reasons provided by an agency (or anyone else) fully exposes the rationale for a decision. Reasons are almost always in some sense post hoc – an attempt to explain a decision after it is made. The stated reasons are unlikely to capture all of the many considerations, large and small, that motivated it.[67] We should note, however, how this requirement of contemporaneous reason-giving in some sense further proceduralizes the reasonableness requirement. The Court seems to be attempting to force agencies to reason within the statute as an integral part of their decision-making process. To comply, agencies will need to structure their internal decision processes in ways that permit ventilation of the relevant considerations and construction of adequate factual predicates for their ultimate decisions.

Providing reasons when issuing a decision may or may not have that desirable effect, but reviewing courts have attempted to make agency processes even more deliberative by pushing back the time at which reasons may be required. It is not just that an agency must, as Judge Carl E. McGowan ruled in the *Automotive Parts* case,[68] provide reasons that reveal how contested issues were resolved. Agencies may also be required to expose their reasoning processes earlier to facilitate participation by parties who have a right to comment on the agency's proposals. In a well-known circuit court case, *United States* v. *Nova Scotia Food Products Corp.*,[69] Judge Murray I. Gurfein invalidated a Food and Drug Administration regulation because the agency's notice of proposed rulemaking had failed to inform parties concerning the scientific methodology by which it proposed to arrive at a final decision. While the court's decision may have been motivated by an underlying suspicion that the rule was substantively unreasonable, at least as applied to the plaintiffs, its explicit rationale was that the plaintiff's right to participate in the rulemaking

---

[67] *See* Karl N. Llewellyn, *The Common Law Tradition: Deciding Appeals* 131 (Boston, Little Brown, 1960) (describing "the horse-sense doubt about how far the postevent document of justification ... can be trusted as evidence of what has gone before"); *see also* James Harvey Robinson, *The Mind in the Making* (Harper and Brothers, NY, 1921).

> Th[e] distinction between "good" and "real" reasons is one of the most clarifying and essential in the whole realm of thought. We can readily give what seem to us "good" reasons for being a Catholic or a Mason, a Republican or a Democrat, an adherent or opponent of the League of Nations. But the "real" reasons are usually on quite a different plane.

[68] *See* discussion in Chapter 2 at 34–35.
[69] 568 F.2d 240 (2d Cir. 1977).

proceeding was fatally impaired by its ignorance about how the agency intended to conduct its scientific analysis.[70]

To be sure, a requirement to reveal reasons, or a proposed reasoning process, as a part of the notice of a proposed rulemaking, is still an example of reason-giving as instrumental to the protection of individual rights. The complaining parties in the *Nova Scotia Food Products* case had a right to participate in the agency's rulemaking proceeding under the Federal APA. Exercising that right implied a right to have adequate notice of relevant facts and methodologies upon which the agency's decision would ultimately be based. Indeed, agencies have been reversed for changing their proposed rules in response to participant comments in ways that the agency's initial notice of proposed rulemaking did not sufficiently contemplate.[71] The rationale in those cases was that the agency's substantial change of course in response to the arguments of outside commentators gave other participants inadequate information upon which to base their comments.[72]

These rationales for reason-giving as instrumental to the protection of legal rights or the facilitation of judicial review do not capture yet another category of reason-giving that is required – even when no one's legal rights are being determined, judicial review is limited, and no law is being made. A prime example here is the RFA. Those analyses have no independent legal effect, they do not determine anyone's legal rights, and no one has any individual, procedural right to participate in developing them. Agencies are required to put together an advisory group of potentially affected parties, but no one has an individual right to inclusion in that group.[73]

To be sure, the common absence of judicial review, or any other monitoring device, concerning agency determinations that RFA analysis is not required may affect agency compliance.[74] Nevertheless, the statutory requirement that agencies explicate how their rules with significant economic impact will affect small entities is clear enough. And where there is external monitoring, as in the OMB review of regulatory impact analyses, compliance is likely to be higher. The critical feature of these cross-cutting analytic requirements, however, is that they are almost wholly procedural. Here, the effort is an attempt to broaden agency reasoning processes to include values or considerations that the statutes for which the agency has principal implementing responsibility do not capture. The idea seems to be that, if agencies can be induced to reason about these matters, they will take them seriously

---

[70] Ibid., at 252. "When the basis for a proposed rule is a scientific decision, the scientific material which is believed to support the rule should be exposed to the view of interested parties for their comment. One cannot ask for comment on a scientific paper without allowing the participants to read the paper."

[71] *Wagner Elec. Corp. v. Volpe*, 466 F.2d 1013 (3d Cir. 1972).

[72] Ibid., at 1019–20.

[73] 5 U.S.C. §§ 609(a), 611 (2012).

[74] Raso, Agency Avoidance of Rulemaking Procedures, 65.

as countervailing considerations when pursuing their basic missions.[75] Save for its role pursuant to the Paperwork Reduction Act,[76] the OMB has no legal authority to impose a different substantive result on a rulemaking agency because it disagrees with the agency's regulatory impact analysis.[77] And other executive monitors – such as the Council on Environmental Quality[78] for environmental impact statements or the Small Business Administration[79] for regulatory flexibility analyses – have even weaker oversight roles. Even under the National Environmental Policy Act, which provides for judicial review of whether an agency has filed the required environmental impact statement and has considered all relevant environmental impacts, the reviewing court is not authorized to consider whether the agency has appropriately factored its environmental impact analysis into its ultimate decision, or, indeed, whether the environmental analysis had any effect on the agency's decision-making at all.[80]

Obviously, a broad range of agency actions carry with them legal requirements for reason-giving, and many of those actions must also satisfy some test of substantive reasonableness. By "substantive reasonableness" I mean that, beyond satisfying the essentially procedural reason-giving requirement that the agency address all relevant issues, the agency must convince the reviewing court that it has not made a decision that is unsupported by the factual record, not committed some clear error of judgment, or abused its discretion. In short, agency action must be both reasoned and reasonable. (We will explore the meaning of reasonableness in more detail in Chapter 5.) But, what about the failure to act? Must agency inaction also be reasoned and reasonable? Or, to put the question in more practical terms: may parties who would be benefited by agency action demand it, with the legal effect that the agency is required to give reasons for its inaction?

In many cases, the answer is easily "yes." Persons or firms who have a right to a license or some public benefit, if they satisfy the relevant statutory criteria, also have a right to agency action where a required action is, as the APA words it, "unreasonably delayed."[81] Whether the delay is reasonable or unreasonable will, absent

---

[75]   For discussion of whether this hope is realized in relation to the National Environmental Policy Act, see Council on Envtl. Quality, *The National Environmental Policy Act: A Study of Its Effectiveness after Twenty-Five Years* (1997), https://ceq.doe.gov/nepa/nepa25fn.pdf (Last accessed May 25, 2018); Eugene Bardach and Lucan Pugliaresi, The Environmental Impact Statement vs. The Real World, *The Pub. Interest* 22 (Fall 1977); and Joseph L. Sax, The (Unhappy) Truth about NEPA, 26 *Okla. L. Rev.* 239 (1973).

[76]   44 U.S.C. § 3508 ("To the extent, if any, that the [OMB] Director determines that the collection of information by an agency is unnecessary for any reason, the agency may not engage in the collection of information.").

[77]   *Envtl. Def. Fund v. Thomas*, 627 F. Supp. 566, 572 (D.D.C. 1986) ("OMB itself admits that it cannot prevent an agency from complying with statutory requirements.").

[78]   42 U.S.C. § 4332(B)–(C).

[79]   5 U.S.C. §§ 602(b), 603(a), 604(a)(3).

[80]   *Marsh v. Or. Nat. Res. Council*, 490 U.S. 360, 371 (1989) ("NEPA does not work by mandating that agencies achieve particular substantive environmental results.").

[81]   5 U.S.C. § 706(1).

an explicit deadline for acting, depend upon the agency's reasons for not acting.[82] Judicial review is also available where agencies fail to use the Section 553 rule-making process by invoking that section's "good cause" exception. On review, the question will be the adequacy of the agency's reasons for avoiding the standard rule-making process.

There are many other situations where agency action would benefit parties, but those parties have no substantive or procedural entitlement to it. The standard cases are those in which someone would benefit by agency enforcement of statutory or regulatory requirements against third parties, or from an agency exercise of its rule-making authority but the agency fails to act after having been petitioned to do so. Should agencies – unlike public prosecutors – be required to justify their failures to act, at least some of the time?

A host of considerations support the immunity of public prosecutors from judicial review for discretionary nonenforcement.[83] Many such prosecutors are elected or are otherwise politically accountable for their actions or inactions. Resource con-straints make it impossible to prosecute all criminal conduct, and revealing prosecu-torial priorities through reason-giving may cause the criminal law to lose much of its in terrorem effect. There are no obviously manageable judicial standards by which to judge whether a prosecutor's allocation of resources is sensible, given the huge number of factors that go into enforcement priorities. Where the underlying reason is lack of sufficient evidence, requiring prosecutors to reveal the weakness of cases might make any judicial decision ordering prosecution self-defeating. Moreover, there are good separation of powers grounds for courts to believe that they have no constitutional authority to force the bringing of lawsuits that they would then adju-dicate. The United States' system of criminal justice is thoroughly adversarial, not inquisitorial. And, even if judges felt that they could provide the remedy requested, there is no obvious way to make the remedy effective. A prosecutor not wishing to prosecute a case need not prosecute it vigorously, and a court has no way to infuse energy into a reluctant prosecutor other than virtually taking over the case itself. The court then becomes a judge in its own cause.

Many of these considerations do not apply to administrative enforcement. At least at the federal level, administrators are not elected. And much administrative enforcement goes forward within administrative adjudicatory fora, not in court. A court order to bring an enforcement action would not, in many cases, produce a lawsuit. On the other hand, the Constitution clearly confers the responsibility to see that the law is faithfully executed on the president and the Executive Branch,

---

[82] *Indep. Min. Co.* v. *Babbitt*, 105 F.3d 502, 505, 507–9 (9th Cir. 1997); *Cutler* v. *Hayes*, 818 F.2d 879, 895 (D.C. Cir. 1987) "Once FDA elected to respond to its legislative directive by establishing the OTC drug review program, the APA imposed an obligation to proceed with reasonable dispatch. We have often intervened to compel an agency unreasonably delaying to speed up its activities, and our authority to do so in appropriate instances is not here in question." (citing 5 U.S.C. § 706[1])

[83] *See, e.g., Inmates of Attica Corr. Facility* v. *Rockefeller*, 477 F.2d 375, 379–83 (2d Cir. 1973).

not the judiciary. Moreover, the problems of manageable standards and remedy are as omnipresent in the administrative enforcement context as they are in trials. For these reasons, there is a general presumption against judicial review where the parties seeking review are attempting to force an administrative enforcement action against particular third parties.[84] Because there is also generally no individual legal right to have a third party made the subject of an administrative enforcement action, there are no procedural rights to a hearing on a request for enforcement. Both of the usual instrumental grounds for requiring administrative reason-giving – protecting individual participation rights and facilitating judicial review – are absent. A few statutes require administrators to investigate complaints and to bring an enforcement action whenever, for example, they have probable cause that a violation has occurred. In these circumstances, denial of a request to prosecute would require a reasoned response, and those reasons would be reviewable for arbitrariness.[85]

Courts have sometimes been willing to provide judicial review where agencies give reasons for failure to enforce that reveal a clear legal error, even though the agency had no obligation to provide reasons in the first place.[86] If courts believe that reason-giving is generally a good thing, even in the absence of a legal requirement to do so, review of voluntary reason-giving in this context may be a strategic blunder. Administrators can avoid review entirely by simply declining to give reasons at all.[87]

There is some suggestion in the jurisprudence that Section 555(e) of the APA might provide a general duty to give reasons pursuant to a petition by any interested party.[88] This would be a bit of a linguistic stretch, given that Section 555(e) seems to speak to petitions in connection with ongoing agency proceedings, not petitions to begin them.[89] Moreover, the practical difficulties with this approach make it rather unattractive as a policy matter. Presumably, were courts to use Section 555(e) as a means for forcing reason-giving in the nonenforcement context, "I do not want to" would not count as giving a reason. Public power is not conferred to enable the exercise of personal preferences. But "resources do not allow prosecution at this time" is good enough on its face. Courts would have no way to challenge that statement without a thorough review of all of the agency's enforcement responsibilities

---

[84]   *Heckler* v. *Chaney*, 470 U.S. 821 (1985).

[85]   *See, e.g., Dunlop* v. *Bachowski*, 421 U.S. 560 (1975).

[86]   *See, S. Cal. Dist. Council* v. *Ordman*, 318 F. Supp. 633 (C.D. Cal. 1970).

[87]   *Compare Med. Comm. for Human Rights* v. *SEC*, 432 F.2d 659 (D.C. Cir. 1970) (reviewing an informal no-action decision, for which the SEC provided reasons) *with Kixmiller* v. *SEC*, 492 F.2d 641 (D.C. Cir. 1974) (refusing to review a similar no-action decision on the basis that, unlike *Medical Committee for Human Rights*, the Commission declined to even consider its staff's no-action decision, whereas the Commission had affirmatively countenanced the no-action decision in *Medical Committee*).

[88]   *Heckler* v. *Chaney*, 470 U.S. 821, 841–2 (1985) (Marshall, J., concurring).

[89]   5 U.S.C. § 555(e) ("Prompt notice shall be given of the denial in whole or in part of a written application, petition, or other request of an interested person made *in connection with any agency proceeding.* Except in affirming a prior denial or when the denial is self-explanatory, the notice shall be accompanied by a brief statement of the grounds for denial.") Emphasis added.

and an assessment of how those responsibilities ought to be carried out in light of always-limited resources. Once again, the problem of unmanageable standards for review intrudes. And if courts are not to go behind the facial reasons provided, using judicial review to force reason-giving becomes something of an empty exercise.

In addition, were courts to take seriously a requirement of reason-giving in every case, including some attempt to see whether the reasons given are substantively reasonable grounds for the agency's decision, courts would go a long way toward allowing petitioners to set agency enforcement priorities. Allowing private parties to seize public enforcement resources to pursue their own private interests hardly seems like a good idea under most circumstances. And agencies might often view honoring the enforcement demands of private petitioners as preferable to using those same resources to defend lawsuits challenging their refusal to enforce.

Congress experimented with something rather like this action-forcing use of Section 555(e) in the original Consumer Product Safety Act.[90] Under that statute, as originally enacted, anyone was allowed to petition the Consumer Product Safety Commission (CPSC) for the adoption of a rule regulating a consumer product safety hazard.[91] If the Commission declined to proceed, reasons were required and the decision was subjected to judicial review.[92] Petitioners quickly seized the Commission's agenda and, pursuant to a petition, the CPSC's first rule dealt with the hazards resulting from swimming pool slides.[93] For swimming pool slides to be the Commission's first priority was bizarre, to put it mildly. To be sure, people can be hurt on swimming pool slides. But, as compared with the detrimental public safety and health potential of chain saws, lawn mowers, lead paint in children's toys, and thousands of other potentially dangerous products, swimming pool slides are pretty insignificant. The legislative mistake was obvious, but operating at its usual glacial pace, Congress took a decade to amend the statute to remove the petitioning process.[94]

Nevertheless, agencies' failure to give a reasoned response to petitions for rulemaking has met with a more generous response from the judiciary than demands that judges review agencies' failure to institute individualized enforcement actions. In the vast majority of cases where petitioners for rulemaking are successful in obtaining a review of agency action, they are successful because Congress has solved the "judicially manageable standards" problem. For example, federal statutes are sprinkled with hundreds of provisions that require regulatory agencies to adopt rules

---

[90] *See generally* Teresa M. Schwartz, The Consumer Product Safety Commission: A Flawed Product of the Consumer Decade, 51 *Geo. Wash. L. Rev.* 32 (1982) describing the failure of the Consumer Product Safety Act's since-repealed public participation provisions.

[91] Ibid., at 45–6.

[92] Ibid., at 46.

[93] Ibid., at 51.

[94] Omnibus Budget Reconciliation Act of 1981, Pub. L. No. 97-35, Title XII, § 1210, 95 Stat. 357, 721 (repealing the Consumer Product Safety Act's § 10, which provided for the public participation discussed in-text).

on particular subject matters within a time certain. The Environmental Protection Agency (EPA) alone has missed hundreds of these deadlines,[95] and a lawsuit by environmentalists demanding that the EPA act is clearly within the APA provision that courts should force agency action that is "unreasonably delayed."[96] Nor, as a practical matter, does the court really have to take on the executive's managerial role of specifying when the agency, now in default, must produce a rule. Courts instead routinely remand the case to the agency so that the plaintiff and the agency can (at least attempt to) establish a timetable, which the court then ratifies.[97] These remedies obviously intrude on agencies' agenda-setting discretion. But Congress, however improvidently, set the agenda by statute.[98]

Statutes may also provide less precise action-forcing obligations. When combined with the APA's Section 555(e), these provisions may provide a court with sufficiently manageable standards for review. But these are much harder cases for courts to adjudicate without interfering in an agency's statutorily conferred discretion to set its own regulatory agenda. In virtually all the cases where judicial review of regulatory inaction is undertaken, prior agency proceedings or factual submissions by the petitioning parties provide a sufficient record upon which to review the agency's refusal or failure to act. Where exercised, this review is generally highly deferential.

The leading case in this area is *Massachusetts v. Environmental Protection Agency.*[99] A group of organizations filed rulemaking petitions with the EPA requesting regulation of greenhouse gas emissions in new motor vehicles pursuant to Section 202 of the Clean Air Act. The EPA requested public comments on this petition and received more than 50,000 responses. It further sought scientific guidance from the National Research Council of the National Academy of Sciences. The EPA ultimately denied the petition and gave two reasons for its decision. One was the purely

---

[95] E.g., Alden F. Abbott, The Case against Federal Statutory and Judicial Deadlines: A Cost-Benefit Appraisal, 39 *Admin. L. Rev.* 171, 181 (1987) (detailing finding that, over the relevant period, "[o]f EPA's approximately 300 deadlines for specific regulatory action ... the agency has met, on time, only 14 percent."); *Public Safeguards Past Due Missed Deadlines Leave Public Unprotected*, Public Citizen 7 (June 2012), www.citizen.org/ documents/public-safeguards-past-due-report.pdf (Last accessed May 25, 2018) (finding that, of EPA's nine rulemakings on the 2011 Unified Agenda with statutory deadlines, only one met its deadline); Chris Mooney, EPA Says It Will Get Back on Schedule in Issuing Rules for Biofuels, *Wash. Post* (Apr. 10, 2015), www.washington post.com/ news/energy-environment/wp/2015/04/10/epa-says-it-will-get-back-on-schedule-in-issuing-rules-for-biofuels/?utm_term=.boae84034cb9 (Last accessed May 25, 2018); Ayesha Rascoe, U.S. Green Groups Sue EPA over Missed Clean Air Act Deadlines, *Reuters Legal* (Apr. 10, 2015).

[96] See, e.g., *Envtl. Def. Fund v. Thomas*, 627 F. Supp. 566 (D.D.C. 1986).

[97] E.g., *Alaska Ctr. for the Env't v. Reilly*, 762 F. Supp. 1422, 1429 (W.D. Wash. 1991). *But see Am. Lung Ass'n v. Browner*, 884 F. Supp. 345, 348–9 (D. Ariz. 1994) (showing the district court determining the specific schedule for EPA's rulemaking process).

[98] See *Nat. Res. Def. Council, Inc. v. Train*, 510 F.2d 692, 713 (D.C. Cir. 1974) ("A federal equity court may exercise its discretion to give or withhold its mandate in furtherance of the public interest, including specifically the interest in effectuating the congressional objective incorporated in regulatory legislation.").

[99] 549 U.S. 497 (2007).

legal conclusion that the Clean Air Act did not give the agency authority to regulate matters that addressed global climate change; the other was a more policy-oriented rationale – i.e., that such regulation, even if the agency had jurisdiction, would be "unwise" at the present time.[100]

When reviewing the EPA's reasons, the Supreme Court sharply distinguished between petitions for individual enforcement actions, not generally subject to judicial review, and petitions for rulemaking. Quoting a prominent circuit court opinion, *American Horse Protection Ass'n* v. *Lyng*,[101] the Court distinguished rulemaking from enforcement on the grounds that "refusals to initiate rulemaking are 'less frequent, more apt to involve legal as opposed to factual analysis, and subject to special formalities, including a public explanation.'"[102] Of course, since the EPA had given extensive reasons for the denial of the petition, the question of whether Section 555(e) actually provided a right to reasons in the absence of ongoing agency process was not really involved. Moreover, because the agency had initiated a comment process that might lead to the adoption of a rule, the petition was arguably "in connection with" an ongoing agency rulemaking process.[103]

Indeed, in most of the cases where one finds courts reviewing an agency's failure to regulate, the courts do not demand reasons, but rather review their adequacy. In *AHPA* v. *Lyng* itself, for example, the petition was to amend an existing rule that the agency had previously described as tentative and subject to revision after further investigation.[104] That investigation had been conducted, the agency had held meetings and conferences to discuss the results, and the agency had drafted new regulations while noting the apparent inconsistency of the current regulation with both the statute and the post-regulation research.[105] Finding that a limited form of judicial review was appropriate in these circumstances, and that the reasons given for the agency's denial of the petition were insufficient, the reviewing court nevertheless contented itself with a simple remand to the agency for further explanation of why its rulemaking process had been aborted. In short, while courts are clearly uncomfortable with unreasoned inaction, their review almost uniformly occurs in situations in which some considerable action has been taken and reasons have been given for not proceeding further. The remedy is almost always a remand for further explanation.[106]

---

[100] Ibid., at 511.

[101] 812 F.2d 1 (D.C. Cir. 1987).

[102] *Massachusetts*, 549 U.S. at 527 (quoting *American Horse Protection*, 812 F.2d at 4) (citing 5 U.S.C. § 555(e)).

[103] 5 U.S.C. § 555(e).

[104] *American Horse Protection*, 812 F.2d at 2.

[105] Ibid., at 2–3.

[106] *See* ibid., at 7 ("The Association seeks an order directing the Secretary to institute rulemaking proceedings. Our cases make clear, however, that such a remedy is appropriate only in the rarest and most compelling of circumstances." (citations omitted)).

Whatever the good sense of limited judicial review of an agency's regulatory agenda or enforcement priorities, the lack of enforceable demands for reasoned administration in these contexts remains troublesome. If the processes of American administrative agencies are to have a legitimate democratic pedigree, they need (see Chapter 7), a plausible attachment to either electoral or deliberative democratic processes. But neither seems to be in play in agency agenda setting, which is rarely subject either to presidential direction, statutory guidance or to other standard processes of citizen participation and reasoned explanation.

Plaintiffs have occasionally convinced courts to review agency inaction for which no reasons were given by convincing the court that the failure to respond to a call for action was tantamount to an action, and therefore subject to review.[107] This stratagem, where successful, converts inaction into an action that has been taken without giving any reasons at all. Having reached the finding that the court has been presented with a reviewable action, but that it has no agency rationale upon which to base its review, the courts do the expected. They remand the case to the agency for articulation of its grounds for refusal of the petition.[108] The question, then, is against what standards the court is to judge the agency's ultimate response? Indeed, this question inheres in all judicial review of whether an agency has met its legal obligation to give reasons. If reasons are required, by what criteria are they to be adjudged adequate or "reasonable"?

REASONABLE REASONS

The demand that administrators act reasonably and give reasons for their actions needs further elaboration if we are to understand exactly what sorts of constraints these legal requirements place on administrative decision-making. Looking generally at the jurisprudence on what this study is calling "reasoned administration," reviewing courts seem to have built an implicit model of administrative rationality that proceeds in at least four steps. First, administrators must demonstrate that they have properly understood the goal or goals that they are meant to pursue – improved public health through the reduction of air pollution, safer motor vehicles or work places, the prevention of the marketing of unsafe or ineffective drug preparations, and so on. Second, administrators need to demonstrate that they have grasped the current state of the world and the degree to which the current situation diverges from the results that the agency is meant to achieve. The EPA, for example, cannot reasonably act to regulate the allowable concentrations of some air pollutant without understanding how that pollutant affects the public's health or welfare – the environmental protection goals EPA is charged with pursuing.

---

[107] *See, e.g., Envtl. Def. Fund v. Ruckelshaus*, 439 F.2d 584 (D.C. Cir. 1971).
[108] E.g., ibid., at 596.

Third, administrators must craft adjudicatory decisions or quasi-legislative rules that conform to the relevant criteria for action specified in their enabling legislation. For example, the Social Security Disability Insurance Program (SSDI) is meant to provide income for workers who become unable to work. That is the statute's broad purpose or goal. But when adjudicating a claim for Social Security Disability benefits, the Social Security Administration must find that specific statutory criteria are met – that the claimant has a clinically determinable impairment, that that impairment will last for at least twelve months, and that the impairment prevents the claimant, given the claimant's age, education, and work experience, from performing any job available in reasonable numbers in the national economy.[109] If the agency fails to find any of those things, an award of benefits should not be made.

Fourth and finally, agencies need to provide a rationale for their decisions that demonstrates that their actions promote the goals of the statute, are based on reasonable factual premises, and have been made within the relevant constraints that bind the agencies' rulemaking or adjudicatory responsibilities.

Many of the most prominent Supreme Court cases could be understood as elaborating this four-step model of administrative rationality. Consider first an agency's goal or mission. The Food and Drug Administration (FDA) is given the responsibility of insuring that all drugs or medical devices marketed in interstate commerce are safe and effective. Under the Federal Food, Drug and Cosmetic Act (FDCA), the definitions of drugs and devices are in essential respects identical. A product is a drug or device if it is "intended to affect the structure or any function of the body of man or other animals."[110] After many years of internal debate, the FDA, during the Clinton administration, adopted regulations concerning the marketing of tobacco products.[111] Its justification for asserting jurisdiction to regulate those products as a "drug" under the FDCA was straightforward: nicotine in cigarettes has pharmacological effects on the human body. Smokers desire those effects. Tobacco products are a means of delivering nicotine to smokers. And cigarette companies market their tobacco products with the intention of creating the pharmacological effects that smokers desire.[112]

In *FDA v. Brown & Williamson Tobacco Corp.*,[113] the Supreme Court found (in a 5:4 split) that the agency had misunderstood its drug and device regulatory mission as applied to tobacco products. As the Court majority saw the matter, the FDA had failed to read its statute within the context of other legislation that specifically

---

[109] The standards for disability determinations under the Social Security Disability Insurance Program and the Supplemental Security Income Program are codified at 42 U.S.C. §§ 401–33, 1381–3f.

[110] 21 U.S.C. § 321(g)(1), (h)(3).

[111] Regulations Restricting the Sale and Distribution of Cigarettes and Smokeless Tobacco to Protect Children and Adolescents, 61 Fed. Reg. 44,396 (Aug. 28, 1996).

[112] *See* Nicotine in Cigarettes and Smokeless Tobacco Is a Drug and These Products Are Nicotine Delivery Devices under the Federal Food, Drug, and Cosmetic Act: Jurisdictional Determination, 61 Fed. Reg. 44,619 (Aug. 28, 1996).

[113] 529 U.S. 120 (2000).

related to tobacco products. Because the FDA would be unable to find that tobacco products were safe under its statute, its regulatory posture should be to ban tobacco products from the market.[114] But, other specific legislation governing the marketing of tobacco – for example, imposing distinctive labeling and advertising restrictions on cigarettes[115] – clearly revealed a congressional presupposition that tobacco products would continue to be marketed. Hence, while looking at the FDCA alone one might conclude that tobacco products were drugs or devices, a broader understanding of the legislative landscape convinced the Supreme Court majority that Congress could not reasonably have intended to include tobacco products in those categories.

Massachusetts v. *Environmental Protection Agency*[116] reveals that agencies may also misunderstand their statutory authority precisely by taking the broad approach to legislative interpretation that the *Brown and Williamson* case seemed to require. This case involved review of a petition asking the EPA to regulate greenhouse gas emissions from new motor vehicles under the Clean Air Act. The agency declined to do so in part on the ground that it did not have authority under that Act to issue mandatory regulations to address greenhouse gases and global climate change. The EPA recognized that greenhouse gases might easily fit the capacious definition of "air pollutant" under the statute, which includes "any air pollution agent or combination of such agents, including any physical, [or] chemical ... substance or matter which is emitted into or otherwise enters the ambient air."[117] However, the agency believed that Congress understood the "air" to be protected as air in the United States, not the global atmosphere. Global warming or climate change was simply not on the legislative agenda when the Clean Air Act was adopted. Moreover, subsequent legislation had both provided funds for (and required inter-agency cooperation in) research about global climate change.[118] Yet, Congress had declined to pass any specific regulatory legislation addressing these matters. Finally, so far as the agency could determine, the only way to reduce greenhouse gases from new motor vehicles was through fuel efficiency standards. But that job had already been assigned to the National Highway Traffic Safety Administration.[119]

The Supreme Court, again 5:4, disagreed. In the majority's view, the sweeping language in the Clean Air Act meant what it said. An air pollutant was any substance entering the ambient air. All such pollutants were covered by Section 202 of the Act.[120] The majority viewed the EPA's invocation of *Brown and Williamson* as inapposite. Here, EPA regulation of greenhouse gases would not in any way require

---

[114] Ibid., at 137.
[115] E.g., Federal Cigarette Labelling and Advertising Act, Pub. L. No. 89-92, 79 Stat. 282 (1965).
[116] 549 U.S. 497 (2007).
[117] 42 U.S.C. § 7602(g).
[118] *Massachusetts*, 549 U.S. at 529–30.
[119] Ibid., at 513.
[120] Ibid., at 528–30.

that they be eliminated. And limitations on these pollutants would not be inconsistent with other governing legislation.[121] That another agency had responsibility for setting fuel economy standards, which might provide one technique for regulating greenhouse gases, did not, in the majority's view, imply any lessening of the EPA's responsibilities to carry out its own regulatory mission.[122]

While *Brown and Williamson* and *Massachusetts* v. *EPA* emphasize different approaches to statutory interpretation – one highly contextual, the other highly textual – they are unified in according little, if any, deference to the respective agencies' views of their legislative mandates.[123] Both agencies had given extensive reasons for their interpretive beliefs. But, while the Supreme Court has been clear that agencies should be accorded deference in interpreting their own jurisdictions under ambiguous or vague statutory mandates,[124] the Court did not find ambiguity in either of these cases. In each case, a majority of the Court simply thought that the statute was clear. When a court takes this approach to statutory interpretation, an agency's reasons must be persuasive in order to be reasonable. In this context, "reasonable" means "correct," as judicially understood. Moreover, issues of statutory interpretation may lie just beneath the surface when a court faults an agency for other aspects of its reasoning process.

Consider the agency's finding of facts concerning whether the current state of the world justifies using its statutory authority. In the *Overton Park* case discussed above, when the Supreme Court found fault with the DOT's explanation for why there were no feasible or prudent alternatives to the taking of a park's land, it did so after providing an interpretation of "prudent"[125] (avoiding the use of parklands save where doing so was "uniquely difficult") that almost certainly came as a surprise to the agency.[126] There were no adequate findings of fact directed to that standard because the agency had not understood "prudent" to be such a limiting concept.[127]

A similar but perhaps a more dramatic example involved the Court's treatment of an Occupational Safety and Health Administration (OSHA) rule concerning workers' exposure to benzene. In explaining why it was reducing the previous exposure level of ten parts per million benzene molecules in the ambient air to one part per million, OSHA provided the following account: Benzene had been determined to be a carcinogen. There was no known exposure threshold for benzene's carcinogenic affects. Hence, any level of exposure to benzene might induce cancer in some workers. The Occupational Safety and Health Act required the agency, when

[121] Ibid., at 530–1.
[122] Ibid., at 531–2.
[123] *But see City of Arlington* v. *FCC*, 133 S.Ct. 1863 (2013) (giving *Chevron* deference to an agency's determination of its own jurisdiction).
[124] Ibid.
[125] 23 U.S.C. § 138(a).
[126] 401 U.S. at 411–16.
[127] 23 U.S.C. § 138(a).

regulating toxic chemical exposures, to protect workers from any significant health hazards even if they were exposed to such a hazard for their whole working lives. The only limitation on that strict standard was that the agency find that the exposure level that it required was technologically and economically feasible. The agency found that the one part per million standard satisfied that criterion.[128]

On judicial review the Supreme Court, in *Industrial Union Department* v. *American Petroleum Institute*,[129] found that OSHA had failed to establish a sufficient factual predicate for its benzene standard. The statute defined an occupational safety and health standard as something that was "reasonably necessary or appropriate to provide safe or healthful employment and places of employment."[130] The Court characterized this definition as requiring that the agency regulate only "significant risks" to worker health or safety.[131] And, although OSHA had provided an extensive analysis of the scientific literature concerning benzene exposures, nothing in that literature demonstrated whether exposure to benzene below ten parts per million had any substantial health effects.[132] In short, there was a critical gap in the agency's reasoning process. The Court was unwilling to allow OSHA to rely on the theoretical possibility of negative health effects just because there was no known threshold for the carcinogenic effects of benzene exposure.

Agency reasoning may also fail by omitting consideration of some relevant fact or by failing to reason persuasively from the facts that the agency has considered. In *Motor Vehicle Manufacturers Ass'n of the United States* v. *State Farm Mutual Automobile Insurance Co.*,[133] the Supreme Court was reviewing a decision by the National Highway Traffic Administration (NHTSA) to rescind its passive restraints rule. Pursuant to that rule, automobile manufacturers were required to equip new vehicles with passenger passive restraint systems that would protect vehicle occupants under specified accident conditions.[134] Any one of several technologies might satisfy the performance standards that the rule prescribed. Automatic lap and shoulder belts, passive interiors, and air bags were all viable alternatives. Virtually all automobile manufacturers informed the agency that they would choose to equip their vehicles with automatic belts, but that, because of passenger concerns about being trapped by belts in a burning vehicle, these automatic belts would be equipped with a release buckle that would permit easy egress from the vehicle.[135]

According to the agency's rationale for rescinding the rule, the manufacturers' choices made it impossible to determine that the rule would provide any significant

---

[128] Occupational Exposure to Benzene, 43 Fed. Reg. 5918 (Feb. 10, 1978).
[129] (*The Benzene Case*), 448 U.S. 607 (1980).
[130] 29 U.S.C. § 652(8).
[131] *The Benzene* case, 448 U.S at 641.
[132] Ibid., at 633–4.
[133] 463 U.S. 29 (1983).
[134] Ibid., at 34.
[135] Federal Motor Vehicle Safety Standards; Occupant Crash Protection, 46 Fed. Reg. 53,419, 53,428 (October 29, 1981).

safety benefits to vehicle occupants.[136] The agency had reliable evidence that automobile passengers routinely failed to use the manual lap and shoulder belts with which all motor vehicles were then equipped. Once the automatic belt was unbuckled, it became, in essence, a manual belt. The agency had no persuasive evidence of how consumers would react to the automatic belt systems. But, if they unbuckled them and made them into manual belts, no safety benefits would be obtained over the status quo, but at considerable cost to car buyers.

The Supreme Court viewed this reasoning as inadequate. While the statute required the agency to regulate in terms of performance rather than design standards, nothing in the statute required the agency to allow manufacturers to use technologies that vehicle owners or passengers could easily defeat. The agency had extensive evidence demonstrating the feasibility and safety effectiveness of air bag technology.[137] And, because air bags were built into the vehicles and were invisible until deployed, there would be no reason to predict that vehicle owners would attempt to defeat the air bag. Why had the agency not considered a performance standard that required an essentially non-defeasible technology? Nothing in the agency's analysis answered that question.[138] As Justice Byron R. White put it in the majority opinion, "[n]ot having discussed" retaining the air bag alternative rather than rescinding the whole rule, the agency had given "no reason at all" for its choice.[139] An unreasoned choice is arbitrary on that ground alone.

The *State Farm* majority also faulted the agency on two other aspects of its reasoning process. Automatic belts did not have to be detachable. A technology called a "continuous, spool-out" belt allowed ingress and egress from the vehicle by simply pulling on the belt to take slack off the spool mechanism.[140] General Motors had done tests and had informed the agency that escape from the continuous spool belt was no more difficult than escape from a detachable belt.[141] Once again, the agency had failed to explain why it did not simply exclude detachable belts but still continue with regulations that could be satisfied with the continuous spool technology.[142] Finally, the majority faulted the agency's reasoning with respect to detachable belts themselves. The agency's analysis noted that, once detached, the automatic belt became a manual belt. Inertia, which the agency had found to be a major factor in the failure of motorists' use of manual belts, would likely cause consumers to detach automatic belts permanently. Hence, NHTSA reasoned, requiring detachable belts might add no safety benefits.

[136] Ibid., at 53,420–2.
[137] *State Farm*, 463 U.S. at 46–8.
[138] Ibid., at 48 ("Not one sentence of its rulemaking statement discusses the airbags-only option.").
[139] Ibid., at 50.
[140] Ibid., at 55.
[141] Ibid., at 56.
[142] Ibid., at 55–7.

But, the majority asked, why would inertia not operate in favor of the belts remaining in their automatic mode if they were ever reattached?[143] After all, the agency had plenty of evidence that most motorists used their belts at least some of the time. The agency had failed to explain why it believed that motorist inertia operated in only one direction. The Court was clear that, after further consideration, the agency could, in a well-reasoned decision, find that the benefits of passive restraints remained too uncertain to justify their cost.[144] But the agency was not going to be allowed to simply invoke "substantial uncertainty"[145] as a ground for rescinding the rule.

Note that, in both the *Overton Park* and the *Benzene* cases, agencies had failed to make findings regarding material facts because they had failed to anticipate the courts' interpretations of their statutes – interpretations that made new factors relevant. The failure to consider relevant factors was somewhat different in *State Farm*, but nevertheless implicated the statute. There, the Court looked carefully at the facts before the agency and the policy alternatives that might have been chosen and demanded, "Why not?" Being reasonable, in the form of considering the "relevant factors,"[146] seems to have required that the agency discuss roads not taken. And those roads were made relevant by the Court's understanding of the overarching goal of the Motor Vehicle Safety Act, to "meet the need for motor vehicle safety."[147]

The Supreme Court's careful parsing of NHTSA's reasoning process in the *State Farm* case may have been motivated in part by a suspicion that the agency's reasons simply pulled a thin technological veneer over a political decision. The Reagan administration had been elected in part on promises to provide regulatory relief to the automobile industry, among others. Rescission of the passive restraints rule seemed to be at least as much the keeping of political promises as an engagement in serious regulatory analysis. While agreeing with the majority's analysis of the agency's consideration of air bags and continuous, spool-out technologies, Justice Rehnquist, writing for himself and three other justices, went out of his way to indicate that a change of administration was a perfectly reasonable basis for an executive agency to reappraise previous policy choices. Politics alone may not be enough to justify administrative decision-making, but according to Justice Rehnquist, agencies are "entitled to assess administrative records and evaluate priorities in light of the philosophy of the administration."[148]

Massachusetts v. *EPA* might have involved a similar judicial concern. The George W. Bush administration was clearly not enthusiastic about initiating climate change regulation pursuant to the Clean Air Act. As in *State Farm*, some members of the

[143] Ibid., at 53–4.
[144] Ibid., at 57.
[145] Ibid., at 52.
[146] Ibid., at 55 (quoting H.R. Rep. No. 89-1776, at 16 (1966)).
[147] Ibid., at 33 (quoting 15 U.S.C. § 1392[a]).
[148] Ibid., at 59 (Rehnquist, J., concurring in part and dissenting in part).

Supreme Court may well have suspected that they were reviewing a decision based on the administration's policy priorities rather than on the considered judgment of the agency charged with administering the statute. Chapter 6 will take a closer look at the issue of politics, or "political reason," in reasoned administration. As we shall see, that issue is closely related to the issue of agencies' discretion to set their own agendas and to the more fundamental question of how reasoned administration should approach issues of vague or multiple and conflicting statutory goals and the problem of political compromise.

Just as failure to consider relevant matters may render an agency's decision-making insufficiently reasoned, so may the consideration of matters that a court finds should play no part in the agency's decision process. The poster child for this proposition is a case that arose in the District of Columbia concerning the building of a highway bridge over the Potomac River.[149] The Secretary of Transportation had approved a route over the river near some small islands that were known locally as the Three Sisters. In announcing his decision, the Secretary revealed that he was not convinced that the bridge was needed in that location but that he was approving the project on the basis of more general considerations about the District of Columbia transportation system. In particular, the Secretary revealed that a substantial part of his thinking was influenced by Representative William H. Natcher, then the head of the Appropriations Subcommittee for the District of Columbia. Congressman Natcher was a great proponent of the Three Sisters Bridge, and he had publicly announced that he would never approve funding for a proposed subway system in the District of Columbia until the Three Sisters project was underway. In the Secretary's view, the District desperately needed a subway system. Hence, all things considered, including Natcher's views and the near dictatorial powers of congressional committee and subcommittee chairs, it was better to proceed with the bridge.

On judicial review, the Secretary's decision was overturned as arbitrary. According to the circuit court, the Secretary may have engaged in a perfectly sensible bit of political reasoning, but the Federal Aid Highway Acts did not make these sorts of political compromises a relevant consideration in the location of the interstate highway system.[150] As the Supreme Court said as far back as the *Illinois Central* cases discussed in Chapter 2, reasonableness review involves, at a minimum, seeing that the agency has engaged with all relevant considerations – and avoided all irrelevant ones.

This approach sounds both sensible and straightforward, but, of course, it is not necessarily so easy to apply. It is not obvious, for example, that when Congress set out the considerations for highway location in the Federal Aid Highway Acts, it intended for those considerations to be a closed set. Federal highway building, which (outside of the District of Columbia or on public lands) involves conditional grants

---

[149] *D.C. Fed'n of Civic Ass'ns* v. *Volpe*, 459 F.2d 1231 (D.C. Cir. 1971).
[150] Ibid., at 1247–8.

to state departments of transportation, is an intensely political process involving bargaining among federal, state, and local authorities. Compromises are inevitable. Whether Congress intended to preclude the Secretary from yielding to powerful political interests in the name of achieving a more balanced transportation plan for the District of Columbia does not have nearly so clear an answer as the reviewing court in the Three Sisters Bridge case seemed to think.

Whether particular factors are excluded from consideration or are a sensible response to a complex reality also sharply divided the Supreme Court in *Massachusetts v. Environmental Protection Agency*. In addition to reasoning that it lacked authority to regulate greenhouse gases under the governing statute, the EPA had also justified its refusal to regulate those pollutants under Section 202 of the Clean Air Act on the basis of a series of broad policy concerns. In its decision declining to act, the EPA pointed out that, in its view, the attempt to regulate greenhouse gases through controlling automobile emissions was a piecemeal (and likely ineffective) approach to the problem of global climate change. Moreover, to act in this fashion would be to ignore the reality that the president and Congress had engaged with climate change through other means – additional support for technological innovation to control greenhouse gases, creation of subsidy programs to encourage voluntary private-sector reduction in greenhouse gas emissions, and the funding of further research on the mechanisms of climate change itself. Finally, EPA suggested that unilateral attempts at regulation by the United States might compromise the country's bargaining position with other countries in ongoing negotiations to develop a comprehensive global response to greenhouse gas issues.

The *Massachusetts* v. *EPA* majority rejected all of these reasons as simply irrelevant to the EPA's job under the Clean Air Act. As the majority read the statute, the EPA was required to form a judgment as to whether chemicals or particulates caused or contributed to air pollution and could reasonably be anticipated to endanger the public health or welfare. If the agency found that a substance had those effects, the statute required the agency to regulate its emission from new motor vehicles. Although the statute required that the EPA exercise judgment about these matters, "the word 'judgment,'" in the majority's view, "is not a roving license to ignore the statutory text."[151] The majority opinion continued, "under the clear terms of the Clean Air Act, EPA can avoid taking further action only if it determines that greenhouse gases do not contribute to climate change or if it provides some reasonable explanation as to why it cannot or will not exercise its discretion to determine whether they do."[152] The majority characterized EPA's stated reasons as a "laundry list of reasons not to regulate" that "had nothing to do with whether greenhouse

---

[151] *Massachusetts* v. EPA, 549 U.S. 497, 533 (2007).
[152] Ibid.

gas emissions contribute to climate change. Still less do they amount to a reasoned justification for declining to form a scientific judgment."[153]

Four members of the Court dissented.[154] In their view, the majority was confused about which considerations were relevant to which questions. The dissenters agreed that EPA was required to act under the statute if it determined that a substance was an air pollutant and was likely to impair the public's health or welfare. And in making that judgment, the dissenters agreed that the agency was bound to focus only on scientific matters and not the broader range of considerations that it had invoked for its failure to act. But, the dissenters argued, there is a prior decision that the agency must make: whether to allocate resources to forming a scientific judgment about a particular alleged air pollutant. With respect to this priority setting or agenda setting question, the dissenters believed that the statute said nothing.[155] And, in deciding how to allocate its limited resources, the dissenters believed that the EPA should consider precisely the sorts of regulatory effectiveness and broad policy concerns that it had articulated. In short, the majority had found the agency's reasons irrelevant and therefore arbitrary because it had mischaracterized the question to which those reasons were addressed. Once again, the determination of the "relevant factors" turned essentially on a disputed question of statutory interpretation.[156]

Abstractly considered, the sorts of demands for and review of reasons that these cases illustrate seem no more than the necessary carrying out of a judicial charge to see that agency action is not arbitrary. Regulators should not be allowed to solve problems that have not been demonstrated to exist. They should be required to provide assurances that they are pursuing problems that are actually within their charge and not excluding, as outside their authority, tasks that their statutes have, in fact, assigned them. Reviewing courts should hardly approve reasoning processes that fail to consider relevant legal requirements, statutory criteria, empirical findings, or opposing arguments, or that consider irrelevant or prohibited ones.

But these cases also illustrate that the project of insuring reasoned administration almost always involves difficult and contestable judgments concerning the reasonableness of an agency's reasons. Courts are not perfect reasoners either, and their capacity to err suggests recharacterizing the reasonableness review question in more institutional terms: Given a generalist jurisdiction and substantial removal from the underlying factual and policy context within which agencies operate, how much deference should courts give to agencies' judgments when asked to determine their reasonableness?

[153] Ibid., at 533–4.
[154] Ibid., at 549 (Scalia, J., dissenting).
[155] Ibid., at 550.
[156] *Motor Vehicle Mfrs. Ass'n of the United States v. State Farm Mut. Auto. Ins. Co.*, 463 U.S. 29, 55 (1983) (quoting H.R. Rep. No. 89-1776, at 16 [1966]).

SUBSTANTIVE STANDARDS FOR OVERSIGHT AND ACCOUNTABILITY

It is hard to argue against the basic model of instrumental rationality that American courts have crafted in cases involving challenges to administrative decisions. It is likewise hard to argue against the basic idea that agencies implementing statutes should be held accountable for behaving reasonably. As we have seen, the substantive due process standard that merely asks whether any state of affairs can be imagined that would justify the agency's action is, in essence, an abandonment of judicial review for reasonableness. Legislation or agency action judged by that constitutional standard virtually never fails to be approved. This approach is quite similar to the so-called Wednesbury[157] standard for reasonableness review in England and much of the Commonwealth.[158] When this standard is applied rigorously, as has historically been true in Australia, judicial review for reasonableness virtually disappears.[159] Once imagined states of the world are abandoned for more serious inquiry into the bases for agency action, disclosure of reasons becomes necessary to facilitate that review.

There is then a progressive logic to reasonableness review. Without some assessment of whether agency reasons are legally sound, factually accurate, and logically coherent, the reasons requirement could become an empty formality. Yet both practical and legal/constitutional considerations argue for a limit on oversight bodies, judicial or otherwise, second-guessing agency decision-making. It seems undeniable that administrators implementing particular statutes will know a great deal more about the subject matter put in their charge than the Congress that delegated authority to them, or generalist courts or executive oversight bodies that review their work product. As a practical matter, de novo redetermination of administrative judgment risks introducing more errors than it corrects. In addition, agency processes may be more open to broad outside participation and more transparent and responsive to data and argument than the reviewing processes of either courts or political overseers. Moreover, as a legal or constitutional matter, the legislature has delegated authority to the administrators, not to the judiciary or to executive branch overseers like the OMB. These bodies are meant to be reviewers, not deciders.

In short, the question of how reasonableness review is to be cabined and structured is unavoidable. In the American administrative law context, this question is often asked as a question of how much deference reviewing courts should accord agency judgments when exercising some form of reasonableness review. But, alas, I know of no topic in administrative law that has generated so much heated controversy while

---

[157] *Associated Provincial Picture Houses, Ltd. v. Wednesbury Corp.* [1948] 1 KB 223 at 230 ("[I]f a decision on a competent matter is so unreasonable that no reasonable authority could ever have come to it, then the courts can interfere ... but to prove a case of that kind would require something overwhelming.").

[158] *See, e.g.,* Abhinav Chandrachud, *Wednesbury Reformulated: Proportionality and the Supreme Court of India,* 13 *Oxford Univ. Commonwealth L. J.* 191 (2015).

[159] Leighton McDonald, Rethinking Unreasonableness Review, 25 *Pub. L. Rev.* 117 (2014).

shedding so little light on the question addressed. Deference doctrines abound in American administrative law jurisprudence, but how they affect judicial decision-making by reviewing courts remains a mystery.

Arguably, the simple fact that courts consistently focus their reasonableness review on the reasons that administrators provide produces a rough form of deference at the remedial phase, whatever level of deference the reviewing court actually accords the agency's judgments. Even before the APA codified reasonableness review in the form of its substantial evidence, arbitrariness, and abuse of discretion standards, reviewing courts tended to ask not whether an agency's decisions were correct, but whether they could be justified in terms of the reasons the agency had provided. The well-known *Chenery* case[160] made clear that judicial review of agency adjudications, in what Chapter 2 characterized as the appellate model of judicial review, was distinct from appeals from the lower-level judiciary. Appellate courts reviewing trial courts on questions of law simply ask whether the trial court's decision was correct. Correctness can be determined on grounds distinct from those that the lower court articulated. Trial court judgments are affirmed if the appeals court agrees with the result, even though it disagrees with the lower court's rationale.

Not so when reviewing administrative actions, said the Supreme Court in *Chenery*.[161] There, the SEC made a ruling concerning the fairness of a corporate reorganization plan and based its decision on what it took to be the common law of fiduciary duties. On appeal, the Supreme Court found that the SEC had misunderstood what the common law of fiduciary duties required. The Court nevertheless recognized that "fairness" under the relevant securities act, the Public Company Holding Act of 1935, might require something more or different than simple compliance with common law fiduciary standards.[162] But it did not supply its own interpretation of fairness. Rather, it remanded the case to the SEC to see whether the Commission, when reconsidering its decision under the possibly unique standards of the securities laws, might provide a rationale that justified its action.[163] The Court declined to supply its own interpretation on the grounds that such action would invade the policy space that Congress had delegated to the Commission in the first instance. A focus on reasons thus helps to preserve administrative policy discretion, even as a reviewing court reverses and remands a decision for further analysis.

Indeed, even when a court provides its own interpretation of an agency statute, remand preserves the agency's discretion to rethink its action in light of the court's statement of the law. If the record before the agency would nevertheless justify the agency's action under this revised interpretation of its statute, the agency can maintain its position by articulating new grounds that are responsive to the reviewing

---

[160] *SEC v. Chenery Corp.*, 318 U.S. 80 (1943).
[161] Ibid., at 87 ("The grounds upon which an administrative order must be judged are those upon which the record discloses that its action was based.").
[162] Ibid., at 89.
[163] Ibid., at 95.

court's view of the law. The *Overton Park* case is a straightforward example. It was clear that the DOT had not thought that the requirement that parkland could be taken only when there was no feasible or prudent alternative required it to determine that avoiding the park would be "uniquely difficult."[164] Yet, on remand, it remained open to the Secretary to attempt to justify routing I-40 through the park, even on this very demanding standard.

Of course, disagreement with an agency's rationale does not always leave open the possibility that the agency could provide an acceptable justification for the same substantive decision. When the Supreme Court in *Brown and Williamson* decided that tobacco products could not be considered drugs or devices under the FDCA, the FDA simply lost jurisdiction over tobacco products. A finding that an agency lacks jurisdiction aborts its actions. But even jurisdictional decisions are not necessarily so conclusive. A finding that the agency has improperly declined jurisdiction does not necessarily require that the agency exercise it. The *Massachusetts v. EPA* decision left open the possibility that the EPA could yet give appropriate reasons for refusing to exercise the jurisdiction the Court insisted that it had.

Even where a reviewing court seems to give an agency on remand a "mission impossible," agencies may find a way to persevere. When the Supreme Court reversed the OSHA's strengthening of its benzene exposure rule, it seemed to foreclose further action.[165] The Court demanded that the agency demonstrate a significant risk when the agency candidly admitted that no good evidence linked benzene exposure below ten parts per million to cancer in humans. Yet, within a few years, on the basis of new epidemiological evidence and animal experiments, the agency was able to reissue the rule in essentially its same form.[166] The Supreme Court's demand for a showing of significant risk forced the agency to engage in much more extensive analysis, indeed to rethink its regulatory approach and to routinely engage in what is now characterized as "quantitative risk assessment." But OSHA's efforts to provide greater health protection for workers exposed to benzene were not thwarted.

This inherently deferential approach is, of course, not always so deferential in effect. Demanding a better justification can not only thwart particular actions, it can skew or virtually dismantle whole programs. Moreover, the fact that a form of review focused on reasons tends to be deferential even when the agency is reversed does not answer the question of how much deference courts should give to agency rationales when deciding whether to reverse and remand, or to affirm, their decisions.

In American administrative law, the question of how courts should reason about reasonableness is often articulated in institutional terms as a question of how much deference courts should accord agency judgments. We hardly lack articulations of

---

[164]   401 U.S. 402, 416 (1971).
[165]   *Indus. Union Dep't v. Am. Petroleum Inst.* (*The Benzene* case), 448 U.S. 607 (1980).
[166]   *See* Occupational Exposure to Benzene, 52 Fed. Reg. 34,460 (Sept. 11, 1987) (codified as amended at 29 C.F.R. § 1910.1028).

deference doctrines, or as the question is also often put, descriptions of the appropriate "scope of review" to be exercised by a reviewing court. The APA itself provides at least four.[167] Its judicial review provisions indicate, first, that courts are supposed to decide for themselves questions of constitutional right, indeed "all relevant questions of law."[168] Here, presumably no deference at all should be paid to an agency's interpretation of its relevant statute. Indeed, the APA suggests that courts are supposed to "determine the meaning or applicability of the terms of an agency action."[169] Read literally, no deference is to be given to agency interpretations of their own regulations or the meaning of their prior decisions. De novo review makes another appearance in the provision instructing the court to invalidate agency action "unwarranted by the facts to the extent that the facts are subject to trial de novo by the reviewing court."[170]

Second, complaints about agency delay are to be judged by a simple reasonableness standard pursuant to the APA's injunction that courts should "compel agency action unlawfully withheld or unreasonably delayed."[171] Reading further, we find a third injunction that all agency actions, findings, or conclusions should be set aside if the reviewing court finds that they are "arbitrary, capricious, an abuse of discretion, or otherwise not in accordance with law."[172] For purposes of this count, I have treated this provision as articulating a single standard, but perhaps this single subsection alone contains four different standards. Finally, where agency action is required to be taken after a hearing pursuant to the APA's formal hearing requirements, or reviewed on the record of a hearing required by some other statute, the court is supposed to invalidate the agency action if it is "unsupported by substantial evidence."[173]

Are these scope of review standards all really different? Justice Scalia, as a circuit court judge, argued that there was actually no difference between the arbitrary and capricious standard and the substantial evidence standard – they were merely applied to agency decisions having different procedural postures.[174] Professor David Zaring has taken the stronger position that the scope of review under virtually any articulation of how a court is to proceed comes down to a basic, and perhaps analytically recalcitrant, question of reasonableness.[175]

---

[167] 5 U.S.C. § 706.
[168] Ibid.
[169] Ibid.
[170] Ibid., § 706(2)(F).
[171] Ibid., § 706(1).
[172] Ibid., § 706(2)(A).
[173] Ibid., § 706(2)(E).
[174] *Assoc. of Data Processing Serv. Orgs., Inc. v. Bd. of Governors of the Fed. Reserve's Sys.*, 745 F.2d 677, 683–4 (D.C. Cir. 1984). ("When the arbitrary or capricious standard is performing that function of assuring factual support, there is no substantive difference between what it requires and what would be required by the substantial evidence test, since it is impossible to conceive of a 'nonarbitrary' factual judgment supported only by evidence that is not substantial in the APA sense.")
[175] David Zaring, Rule by Reasonableness, 63 *Admin. L. Rev.* 525 (2011).

The federal courts have not been hesitant to supply further refinements to the APA list. Indeed, the Supreme Court has altered what would seem to be the plain meaning of some of those provisions. In the famous *Chevron* case,[176] the Court reinterpreted the injunction to decide questions of statutory interpretation to mean that courts should decide for themselves whether a statutory provision is ambiguous. If not, the court should apply the statute's plain meaning. However, if the statute appears ambiguous,[177] the court should uphold an agency interpretation so long as it is "reasonable." The circuit court cases, Supreme Court cases, and academic commentary parsing and dissecting this so-called *Chevron* doctrine would fill a small library. In an attempt to understand Supreme Court practice in this regard, Professors William Eskridge and Lauren Baer did a comprehensive study of all Supreme Court cases involving statutory interpretation decided between 1983 and 2005 – 1,014 cases in all.[178] They found that the Supreme Court actually uses seven different scope of review doctrines when reviewing agency interpretations of statutes. And, oddly enough, given the importance attached to *Chevron* in the legal literature, the authors found that case was applied in only 8.3 percent of Supreme Court cases evaluating agency statutory interpretations.[179] Indeed, although given seven different deference doctrines to choose from, the Eskridge-Baer study found that in the majority of cases – 53.6 percent of them – "the Court does not [explicitly] apply any deference regime at all."[180] Moreover, when Eskridge and Baer attempted to analyze when a particular deference doctrine is invoked, their remarkably extensive data offered "no clear guide as to when the Court will invoke particular deference regimens, and why."[181]

Is all of this effort at articulating what reasonableness review means in different contexts simply meaningless? Surely that would be too strong an assertion. When a court indicates that it is authorized to overturn an agency decision only if "clearly erroneous," it is surely telling us something different about its intentions concerning the intensity of its review than when it tells us that the agency's views are to be accorded deference only if they have "the power to persuade."[182] The articulation of some deference doctrine or description of the court's scope of review surely sets a tone and provides some information about a reviewing court's approach. But whether these articulated standards have any particular analytic bite is a different question.

Considerable evidence suggests that they do not. Paul Verkuil compared the win-loss rate on judicial review of three different agencies whose decisions were

---

[176] *Chevron, U.S.A. Inc. v. Nat. Res. Def. Council, Inc.*, 467 U.S. 837 (1984).
[177] The real problem is, in practice, usually vagueness.
[178] William N. Eskridge, Jr. and Lauren E. Baer, The Continuum of Defense: Supreme Court Treatment of Agency Statutory Interpretations from Chevron to Hamdan, 96 *Geo. L.J.* 1083 (2008).
[179] Ibid., at 1100.
[180] Ibid.
[181] Ibid., at 1091.
[182] *Skidmore v. Swift & Co.*, 323 U.S. 134, 140 (1944).

subjected to three quite different articulations of the scope of judicial review.[183] His findings were not just that the apparent stringency of the review required was not predictive of outcomes; outcomes seemed paradoxical when viewed simply in terms of the articulated standard of review. In the areas he studied, a more stringent test for reasonableness was more likely to be associated with judicial approval of agency action than was a less stringent test applied to a different agency or function. Context – meaning here which agency or agencies are performing which type of function – obviously mattered more than nominal deference regimes. And David Zaring, once again, found that courts remand agency decisions at roughly the same rates no matter what the articulated review standard.[184] Other empirical research suggests that whether a particular federal judge will view an agency's actions as reasonable or unreasonable is almost fully predictable, not by parsing doctrine, but by simply knowing whether the judge was appointed by a Democrat or a Republican and whether the plaintiff was a regulated party or a regulatory beneficiary.[185]

Judges are hardly unaware that doctrine does not determine outcomes. In a symposium celebrating the fiftieth anniversary of the APA, Judge Patricia Wald lamented that, a half-century after that statute's enactment, judges were still struggling to understand how its judicial review provisions were to be applied.[186] Other judges have attempted to explain their practice, not by invoking particular standards for review, but by explaining that the judge varied his or her intensity of review depending on a host of contextual "danger signals" that might suggest that an agency action was not well-considered.[187]

The unruliness of reasonableness review and the difficulty of capturing its essence in verbal formulae is hardly limited to American courts and American administrative law. In an article on reasonableness review under Australian law, the author wisely suggests, "[t]he application of any ground of review based on the determination of 'reasonableness' or 'unreasonableness' will inevitably depend as much on background judicial attitudes and sensibilities concerning the judicial role as the verbal formulae within which doctrine is developed."[188]

---

[183] Paul R. Verkuil, An Outcomes Analysis of Scope of Review Standards, 44 *Wm. & Mary L. Rev.* 679 (2002).

[184] David Zaring, Reasonable Agencies, 96 *Va. L. Rev.* 135, 137 (2010). *But see* Ronald M. Levin, Hard Look, Review, Policy Change, and Fox Television, 65 *U. Miami L. Rev.* 555, 574–5 (2011) (suggesting caution in interpreting Zaring's conclusions).

[185] Thomas J. Miles and Cass R. Sunstein, Do Judges Make Regulatory Policy? An Empirical Investigation of Chevron, 73 *U. Chi. L. Rev.* 823 (2006). For a survey of the empirical literature and yet another empirical test for what explains judicial decision-making, see Jason J. Czarnezki, An Empirical Investigation in Judicial Decisionmaking (if consistent with original), Statutory Interpretation and the Chevron Doctrine in Environmental Law, 79 *U. Colo. L. Rev.* 767 (2008).

[186] Patricia M. Wald, Judicial Review in Midpassage: The Uneasy Partnership between Courts and Agencies Plays On, 32 *Tulsa L. J.* 221, 258 (1996).

[187] *Greater Boston Television Corp.* v. FCC, 444 F.2d 841, 851–2 (D.C. Cir. 1970).

[188] McDonald, Rethinking Unreasonableness Review, at 126.

These doctrinal difficulties suggest that if we are to evaluate the utility of legal demands for administrative reasonableness and reason-giving, particularly backed by a monitoring system that features judicial review of administration action, we should perhaps ask different questions. First, we need to have, or attempt to obtain, some appreciation of what the effect of the legal demand for reasonableness has on the administrators subject to those requirements. If we expect the demand for reasoned administration to have positive consequences, what are the conditions under which we should expect those consequences to obtain and what do we know about whether we are actually getting them? Can reasonableness be given some more determinate content by specifying the analytic methodology that agencies are to employ in making policy decisions? Is this approach likely to merely substitute the "rational" for the "reasonable"? Or, as Chapter 1 suggests, is reasoned administration a fundamental presupposition for the maintenance of liberal democracy in modern administrative states? Does that political value, or some other important normative basis for legal requirements of reason-giving and reasonableness, justify this approach to administrative legality, whatever the difficulties of its application and its consequences for effective and responsible administration? Subsequent chapters explore all of these questions.

4

Reasonableness, Accountability, and the Control of Administrative Policy

INTRODUCTION

The American jurisprudence of judicial review of administrative action seems to imagine a fairly straightforward process of instrumentally rational action that the courts monitor and enforce. Other monitors – the Office of Management and Budget (OMB), Congress, other agencies and affected publics – also play a significant part in holding agencies accountable for various reason-giving and reasonableness requirements. All of these accountability regimes seem directed at insuring that administrators, in fact, engage in a process of reasoned decision-making – one that gives consideration to the various constraints on, criteria for, and potential effects of, agency action.

The crucial question, of course, is to what degree these demands actually shape agency behavior. It would certainly be surprising if all of these requirements for reasoned administration had no effect on how agencies behave, or who has influence on their decision-making. It seems equally implausible to imagine that responding to requirements for reasoned administration has only the desired effects and no unwanted side effects. As we shall see, neither of these implausible results obtains. On the other hand, demonstrating exactly how legal requirements for reasoned administration affect the administrative state's processes and outcomes, and determining whether we have achieved an appropriate balance between desired effects and unwanted side effects, is a quite uncertain business.

In addressing these issues, this chapter will focus on three more specific questions: (1) How do legal requirements for reasoned administration affect the internal organization and processes of agencies that are subject to their demands? (2) How do these demands, and agency responses to them, empower different internal and external actors in an agency's legal environment? (3) Finally, what can be said about how reasoned administration as a legal requirement affects agency outputs and the quality or character of agency decision-making?

ORGANIZATION AND PROCESS

There are not that many ways to organize an administrative agency, or a firm for that matter. Organization by specialized function, subject matter, geography, or clientele pretty much exhausts the universe of organizational alternatives. Indeed, most bureaucratic organizations use all of these techniques. If legal requirements for reasoned administration affect agency organization and process, one might expect to find both specialized offices to respond to particular legal demands and internal processes of coordination that attempt to make certain that all the reason-giving I's are dotted and T's are crossed.

There is considerable evidence that agencies' organizations and processes respond to legal requirements for reasoned administration in precisely these ways. I will here use the organization and rulemaking processes of the Environmental Protection Agency (EPA) as an example.[1]

The EPA is a large agency with an enormous range of substantive responsibilities. Its actions often have substantial effects across the whole economy, and many of its policies provoke continuing controversy.[2] The EPA Administrator is a popular defendant in judicial proceedings to review EPA rules.[3] Moreover, because of the significance of its rulemaking, the EPA is closely monitored by OMB, Congress, and affected interests including regulated firms, environmental advocacy organizations, state and local governments, and other federal agencies. In response, the EPA has created an internal structure that reflects the challenges to the accomplishment of its basic mission that these overlapping accountability regimes pose.

First, the agency's Office of General Counsel (OGC) has a large staff and a very prominent position within the agency hierarchy. As is true in most agencies that are large enough to have their own internal legal staff, the EPA General Counsel has a hierarchical position just below of the offices of the Administrator and Deputy Administrator. The General Counsel's Office has authority in the agency, not just because it is obviously important to defend the EPA against successful legal challenges, but also because only two individuals in the agency, the Administrator and Deputy Administrator, hold higher rank. Agency policymakers must satisfy the

---

[1] The discussion that follows concerning the Environmental Protection Agency is based on analysis of information available on its website at www.epa.gov (Last accessed May 17, 2018). The EPA site is quite elaborate and informative. By clicking on "About EPA," interested parties can get an organization chart for the Agency and then by clicking on different sub-organizations and regions, additional information is provided concerning the functions of those offices.

[2] *E.g., Michigan v. EPA*, 135 S. Ct. 2699 (2015); Brady Davis, The EPA's Lead-in-Water Rule Has Been Faulted for Decades. Will Flint Hasten a Change?, Wash. Post (May 5, 2016), available at: www .washingtonpost.com/national/health-science/epas-lead-in-water-rule-has-been-faulted-for-decades-will-flint-hasten-a-change/2016/05/04/8d25bb12-0de9-11e6-bfa1-4efa856caf2a_story.html (Last accessed May 17, 2018).

[3] *E.g., Michigan*, 135 S. Ct. 2699; *Util. Air Regulatory Grp. v. EPA*, 134 S. Ct. 2427 (2014); *Massachusetts v. EPA*, 549 U.S. 497 (2007); Order in Pending Case, *North Dakota v. EPA*, 136 Sup. Ct. 999(2016) (No. 15A793) (granting stay of EPA rule in pending lower court litigation).

OGC or be prepared to burden the top two political appointees with resolving the conflict. This high position in the agency hierarchy may be particularly important where the analytic legal requirements are not subject to judicial review. Demanding compliance with those requirements expresses rule-of-law values, but lacks the characteristic legal counselor's threat, "Follow my advice or you are likely to get sued."

Consistent with these rule-of-law values, the OGC reviews proposed agency actions and advises on their legality in areas that go well beyond what might be regarded as necessary because of possible judicial review. To be sure, OGC provides legal advice to the agency in respect of virtually any action that might be challenged in court. But, in addition, OGC has a division titled the "Cross-Cutting Issues Law Office." This office is responsible for advice concerning a host of framework statutes, such as the Paperwork Reduction Act, the Regulatory Flexibility Act, the Data Quality Act and the Unfunded Mandates Reform Act. Of the statutes just listed, only the Regulatory Flexibility Act, as amended, subjects the agency's compliance with its provisions to meaningful[4] independent judicial review.[5] The Cross-Cutting Issues Law Office also deals with a host of executive orders imposing analytic requirements on federal agencies, including the executive order requiring regulatory impact analysis.[6] Even if not subject to judicial scrutiny, some of these analytic requirements are subject to OMB oversight,[7] but many others – for example, the requirement to analyze effects on American federal structure[8] – have no formal review process attached to them.

Other groups within the EPA Office of the Administrator also have responsibilities for compliance with analytic requirements that derive from EPA's mission-oriented statutes, as well as framework statutes and cross-cutting executive orders. The Office of Regulatory Policy and Management,[9] for example, provides advice and support to all elements of the agency concerning compliance with the Regulatory Flexibility Act, the Data Quality Act, and certain executive orders such as the requirement for annual publication of agency regulatory agendas.[10] Another group within the Office of the Administrator, the National Center for Environmental Economics,[11] is charged with helping the agency perform sound economic and risk analysis. It

---

[4] The Unfunded Mandates Reform Act permits a (nearly meaningless) modicum of judicial review. *See* 2 U.S.C. § 1571 (2012). The availability of judicial review under the Data Quality Act (also known as the Information Quality Act) is somewhat contested. Litigants have attempted to force judicial review under the Data Quality Act, but courts have found judicial review is unavailable. *E.g., Harkonen* v. *U.S. Dep't of Justice*, No. C 12-629 CW, 2012 WL 6019571, at *16 (N.D. Cal. Dec. 3, 2012), *aff'd*, 800 F.3d 1143 (9th Cir. 2015); *Salt Inst.* v. *Thompson*, 345 F. Supp. 2d 589, 603 (E.D. Va. 2004), *aff'd sub nom. Salt Inst.* v. *Leavitt*, 440 F.3d 156 (4th Cir. 2006).

[5] 5 U.S.C. § 611.

[6] Exec. Order No. 12,866, 58 Fed. Reg. 51,735 (Oct. 4, 1993).

[7] For instance, the Paperwork Reduction Act. *See* 44 U.S.C. § 3508.

[8] Exec. Order No. 13,132, 58 Fed. Reg. 43,255 (Aug. 4, 1999).

[9] This group sits within the Office of Policy.

[10] Exec. Order No. 12,866, § 4.

[11] Also within the broader Office of Policy.

provides regulatory review support for economically significant rules subject to Executive Order 12,866, as well as guidance on quantitative risk assessment.

Internal agency processes for review of proposed rules and other decisions attempt to ensure that the review and support offices that respond to legal demands for reasoned administration are integrated into the agency decision process. If the agency is to assure itself that its ultimate decisions will comply with the multiple demands for reasoned administration that it faces, it must require that these specialized support and advice institutions are consulted whenever and wherever their inputs are relevant. This major coordination problem is dealt with, in part, by internal operational manuals that provide step-by-step instructions concerning the formulation of rules and policies or the issuance of permits.[12]

The demand for reasoned and reasonable decision-making also affects processes involving outside parties. The EPA rules, for example, often go through multiple rounds of notice and comment. While the agency can bring considerable expertise to bear on actions that promote its primary missions, the world is always much more complex than it can anticipate. Affected interests have much of the "local knowledge" that bears on the agency's proposals and, particularly, how those proposals will likely function – or malfunction – when implemented. Commenters in rulemaking proceedings raise new issues that, under applicable legal doctrine, require a response. Providing that response may require the agency to seek additional information through another round of notice and comment. And, as we have seen, responsiveness to comments may significantly alter proposals in ways that raise new issues for consideration. Here again, an additional round of notice and comment rulemaking is required.

From this brief description, it seems reasonable to conclude that the EPA, and by analogy most other agencies, organize themselves and structure their processes for decision-making, at least in part, in response to legal requirements for reasoned

---

[12] For an early but extensive discussion of the EPA's internal rulemaking processes, *see* Thomas O. McGarity, The Internal Structure of EPA Rulemaking, 54 *L. & Contemp. Probs.* 57 (1991). The number of manuals and guidance documents dealing with various parts of rulemaking, permitting and other processes at EPA is quite staggering. Consulting one of them – such as, Guidance on Considering Environmental Justice during the Development of Regulatory Actions, Envtl. Prot. Agency (May 2015), available at: www.epa.gov/sites/production/files/2015-06/documents/considering-ej-in-rulemaking-guide-final.pdf (Last accessed May 17, 2018) – leads into a thicket of other manuals and guidance documents that also relate to the rulemaking, permitting, and other processes. Scanning these documents leads one to wonder how the EPA staff ever finishes reading the instructions for how to do anything, much less actually does anything. For an example from another substantial agency, see the Department of Transportation's 47-page staff manual that outlines all the analytic requirements potentially applicable to DOT rulemaking. Neil Eisner, Rulemaking Requirements, Dep't of Transp. (Mar. 2012), available at: www.transportation.gov/regulations/rulemaking-requirements-2012 (Last accessed May 17, 2018). It should be emphasized that this lengthy manual is only an outline of potentially applicable requirements. DOT cautions that the manual cannot be used as a guide without consulting the various statutes, executive orders, agency rules, and guidance documents to which it refers. *See* Rulemaking Requirements: Overview, Dep't of Transp. (Feb. 5, 2015), available at: www.transportation.gov/regulations/rulemaking-requirements (Last accessed May 17, 2018).

administration. It is, of course, impossible to know to what extent many of these organizational forms and process initiatives would exist in the absence of legal requirements imposed on the agencies by statute, executive order and, in rare cases, the Constitution. The people who work in, and manage, public administrative agencies are hardly immune from usual human desires for authority, legitimacy, and respect. On Charles Tilly's account, as described in Chapter 1, we establish and negotiate virtually all of our human relationships through providing reasons. EPA engineers would give reasons to each other and to their fellow engineers outside the agency as a way of demonstrating that they are competent practitioners. EPA managers are likely to give reasons for decisions to lower-level personnel as a means of educating them about desired performance and motivating their production of usable information and sensible action. Because all regulatory agencies rely importantly on voluntary compliance by those whose conduct they regulate, reasons are a way of convincing the burdened or recalcitrant that the agency knows what it is doing and has taken their interests into account.

In short, it seems highly likely that the agency organization and process structures that we have been discussing are not simply artifacts of legal requirements for reasoned administration. On the other hand, it seems equally reasonable to believe that these organizational structures and processes often take the specific form that they do in response to legal demands. The demands of the legal culture are only one of the accountability regimes within which agencies function, but the fingerprints of those legal demands are easy to discern in the ways that agencies organize their personnel and instruct them how to pursue their missions.

THE DEMAND FOR REASONS AND THE STRUCTURE
OF ORGANIZATIONAL INFLUENCE

Organizational sociologists have long understood that institutional "boundary keepers" have significant authority in shaping organizational policies. In any organization, certain personnel function as boundary keepers. They explain the organization's actions to external audiences and protect the organization from external threats, while simultaneously explaining the external world's demands and expectations to internal decision-makers.[13] As the discussion on agency organization and process demonstrates, administrative agencies organize themselves internally to ensure that the relevant expertise is brought to bear on issues about which they are required to provide reasoned decisions, particularly when external monitors review those reasons. To take some obvious examples: judicial review empowers lawyers; OMB

---

[13] In organizational sociology and law, these boundary keepers are also called "gatekeepers." *See generally* John C. Coffee, Jr., *Gatekeepers: The Professions and Corporate Governance* (2006) (discussing the development and potential reform of various corporate gatekeeper roles); Reinier H. Kraakman, Gatekeepers: The Anatomy of a Third-Party Enforcement Strategy, 2 *J. L. Econ. & Org.* 53 (1986) (discussing liability regimes for gatekeepers).

review of cost-benefit analyses empowers economists; the National Environmental Policy Act's requirement for environmental impact statements empowers environmental analysts. These are the people whose expertise is relied upon to assure agency decision-makers that the evidence, methodology, and rationale offered in support of an agency's actions are sufficient to withstand external scrutiny.

The dominant professionals in any administrative agency are usually, of course, those who have the expertise that coincides with the agency's central mission. Because the relevant statutes largely presume engineering solutions for safety and health risks, the line personnel responsible for developing policy at agencies like the EPA or the National Highway Traffic Safety Administration (NHTSA) are engineers. Their counterparts who implement the Endangered Species Act at the Fish and Wildlife Service are biologists. But missions are pursued subject to constraints that can reorder hierarchies of professional influence. As David Harfst and I explained in our study of rulemaking at NHTSA,[14] that agency's failure to convince reviewing courts that its rules were reasonable and practicable led to a massive reorganization within the agency. The authority of the general counsel's office substantially increased, and an economist who specialized in cost-benefit analysis replaced a safety engineer as the head of the rulemaking office.

The NHTSA story is hardly unique. Moreover, structural changes in agency organization and process are not essential for these boundary keepers to have substantial influence. For example, years after the Supreme Court's determination that the Food and Drug Administration (FDA) did not have authority over tobacco products under its basic statutes,[15] Congress passed legislation that provided the FDA with special and more limited regulatory authority over tobacco.[16] But in 2014, a cost-benefit analysis that the agency's economists prepared cast doubt on the agency's major rulemaking efforts pursuant to that new authority.[17] Because the economists insisted that the agency consider the loss of enjoyment that its rule would impose on smokers as a part of the costs of the rule, the welfare gain was relatively modest when those costs were compared with the rule's anticipated health benefits.[18] This analysis

[14] Jerry L. Mashaw and David L. Harfst, *The Struggle for Auto Safety* (1990).

[15] *FDA v. Brown & Williamson Tobacco Corp.*, 529 U.S. 120 (2000).

[16] Family Smoking Prevention and Tobacco Control Act, Pub. L. No. 111-31, Div. A, 123 Stat. 1776 (2009) (codified at 21 U.S.C. §§ 387-87t).

[17] Preliminary Regulatory Impact Analysis, Deeming Tobacco Products to be Subject to the Food, Drug, and Cosmetic Act, Food & Drug Admin. (Apr. 2014), available at: www.regulations.gov/document?D=FDA-2014-N-0189-20877 (Last accessed May 17, 2018); Micah Berman, Cost-Benefit Analysis, the FDA, and Tobacco, *Yale J. on Reg.: Notice & Comment* (Sept. 16, 2014), http://yalejreg.com/nc/cost-benefit-analysis-the-fda-and-tobacco-by-micah-berman/ (Last accessed May 17, 2018).

[18] Sharon Begley, FDA Calculates Costs of Lost Enjoyment If E-Cigarette Rules Prevent Smoking, Reuters (June 2, 2014); Sabrina Tavernise, In New Calculus on Smoking, It's Health Gained vs. Pleasure Lost, N.Y. Times (Aug. 6, 2014), available at: www.nytimes.com/2014/08/07/health/pleasure-factor-may-override-new-tobacco-rules.html (Last accessed May 17, 2018).

made the rulemaking proposal harder to defend and provoked reconsideration of the FDA's proposed policy.[19]

These are anecdotal examples, but a vast literature in organizational sociology documents the way structure and process in organizations affects norm creation and transmission within them – that is, agency culture. On the basis of that literature, Professor Jodi Short has argued that legal requirements for reason-giving are critical to the maintenance of a culture of technical and scientific reasonableness within federal administrative agencies.[20] There is also evidence that the threat of judicial review may be a crucial determinant of agency compliance with procedural and analytic requirements.[21] Demands for analysis and reason-giving create a complex regime of checks and balances within administrative organizations that promote reasoned administration – all things considered – and that also explain, in part, the torpidity of many administrative processes.

Analytic requirements can also result in making insiders out of outsiders. The Regulatory Flexibility Act requires that when certain agencies adopt policies that have significant effects on small public or private entities, they must "assure that small entities have been given an opportunity to participate in the rulemaking."[22] The Federal Highway Act requires that the Federal Highway Administration (FHWA) assure itself that federal aid funds are expended for highway construction in accordance with local land use planning.[23] Many, perhaps most, modern regulatory statutes demand that agencies consult with other agencies, outside advisory committees, or state and local officials.

Even in the absence of statutory consultation requirements, the overlapping jurisdictions of federal agencies and the potential agency role as commenters on each other's policies in rulemaking proceedings often lead to intense interagency cooperation in rule development. Rather than respond to critical comments from sister agencies, rulemaking agencies often develop their regulations in interagency

---

[19] Celia Wexler, *How Much Is the 'Lost Pleasure' from a Cigarette Worth?*, LiveScience (June 24, 2014, 5:15 PM), available at: www.livescience.com/46503-value-of-lost-pleasure-from-smoking.html (Last accessed May 17, 2018).

[20] Jodi L. Short, The Political Turn in American Administrative Law: Power, Rationality and Reasons, 61 *Duke L.J.* 1811, 1861–78 (2012).

[21] Connor Raso, Agency Avoidance of Rulemaking Procedures, 67 *Admin. L. Rev.* 65 (2015).

[22] 5 U.S.C. § 609(a). For the EPA's approach to implementation for the Regulatory Flexibility Act, see Final Guidance for EPA Rule writers: Regulatory Flexibility Act as Amended by the Small Business Regulatory Enforcement Fairness Act, Envtl. Prot. Agency (Nov. 2006), available at: www.epa.gov/sites/production/files/2015-06/documents/guidance-regflexact.pdf (Last accessed May 25, 2018).

[23] 23 U.S.C. §§ 134–5. For a description of the extraordinary local involvement in the routing decision that was at issue in the *Overton Park* case, see Peter L. Strauss, Revisiting Overton Park: Political and Judicial Controls Over Administrative Actions Affecting the Community, 39 *UCLA L. Rev.* 1251 (1992).

working groups that attempt to satisfy each affected agency's concerns.[24] OMB also plays a coordinating role in attempting to assure widespread, interagency consultation.

Once again, it is hard to sort out the specific influence of reason-giving and reasonableness requirements on the way authority is distributed in administrative agencies. Good administration would require that a responsible agency seek out the best possible information on both the effects and side effects of its proposed policies. "Stakeholder buy-in" as the management gurus might put it, is critical to success in virtually any organization, public or private. Hence, while the requirements for reasoned administration along multiple dimensions of reasonableness surely play a part in who has authority within agency policymaking processes, the extent of that influence is very difficult to measure.

The foregoing discussion has concentrated on agency policymaking by rule. But, of course, agencies make policies with legal effect through adjudication as well, both through the content of their adjudicatory opinions and by the types of enforcement proceedings that they are prepared to initiate. Because virtually every agency adjudication that has legal effects on the rights, privileges, or immunities of individuals or firms is subject to judicial review, these adjudications will be subject to justification in the form of a written opinion. Who within the agency is empowered by a demand for reasons justifying agency adjudicatory decisions depends, then, on what sorts of reasons are relevant.

To take a straightforward example, the Federal Trade Commission (FTC) has authority to pursue firms for violations of the antitrust laws.[25] FTC antitrust enforcement actions might be divided roughly into two categories: conduct cases and structure cases. In the first type, the basic questions are: (i) what sorts of evidentiary facts can be produced concerning the parties' conduct, and (ii) whether that evidence will be sufficiently substantial to establish a violation of a well-established legal norm.[26] These sorts of determinations will be made largely on the advice of the agency's lawyers. Structure cases, by contrast, involve issues of how particular mergers or acquisitions, or firm sizes and structures, do or do not amount to monopolization of a relevant market, or a significant lessening of competition through abuse of a dominant position.[27] Here, economic theory plays an enormous role. Hence, what sorts of cases are worth bringing – and on what theory they should be prosecuted – depends importantly on the opinions of the agency's economists. And,

---

[24] American administrative agencies are not only interested in rules that their counterparts in other departments or independent commissions adopt that may obliquely bear on their own functions; they often have joint jurisdiction over the same questions. *See generally* Jacob E. Gersen, Overlapping and Underlapping Jurisdiction in Administrative Law, 2006 *Sup. Ct. Rev.* 201 (analyzing interpretive issues related to shared jurisdiction among administrative agencies).

[25] *See* 5 U.S.C. § 45.

[26] E.g., *FTC v. Superior Court Trial Lawyers Ass'n*, 493 U.S. 411 (1990).

[27] E.g., *FTC v. Sysco Corp.*, 113 F. Supp. 3d 1 (D.D.C. 2015).

of course, the agency's experience with satisfying courts that its case has been proven and appropriately rationalized will have an impact on the agenda-setting decisions of upper-level agency management. Judicial review impacts what sorts of cases FTC leadership brings and, hence, whose expertise will be most relevant to the agency's enforcement practices.[28]

Administrative agencies also carry out their statutory responsibilities in a host of ways that do not entail either rulemaking or formal adjudication. State agency personnel, by contract with the Social Security Administration, make over three million initial decisions on social security disability pension applications each year. The decisions of insurance company contractors, on the payment of provider claims under the Medicare program, number in the hundreds of millions. Most of these initial decisions are never appealed to a hearing stage at which extensive reasons for decisions would be required. Most agencies receive a constant barrage of questions concerning the application of their statutes and regulations, and in the digital age, agency websites bristle with answers to "frequently asked questions" (FAQs). There is reasoning in these initial decisions or interpretive responses, but they are generally provided in a very cursory fashion. Serious reason-giving is generally reserved for conflict that rises to the level of formal adjudication or when policies with legal effect are made by rule.

These practices hardly undermine the legitimation of agency action by reason-giving. Informal decision-making of these sorts does not make policy. And if mass administrative justice and responsiveness to questions by affected parties are to function at all effectively, elaborate reason-giving cannot be required. On the other hand, there is a vast domain of policy-making by so-called "guidance documents" that lies outside the analytic and reason-giving structure that we have been discussing. We will return to the question of policy by guidance when we discuss reform proposals in Chapter 8.

THE ROLE OF OUTSIDE MONITORS

Legal requirements for reasons and reasoned analysis obviously empower outside monitors who are authorized to determine whether an agency's actions are indeed reasonable. Beyond the federal judiciary, the other constitutionally empowered monitors are Congress and the President. I will here concentrate on their roles, although numerous specific statutes make agencies subject to the review or approval of some other administrative entity for one or another of its functions.[29] Under the Endangered Species Act, for example, agencies engaged in substantial projects

---

[28] For a discussion of the competition between lawyers and economists concerning regulatory policy at the FTC, see Robert A. Katzmann, *Regulatory Bureaucracy: The Federal Trade Commission and Antitrust Policy* (1980).

[29] *See* Gersen, Overlapping and Underlapping, 201.

affecting the environment may be required to obtain an opinion from the Fish and Wildlife Service.[30] If this "biological opinion" determines that the project is likely to have deleterious effects on the habitat of an endangered species, that opinion triggers further analytical requirements designed to demonstrate that the project agency has engaged in the necessary planning to mitigate the impact of its project on the relevant species.[31] Many agency rules may be adopted only after consultation with expert advisory committees. When adopting health and safety standards the Occupational Health and Safety Administration must consult with the National Institute of Occupational Safety and Health; and so on, and on. Much administrative rulemaking is formally structured to be deliberative even before the participation of affected publics though notice and comment rulemaking.

Congressional Oversight

Consider first the US Congress. Congressional legislation establishes substantive criteria for agency action that, in turn, determine in many circumstances what sorts of reasons are required to be given. Statutes further prescribe by what standards agency action is to be judged as reasonable or unreasonable. The United States government is in many respects a government of statutes. But whether Congress is an effective monitor with respect to agency performance in relation to its statutory standards is controversial. The constitutional propriety of congressional demands for explanation from the executive branch can hardly be questioned. Congressional requirements for reports and explanations from government department heads began during the administration of George Washington.[32] Save for limited exceptions for information covered by executive privilege, Congress can demand an explanation from any agency any time,[33] and it has imposed continuous reporting requirements in a multitude of general and agency-specific statutes.[34]

But the ability of Congress to overturn agency decisions that it thinks are unjustified is limited to passing new legislation. Congressional attempts to override agency decisions by the vote of either one or both houses of Congress, without submission

---

[30]   16 U.S.C. § 1536(a)-(b); 50 C.F.R. § 402.01(a) (2016).

[31]   For a discussion of the legal effect of the biological opinion required under the Endangered Species Act, see *Bennett* v. *Spear*, 520 U.S. 154 (1997).

[32]   E.g., An Act to Establish the Treasury Department, ch. 12, § 2, 1 Stat. 65, 66 (1789) (requiring the Treasury Secretary "to make report, and give information to either branch of the legislature, in person or in writing [as he may be required], respecting all matters referred to him by the Senate or House of Representatives, or which shall appertain to his office.").

[33]   For discussion of executive privilege and its limits in United States constitutional law, see *United States* v. *Nixon*, 418 U.S. 683 (1974).

[34]   Indeed, these reporting requirements have grown so numerous that efforts have been undertaken to cut back on duplicative and unnecessary reports. Beth Cobert, Calling on Congress to Eliminate Outdated and Duplicative Reporting Requirements, White House Blog (June 25, 2014, 9:09 AM), available at: www.whitehouse.gov/blog/2014/06/25/calling-congress-eliminate-outdated-and-duplicative-reporting-requirements (Last accessed May 25, 2018).

to – and agreement by – the President, were determined to be unconstitutional (absent a two-thirds majority in both houses to override a presidential veto).[35] The operational history of the Congressional Review Act (CRA),[36] which requires the submission of major rules for review by the Government Accountability Office (GAO) and subjects those rules to congressional veto by statute, demonstrates how difficult this process may be.[37] Prior to 2017, the CRA procedure was used only once to overturn a rule.[38] It was effective in that instance because a rule adopted in a Democratic administration was subject to congressional review in the new Republican administration with a decidedly different regulatory philosophy.[39] The same dynamic occurred after the elections of 2016. A unified Republican Congress used the CRA to rescind fourteen rules adopted during the late stages of the Obama administration. But the CRA is self-limiting. It may only be used to rescind rules within the first sixty legislative days of their adoption.

The political science literature on whether Congress is an effective monitor of agency action using its more informal investigatory and public hearing processes is substantial. To say the least, opinion is divided. On one end of the spectrum are researchers who might be characterized as the "structure and process school." They seem to believe that virtually every aspect of agency organization and procedure can be explained as a device for monitoring agency behavior either by Congress or its surrogates.[40] At the other end are those who emphasize the episodic nature of congressional oversight and its focus on scandal rather than routine policymaking, along with the weak political incentives of representatives and senators to spend their time monitoring agency behavior. These commentators tend to conclude that congressional oversight is largely ineffectual.[41] This position is countered by yet another

---

[35] *INS v. Chadha*, 462 U.S. 919 (1983).

[36] Pub. L. No. 104-121, Tit. II, § 251, 110 Stat. 868 (1996) (codified at 5 U.S.C. §§ 801–8).

[37] In 2006, the GAO informed Congress that, on the 610 major rules reported to the GAO under the CRA in the previous decade, only 28 had been subject to one or more resolutions of disapproval, and only one rule was ultimately disallowed. *10th Anniversary of the Congressional Review Act: Hearing Before the* H. Subcomm. On Commercial and Admin. Law, 109th Cong. (2006) (prepared statement of J. Christopher Mihm, Managing Director, Strategic Issues, Gov't Accountability Office), available at: www.gpo.gov/fdsys/pkg/GAOREPORTS-GAO-06-601T/pdf/GAOREPORTS-GAO-06-601T.pdf (Last accessed May 25, 2018).

[38] Ibid.

[39] The Bush-era Congress nullified the Labor Department's ergonomics rule, which was formulated under President Clinton. S.J. Res., Pub. L. No. 107-5, 115 Stat. 7 (2001); *see also* Ergonomics Program, 65 Fed. Reg. 68,262 (Nov. 14, 2000) (providing the final text of the rule, prior to congressional nullification).

[40] *See* Mathew D. McCubbins et al., Structure and Process, Politics and Policy: Administrative Arrangements and Political Control of Agencies, 75 *Va. L. Rev.* 431 (1989); Mathew D. McCubbins et al., Administrative Procedures as Instruments of Political Control, 3 *J. L. Econ. & Org.* 243, 246 (1987) ("[M]ost administrative law ... is written for the purpose of helping elected politicians retain control of policymaking.").

[41] *See* Bernard Rosen, *Holding Government Bureaucracies Accountable* (1982); *The Federal Trade Commission Since 1970: Economic Regulation and Bureaucratic Behavior* 34 (Kenneth W. Clarkson and Timothy J. Muris eds., 1981) ("The ability of Congress to monitor individual FTC activities effectively is limited.").

strand in the literature that suggests agencies may be almost-perfectly attuned to the preferences of the relevant congressional committees and subcommittees in their political environment and that they anticipatorily monitor their own behavior to avoid getting into political trouble.[42] The middle ground believes that the efficacy of congressional oversight depends on political salience, and, hence, that congressional oversight is sometimes effective and sometimes not.[43] We will be content here to note that: (i) agencies are created and funded by congressional statute, (ii) they are subject to legitimate congressional demands for explanation about almost anything, and (iii) that agency legal obligations to provide reasons both to Congress and to others are themselves largely the product of legislation. In this context it is surely fair to say that no institutional actor in the American constitutional system is better situated to shape — and to insist on — reasoned administration than the Congress of the United States.

But Congress is not a court, and senators and representatives are not judges.[44] Hence, congressional demands for explanation – from committees, subcommittees and individual members – diverge markedly from those administrators face in judicial review proceedings. First, Congress is often intensely concerned with agency agenda-setting and enforcement, two areas largely immune from judicial review. When General Motors (GM) cars were found to have ignition switch problems that could result in unexpected engine shutdowns and deactivation of the vehicle's airbags, no court would have ordered NHTSA to take prompt action to initiate a recall proceeding. But Congress, sensing a public outcry, was quick to demand explanations and enforcement action.[45]

When Ford Pinto fuel tanks were found to cause vehicle fires in rear-end collisions, it was Congress that demanded an explanation of why NHTSA had no fuel tank integrity standard that would have forbidden Ford's particular design. And perhaps sensing a lack of sufficient urgency on this matter, Congress intervened by statute to force the prompt adoption of an agency rule that had been proposed, but never finalized.[46] Examples could be multiplied ad infinitum concerning other agencies as well. While courts seldom intervene concerning agencies' agenda-setting or enforcement priorities, these topics are high on Congress' list of items for agency oversight.

Second, reasonableness in the context of congressional oversight is based on "political reason," not the instrumental rationality analysis normally pursued in

---

[42] *See* Mathew D. McCubbins and Thomas Schwartz, Congressional Oversight Overlooked: Police Patrols Versus Fire Alarms, 28 *Am. J. Pol. Sci.* 165 (1984).

[43] *See* Joel D. Aberbach, *Keeping a Watchful Eye: The Politics of Congressional Oversight* (1990).

[44] At least most of the time. U.S. Const. art. 1, § 3, cl. 6 ("The Senate shall have the sole Power to try all Impeachments.").

[45] Jeff Bennett and Joseph B. White, Congress to Investigate GM Recall, Wall. St. J. (Mar 10, 2014 9:54 PM), available at: www.wsj.com/articles/SB10001424052702304020104579431141203677528 (Last accessed May 25, 2018).

[46] See Mashaw and Harfst, The Struggle for Auto Safety, at 233.

judicial review. "What we did was legal, indeed required by our statute," may be a perfectly correct but, nevertheless, insufficient response to a congressional committee overseeing an agency's actions. For example, when the FDA began the rulemaking process to ban saccharin – then the only available no-calorie artificial sweetener – from food products due to its potential carcinogenicity,[47] the American public was livid.[48] The FDA Commissioner explained to Congress that the banning of this relatively mild carcinogen was required by the so-called Delaney Clause in the food additives sections of the Food, Drug and Cosmetic Act,[49] but Congress was not mollified.[50] However good the legal argument, decimating the diet-food industry and depriving American dieters of low-calorie foods and drinks was politically unreasonable, whatever the statute said.

The NHTSA experienced a similar congressional uproar over its passive restraints rule when, because of judicial invalidation of part of the rule, ignition interlocks which disabled vehicles unless all passengers were "buckled up," became the only feasible compliance technology. The American motoring public was up in arms.[51] That ignition interlocks: (i) might have saved 10,000 lives per year, (ii) were cheap (indeed, at the time, they may have been the most cost-effective automotive safety technology ever devised), and (iii) had survived judicial review, availed the agency nothing. The statute said that the agency was to "meet the need for auto safety," but in Congress' view, the law contained an implicit caveat to "be reasonable about it." And the implicit message here was that Congress intended something more than a technocratic judgment that a safety requirement met the explicit statutory requirements that a performance standard was "reasonable" and "appropriate" for the type of motor vehicle regulated. "Reasonable" here meant something like, "don't do things that are wildly politically unpopular." An amendment to the Motor Vehicle Safety Act promptly eliminated ignition interlocks from the potential universe of the NHTSA safety technologies.[52]

Political legitimacy demands the exercise of "political reason," which entails considerations beyond the single-minded, instrumentally rational pursuit of an agency's core mission. Whether and how such "political" considerations can be translated into forms that fit an agency's understanding of its statutory obligations and incorporated

[47] Saccharin and Its Salts: Proposed Rulemaking, 42 Fed. Reg. 19,996 (Apr. 15, 1977).

[48] Peter Milius, Pending FDA Saccharin Ban a Bitter Dose for Many in U.S., Wash. Post, Apr. 4, 1977, at A2.

[49] 21 U.S.C. § 348(c)(3)(A) (2012). ("[N]o additive shall be deemed to be safe if it is found to induce cancer when ingested by man or animal, or if it is found, after tests which are appropriate for the evaluation of the safety of food additives, to induce cancer in man or animal."); see Richard A. Merrill, Food Safety Regulation: Reforming the Delaney Clause, 18 Am. Rev. of Pub. Health 313 (1997).

[50] E.g., Moratorium on Saccharin Ban: Hearing Before the Subcomm. on Health and the Env't of the H. Comm. on Interstate and Foreign Commerce, 95th Cong. 65–6, 97 (1977).

[51] Stephen R. Kratzke, Regulatory History of Automatic Crash Protection in FMVSS 208 (SAE Technical Paper 950865), in Seat Belts: The Development of an Essential Safety Feature 53 (2003).

[52] See 49 U.S.C. § 30124.

into its reasoning is addressed in Chapter 6. The NHTSA's response to the ignition interlock fiasco reveals that translating political into technocratic reasons is certainly possible. A reader of the NHTSA's subsequent rulemaking proposals, and other issuances, will find that "public acceptability" has become a regular topic for discussion when the agency is considering or explaining its policy choices. Presumably a safety technology is not "reasonable" or "appropriate" if the public hates it.

Presidential Control?

Oddly enough, the President's power to contribute to reasoned administration through independent action remains constitutionally controversial.[53] I say "oddly enough" because the President is the only institutional actor clearly given an oversight role in the text of the Constitution. Not only does the Constitution charge the President with seeing that the laws are "faithfully executed"[54]; it specifically empowers the President to appoint the heads of all government departments and to demand reports in writing from those department heads.[55]

The legal controversies about the President's role in administration are, in substance, controversies about the President's independent role in policymaking. They reflect a continuous struggle between Congress and various presidents over the control of federal administrative officials. Administrative agencies serve two principals, neither of which is a political lightweight.

This contest began in the earliest days of the Republic. A gap in the Constitution – the failure to specify who removes officers of the federal government once appointed – provoked many days of congressional debate in the first Congress. Opinions ranged from those who thought the President could remove any officer that he had appointed, to those who thought that the President could remove officers he appointed only with the consent of the Senate, to those who thought this constitutional gap should simply be filled by legislation that specified whatever removal authority that Congress thought appropriate. The resolution of this issue in the "Decision of 1789" actually papered over the problem and resolved nothing. It was a "resolution" that set a pattern for over two hundred years of continuing controversy.[56]

Courts determined early that officers sued for damages could not escape liability by invoking a presidential direction where that direction conflicted with the officer's

---

[53] *Compare* Elena Kagan, Presidential Administration, 114 *Harv. L. Rev.* 2245 (2001) (applauding presidential control of administrative action) *with* Peter M. Shane, *Madison's Nightmare: How Executive Power Threatens American Democracy* (2009) (making arguments basically consistent with the title of the book).

[54] U.S. Const. art. 2, § 3.

[55] Id., art. 2. § 2, cl. 1–2.

[56] On the Decision of 1789, see Jerry L. Mashaw, *Creating the Administrative Constitution: The Lost 100 Years of American Administrative Law* 38–40 (2012).

statutory authority (see Chapter 2). But these Supreme Court rulings said nothing about presidential direction where the officer's statutory instructions were not clear. Hence, when a lower court interfered with Thomas Jefferson's instructions to customs officers, he sent those officers further instructions – to ignore the courts.[57]

The contest over presidential control of administration returned to congressional fora and created a constitutional crisis during the "Bank War" of the 1830s, which concerned the rechartering of the Second Bank of the United States.[58] In practical terms, Jackson won the Bank War; the Second Bank of the United States was history. But the battle over presidential direction, including presidential power to appoint and remove, raged on.

That battled flared again roughly three decades later. After Abraham Lincoln's assassination, the Republican majority in Congress trusted Lincoln's department heads, but pointedly did not trust Andrew Johnson, Lincoln's successor in the presidency. Congress proceeded to pass the Tenure of Office Act,[59] which required that presidents seeking to remove any department head that they had appointed obtain the Senate's advice and consent. Johnson ignored the statute, was impeached, and narrowly escaped conviction. He was apparently acquitted on the technical ground that the officer he removed had been appointed by Lincoln, not by him.[60] The case was resolved based on Congress' faulty drafting, but the constitutional ambiguity remained unresolved.

The legal struggle moved back to the Supreme Court in the 1920s. The Court determined that, as a constitutional matter, Congress could not limit the President's power to remove executive officers by making removal contingent on the Senate's advice and consent.[61] But within ten years, the reach of that decision was cast in doubt. *Humphrey's Executor v. United States*[62] concerned President Franklin D. Roosevelt's removal of an FTC Commissioner on the simple ground that the Commissioner and he did not agree on FTC policy. The Federal Trade Commission Act (FTCA) had made commissioners removable only for cause, such as malfeasance or nonfeasance in office, and not because of policy disagreements.[63] The President's attorneys argued that these statutory restrictions on the President's removal power were unconstitutional, but the Court rebuffed them. The Court ruled that quasi-judicial and quasi-legislative officers, like FTC commissioners, could be made removable only for cause to ensure their independence from presidential control. Apparently, Congress' error in the prior *Myers* case (although one cannot tell it from the Court's opinion) was to insert itself into the appointment and removal process in a way that

---

[57] *See* id., at 107–8.
[58] *See* id., at 156–63.
[59] ch. 154, 14 Stat. 430 (1867).
[60] *See* id., at 234–5.
[61] *Myers v. United States*, 272 U.S. 52 (1926).
[62] 295 U.S. 602 (1935).
[63] Id., at 622.

went beyond the Senate's textually based advice and consent authority concerning high-level appointments.

The battle over appointments and removals continues. In the past several decades, "for cause" removal has been approved even for officers exercising the quintessential executive function of criminal prosecution.[64] Yet congressional removal of the Comptroller General, long thought to be an officer of Congress, was held unconstitutional even though the removal authority required presidential consent.[65] And, after winning judicial approval in *Humphrey's Executor*, "for cause" removal was cut down to size in the twenty-first century. The Court found unconstitutional a "for cause" removal provision which protected an officer who could only be removed by yet another administrative officer whom the President could also only remove for cause.[66] For reasons that left the dissenting justices, and many commentators, mystified, the majority decided that "for cause" removal was constitutional, but double "for cause" removal was not.[67] The waters here are truly murky.

Lying just beneath the surface of this controversy over appointments and removals is the critical question: what authority does the President have to influence administrative policy by requiring that administrators take account of considerations other than criteria for action specified in the agencies' governing legislation? For now, we will concentrate on the way in which presidents have empowered themselves by demanding various forms of regulatory analysis prior to the adoption of major administrative rules – and have subjected those analyses to monitoring by the OMB, or other entities in the Executive Office of the President (EOP).

Regulatory Impact Analysis

Contemporary concerns about presidential direction of agency rulemaking and its effects on regulatory policy cluster around a series of analytic requirements that date back to the 1970s. These requirements emerged from widespread concern that the veritable orgy of regulatory statutes passed in the 1960s and early 1970s imposed unreasonable costs on the American economy. Presidents had long had substantial control over agency budgetary requests through the Bureau of the Budget, now the OMB. But administrative agencies had no "regulatory budget" constraining the costs that they might impose on the economy in the name of, for instance, environmental, worker, or consumer protection. In the midst of economic troubles that generated terms like "stagflation" and "the misery index," it seemed sensible to construct some means to assure that agencies were paying attention to their regulatory actions' economic effects.

[64] *Morrison v. Olson*, 487 U.S. 654 (1988).
[65] *Bowsher v. Synar*, 478 U.S. 714 (1986).
[66] *Free Enter. Fund v. Pub. Co. Accounting Oversight Bd.*, 561 U.S. 477 (2010).
[67] Id., at 495–6.

Regulatory impact analysis is, in essence, the mirror image of the environmental impact analyses required by the National Environmental Policy Act (NEPA) of 1970. Under the NEPA statute, agencies pursuing infrastructure and other projects designed to promote economic growth are required to consider the environmental consequences of their actions. Following this template, multiple Presidents have demanded, by executive order as discussed in Chapter 3, that agencies pursuing major policies by rule consider those policies' economic effects by providing cost-benefit and cost-effectiveness analyses of the proposed regulations.

Regulatory-impact analysis requirements began in a mild way with President Gerald R. Ford's executive order requiring "inflation impact statements" to accompany any major agency proposals for legislation or regulation.[68] President Jimmy Carter made these analyses more demanding by requiring that the agencies prepare cost-effectiveness analyses, which were to include "a detailed explanation of the reasons for choosing one alternative over the others."[69] The Carter analyses were made available to the public and were subject to review by an entity known as the Regulatory Analysis Review Group in the EOP.

President Ronald Reagan gave the regulatory-impact analysis something like its contemporary form with Executive Order 12,291.[70] That order not only required that agencies do cost-benefit as well as cost-effectiveness analyses; it mandated that agencies, to the extent permitted by their statutes, be guided by that order's stated policy goals. Those goals included: (i) only adopting policies justified by benefits that exceeded their costs, and (ii) choosing, from among possible regulatory policies, the policy least burdensome on the national economy. All such analyses were made reviewable by the Office of Economic and Regulatory Affairs (OIRA) in OMB, an office created by the Paperwork Reduction Act (PRA) of 1980.[71]

The OIRA's review of regulatory analyses does not include the authority to prevent agency adoption of a proposed regulation with which the OIRA disagrees. The practical effect of OIRA disagreement is nevertheless similar to its permit authority under the PRA. The OIRA reviews all agency budgetary requests, all agency proposals for legislation and agency congressional testimony concerning budgetary and

---

[68] Exec. Order No. 11,821, 3 C.F.R. § 926 (1971–1975). On the development of presidential oversight through the EOP, see generally Jerry L. Mashaw et al., *Administrative Law: The American Public Law System* 326–44 (7th edn. 2014).

[69] Exec. Order No. 12,044, § 3(b)(1), 3 C.F.R. § 152 (1979).

[70] 46 Fed. Reg. 13,193 (Feb. 17, 1981).

[71] The PRA required all agencies whose regulations required additional record keeping or reports from regulated parties to provide an analysis demonstrating both the necessity of those information requirements and that the agency had imposed only those paperwork burdens that were absolutely essential to carrying out its legislative tasks. The OIRA was to review each of these analyses and determine whether the agency should be authorized to impose the contemplated paperwork burden. *See* 44 U.S.C. § 3507(a). Without an OIRA authorization, agencies can still request information from outside parties, but provision of that information is not legally required.

legislative matters.[72] Whether an agency's budgetary requests or legislative proposals become a part of the "President's Program" is crucially important to an agency's substantive authority and fiscal resources. Moreover, no agency head normally wants to be viewed as seriously out-of-step with the President's policy priorities or at loggerheads with the White House. OMB objections to an agency's reasoning in its regulatory analyses carry serious political weight.

Each President since Reagan has revised the Reagan program in various ways to emphasize that particular administration's concerns. We need not here pursue the substantive and procedural details of those various programs. Suffice it to say that no President has thought it advisable to eliminate regulatory impact analysis. When combined with the executive-order-based requirement that agencies prepare annual regulatory agendas,[73] the political effect of regulatory analysis is to give the EOP, through the OMB, substantial influence, if not control, over major agency regulatory initiatives.

The OMB looks at regulatory activity across the whole of the executive establishment, and is charged with assuring that regulatory programs do not make unreasonable demands on national resources. The OMB's perspective on regulation is institutionally distinct from line agencies charged with more focused missions to promote, for instance, health, safety, or environmental preservation. The line agencies and the OMB are natural antagonists. Agencies and their allies often view the OMB as overly cautious about regulation. Regulated industries, by contrast, may view the OMB as their last hope for "reasonable" public policy.

These institutional and interest group policy cleavages echo in legal conflicts about the constitutionality of presidential demands for regulatory analysis. The Reagan program was immediately attacked as an unconstitutional presidential power grab.[74] And prominent legal scholars have warned that the OMB review process can easily step over the line from oversight of the reasonableness of agency policy to presidential decision-making.[75] These critics emphasize that the Constitution gives the President the authority to see that the laws are faithfully executed, not to require them to be executed in line with a particular administration's policy preferences. Modern statutes dealing with domestic matters generally delegate decisional authority to agency heads, not to the President. And where authority is delegated clearly matters to Congress. Putting pesticide regulation in the Department of Agriculture is very different from putting it in the EPA. Presidential policy direction arguably upsets hard-fought legislative compromises over who decides what.

---

[72] *See Open Government Plan*, Office of Mgmt. & Budget 1 (Apr. 7, 2010), available at: www.whitehouse .gov/sites/default/files/microsites/100407-omb-opengov-plan.pdf (Last accessed May 25, 2018).

[73] Exec. Order No. 12,866, § 4, 58 Fed. Reg. 51,735 (Oct. 4, 1993).

[74] Morton Rosenberg, Beyond the Limits of Executive Power: Presidential Control of Agency Rulemaking under Executive Order 12,291, 80 *Mich. L. Rev.* 193 (1981).

[75] Peter L. Strauss, Presidential Rulemaking, 72 *Chi.-Kent L. Rev.* 965 (1997).

Supporters of presidential control have argued that objections to presidential direction ignore the fact that public policy initiatives increasingly are accomplished through administrative actions under existing statutes, not by passing new legislation.[76] Hence, as a matter of democratic accountability, the President should be – and generally is in the popular mind – held politically responsible for agency policy. Given these realities, it is only fitting that presidents systematically monitor what administrators do and direct their exercise of policy discretion, so long as those directions do not conflict with the agencies' statutory mandates. On this view, centralized control and direction in the Executive Branch furthers basic constitutional commitments.

It is also worth noting that prior to the Trump administration the analytic requirements imposed by presidential executive orders remained, at least formally, within the tradition of reasoned administrative action. They merely broadened the considerations about which agencies must reason to the extent consistent with agencies' governing statutes. President Donald Trump's directives are different. They are explicitly deregulatory. His Executive Order 13,771, "Reducing Regulation and Controlling Regulatory Costs"[77] purports to require that any agency proposing a new regulation identify two regulations for repeal. The repealed regulations must reduce regulatory costs by at least as much as the proposed new regulation adds regulatory burdens. Trump's EO further authorizes the OMB to provide each agency with a "regulatory budget" for each fiscal year and prohibits agencies, to the extent permitted by law, from exceeding that budget when adopting new regulations. Whether these instructions can qualify as "legal" reasons for agency regulatory choices remains to be seen. Whether these instructions should be understood as fulfilling the constitutional duty of overseeing faithful execution of the law is equally problematic.

Chapter 6 will return to the issue of the relationship between politics and reasoned administration. For present purposes, the important point may be that regulatory impact analysis, combined with other crosscutting analytic requirements, substantially broadens the demands of reason-giving and reasonableness, at least for major policy decisions adopted by rule. The means-ends rationality that inhabits the basic model of reasoned decision-making under particular statutes has been expanded to require something like synoptic or comprehensive rationality. Where these analytic requirements apply, agencies must now provide reasoned analysis of not just how their policies further their statutory missions, but how they affect the economy, the environment, the paperwork burden of affected parties, the position of small entities subject to their rules, income distribution, and even the structure of federalism in the United States. Whether this burden of justification can be borne and still produce effective governance is something that we will take up in the next section. But

---

[76] *See* Kagan, Presidential Administration.
[77] 82 Fed. Reg. 9339, Feb. 3, 2017.

before leaving the question of how reason-giving and reasonableness requirements empower actors in administrative agencies' policy spaces, we should also look at how these requirements impact the influence of affected, non-governmental parties who are neither inside the agency nor a part of the EOP.

Reason and the Role of Outsiders

As we have seen, statutory requirements for reasoned administration, embellished by judicial construction, include requirements for responsiveness to the submissions of participants in agency processes. These responses are also meant to explain to parties who are disappointed by an agency policy choice, or an agency decision on their particular case, why the agency action is a legitimate exercise of public authority. There seems little doubt that these requirements for reason-giving and for substantive reasonableness in agency decision-making both empower outsiders and legitimate administrative governance.

Where agency adjudication is concerned, study after study has demonstrated that procedural rules that give participants a sense of control over the decision process – including adequate notice of issues, adequate opportunity to present facts and arguments, and opinions that explain official decisions – give participants a sense that they have been treated fairly and that the decisions are legitimate.[78] To be sure, participants in administrative adjudications who lose their cases often appeal. But, most losing parties do not. And the opportunity to appeal does more than provide disappointed participants with the opportunity to correct error. The simple existence of that appeal opportunity reinforces the participants' sense that administrative decision-makers must duly attend to their evidence and arguments.

Imbalances in litigant resources to exercise hearing rights or appeal opportunities to some degree diminish the luster of this happy picture. But many administrative adjudicatory processes are tailored to take account of litigant capacities.[79] In short, requirements for an adjudicatory hearing prior to administrative action are meant to protect the influence of directly affected outsiders on administrative decision-making. Reasoned administration in adjudication demands that administrators both listen to the litigants' point of view and provide a rationale that is respectful of the facts and arguments put forward in the adjudicatory process. No system is perfect,

---

[78] See E. Allan Lind and Tom R. Tyler, The Social Psychology of Procedural Justice (1988); John Thibaut and Laurens Walker, Procedural Justice: A Psychological Analysis (1975).

[79] For example, the Supreme Court, in the seminal case of Goldberg v. Kelly, 397 U.S. 254 (1970) required as a constitutional matter that pre-termination hearings provided to disappointed applicants for welfare benefits include an opportunity for oral contest. This requirement was premised on the potentially limited reading and writing skills of welfare clientele. Id., at 269. Similarly, claimants seeking hearings after denial or termination of disability benefits under the Social Security Act are provided an audience before an administrative law judge who has the responsibility to develop all aspects of the case. The government is not represented in these hearings, although the claimant may be. See Jerry L. Mashaw, Bureaucratic Justice: Managing Social Security Disability Claims (1983).

and reform of administrative adjudication is always on the agenda. But, if fairness to participants through the provision of significant participant influence over outcomes is the goal, reasoned administration in its adjudicatory form is generally a success.

The rulemaking story is more complicated. When rulemaking became an important agency function in the late 1960s and 1970s, it combined with an increasingly "hard look" judicial review and a series of beneficiary friendly changes in standing, finality, and ripeness doctrines (see Chapter 2). These changes facilitated review of agency action by parties seeking regulatory benefits in addition to those attempting to avoid regulatory costs. After several decades of concern about regulatory capture of administrative agencies by regulated firms, these changes were predicted to usher in a new era of participatory rulemaking.[80] The openness of the rulemaking process – its availability to any interested party, the low cost of participation by comparison with formal adjudicatory proceedings, and the dialogic implications of requirements that agencies respond to all material issues raised – suggested the creation of a deliberative democratic process at the micropolitical, administrative level. And, unlike the general legislative process characterized by bargaining, logrolling, strategic actions for partisan advantage, and the like, the rulemaking process was bounded by subject matter jurisdictions and criteria for action that seemed to make political ideology and interest group preferences irrelevant to decisional outcomes. Agency rulemaking processes could thus be the home of reasoned administration, the instrumentally rational pursuit of legislatively specified goals, while at the same time providing a forum for democratic deliberation about the pursuit of public purposes.

This rosy vision was, of course, not universally shared, and subsequent events revealed that the skeptics had a point. Many of the new health, safety, and environmental and consumer protection programs were designed to provide diffuse benefits to the general public by regulating the conduct of parties who would bear relatively concentrated regulatory costs. Moreover, regulated firms – and industry or commercial associations – tended to have considerably greater resources to back their intense interests relative to the so-called public interest organizations that grew up around the new regulatory programs – and that sometimes had been instrumental in their creation. And while participation in informal rulemaking processes was cheap compared with the costs of contested formal adjudication, *effective* participation in rulemaking demanded a level of technical expertise that tended to be in short supply outside of regulated firms or industries.

As a result, participation in agency rulemaking is lopsidedly populated by regulated parties, their trade associations, and industry-funded think tanks often

---

[80] Nina A. Mendelson, Rulemaking, Democracy and Torrents of E-mail, 79 *Geo. Wash. L. Rev.* 1343–45 (2011) (citing sources that espouse this view).

committed to deregulatory or anti-regulatory agendas.[81] Moreover, notwithstanding the protests of its defenders, the OIRA rulemaking review process, even pre-Trump, has had a similar cast.[82] On its website, the OIRA reveals all meetings that it has held with persons interested in rules under OIRA review. Overwhelmingly these meetings are with regulated parties or their representatives. Many observers believe that this reinforces the OIRA's skeptical view of regulation and results in weakening, or abandonment, of regulatory agency initiatives submitted for regulatory impact analysis review. But, because the OIRA does not publish the content of its discussions with affected parties, or routinely reveal its comments on – and changes to – agency rulemaking proposals, documenting these effects is extremely difficult. We know that many agency proposals are withdrawn, that many languish for years in the OIRA review process (notwithstanding the OIRA's own timeliness rules), and that large numbers of rulemaking proposals are changed to limit the stringency of regulatory requirements. Whether this results from industry influence at the OIRA remains an open question.

Reasonableness review by the judiciary also clearly leverages the influence of rulemaking participants, as was anticipated. But the same factors that lead to lopsided participation in the rulemaking process, both at the agency and the OIRA levels, promote lopsided participation in judicial review as well. The limited capacity of potential beneficiaries to force regulatory action has already been discussed. But even when agencies adopt a rule subject to judicial review, agencies cannot be faulted for failure to give good reasons for resolving issues that were never raised. Hence, limited participation by regulatory beneficiaries in rulemaking proceedings limits the claims that they can make in a judicial review proceeding – should they have sufficient resources to engage in litigation at all.

Moreover, at the remedy phase, judicial review has uneven effects for regulatory beneficiaries. If a regulated party convinces a court that an agency's rule is unreasonable, the rule generally cannot go into effect. At the very least, the regulated party has achieved delay in the implementation of unwanted regulatory requirements. Where regulatory beneficiaries successfully convince a court that a rule is unreasonable (presumably in its leniency), implementation is also delayed – not exactly what the plaintiffs wanted. Regulatory beneficiaries also have limited capacity to force reissuance of more stringent requirements. Professor Wendy Wagner's empirical study

---

[81] *See* Susan Webb Yackee, Reconsidering Regulatory Capture During Regulatory Policymaking, *in* *Preventing Regulatory Capture: Special Interest Influence and How to Prevent It* 292–325 (Daniel Carpenter and David A. Moss, eds., 2013); Wendy Wagner, The Participation-Centered Model Meets Administrative Process, 2013 *Wis. L. Rev.* 671.

[82] *See* Stephen Croley, White House Review of Agency Rulemaking: An Empirical Investigation, 70 *U. Chi. L. Rev.* 821 (2003); David M. Driesen, Is Cost-Benefit Neutral?, 77 *U. Colo. L. Rev.* 335 (2006); Lisa Schultz Bressman and Michael P. Vandenbergh, Inside the Administrative State: A Critical Look at the Practice of Presidential Control, 105 *Mich. L. Rev.* 47 (2006); Sidney A. Shapiro and Christopher H. Schroeder Beyond Cost-Benefit Analysis: A Pragmatic Orientation, 32 *Harv. Envtl. L. Rev.* 433 (2008).

of EPA regulatory decision-making has documented both the extreme imbalance in regulated party versus regulatory beneficiary participation in the EPA's rulemaking process and the uncertain, even ultimately unhelpful, relief that judicial remand provided for regulatory beneficiaries.[83] In Professor Wagner's studied subset of EPA rules, only one of the rules invalidated because of the agency's inability to justify its weak stance toward a particular regulatory problem had, at the time of her writing, been reissued. That reissue took a decade.[84]

These empirical findings raise serious questions about the democratic pedigree of administrative decision-making. If we imagine that agency policy-making is a micro-political process in which agencies implementing the will of the people as represented in their governing statutes nevertheless have broad discretion to set alternative agendas for action and choose among alternative implementing policies, skewed representation of citizen views and interests is prima facie troubling. Basic ideas of representative democracy imagine that, with some distortion to be sure, the people are represented by their elected representatives. Does that representation flounder when agencies exercising delegated authority operate in an evidentiary and argumentative context that dramatically over-represents some affected interests? Can the culture of reason-giving that I have been describing compensate for these obvious participatory imbalances?

These questions raise deep theoretical issues about the way we should understand both representation and democracy in our modern administrative state. I will here only note these issues and return to them in more detail in Chapter 7.

REASONS AND THE QUALITY AND QUANTITY OF AGENCY POLICYMAKING

The resource demands of reasoned administration in contemporary American administrative law are formidable. For the past several decades academic studies have debated the extent of the "ossification" of the rulemaking process as a result of both OMB oversight and judicial reasonableness review. Controversy rages on, in part because neither quantitative nor qualitative claims concerning agency policy outputs have an objective baseline of regulatory performance against which to compare an agency's actual conduct.

It is perhaps not too much of a simplification to say that students of particular agency functions and particular subject matter areas often find agencies underperforming in terms of the number of substantive rules promulgated, the timeliness of agency decision-making, and the regulatory content of the rules adopted. More quantitative analysts, who look across multiple agencies and attempt to evaluate matters by looking at generally available statistical evidence – such as the numbers

---

[83] Wendy Wagner *Revisiting the Impact of Judicial Review on Agency Rulemakings: An Empirical Investigation*, 53 *Wm. & Mary L. Rev.* 1717 (2012).

[84] Ibid., at 1751.

of rules adopted, the numbers of pages published in the Federal Register, the estimated costs and benefits of rules adopted, and the average times between proposal and adoption of final rules – are often skeptical that ossification is a serious problem.[85] While many of these quantitative analyses are methodologically clever, I tend to think that the more qualitative literature has the better of the argument.[86]

There are a number of reasons to believe that legal demands for reasoned administration both limit regulatory output and change its character. For one thing, information demands from these requirements have grown significantly over time while the resources devoted to agency policymaking have not kept pace. No obvious technological advances allow regulatory or other agencies to produce more defensible decisions in the face of more demanding analytic requirements and reduced resources. Second, significant evidence shows that agencies attempt to avoid using the policymaking techniques that are more resource-intensive.[87] Rulemaking itself may be difficult, but many agencies avoid even more resource-intensive formal adjudication through the use of bright-line rules that eliminate the need for many adjudicatory hearings.[88] And agencies can sometimes get much of the policymaking effect of rules by issuing various forms of guidance documents that are not subject to the same demands for reason-giving and review.[89] These avoidance techniques are designed to absolve the agencies of requirements to demonstrate their actions' reasonableness that they find too demanding to fulfill and still carry out their statutory responsibilities.

But the efficacy of retreat to various guidance documents depends on an agency's other authority. Because no new pharmaceutical can be marketed without FDA approval, that agency's informal guidelines concerning the requirements for demonstrating a drug's safety and effectiveness are almost certain to be followed, even though they have no independent legal effect. No manufacturer wants to spend millions on drug development and testing to have its application for the new

---

[85] *See, e.g.,* Cary Coglianese, Empirical Analysis and Administrative Law, 2002 *U. Ill. L. Rev.* 1111; Anne Joseph O'Connell, Political Cycles of Rulemaking: An Empirical Portrait of the Modern Administrative State, 94 *Va. L. Rev.* 889, 932 (2008) ("The administrative state, at least on a macro level, does not seem to be substantially ossified."); Jason Webb Yackee and Susan Webb Yackee, Administrative Procedure and Bureaucratic Performance: Is Federal Rulemaking "Ossified"?, 20 *J. Pub. Admin. Research & Theory* 261 (2010).

[86] For perhaps the most informative exchange on this topic, see Jason Webb Yackee and Susan Webb Yackee, Testing the Ossification Thesis: An Empirical Examination of Federal Regulatory Volume and Speed, 1950–1990, 80 *Geo. Wash. L. Rev.* 1414, 1421 ("[E]vidence that ossification is either a serious or widespread problem is mixed and relatively weak.") (2012); and Richard J. Pierce, Jr., Rulemaking Ossification Is Real: A Response to Testing the Ossification Thesis, 80 *Geo. Wash. L. Rev.* 1493, 1495 (2012) ("[T]he Yackees' specific findings do not support their broad conclusion.").

[87] *See* Magill, *supra* at note M. Elizabeth Magill, Agency Self-Regulation, 77 G.W. L. Rev. 859 (2009).

[88] The Supreme Court approved these techniques very early in what we might call the "rulemaking era." *See, e.g., United States v. Storer Broadcasting Co.,* 351 U.S. 192 (1956); *Federal Power Comm'n. v. Texaco, Inc.,* 377 U.S. 33 (1964); *see also Weinberger v. Hynson,* Westcott and Dunning, Inc. 412 U.S. 609, 620–1 (1973) (citing *Storer* and *Texaco* approvingly).

[89] See Chapter 3 for a discussion of these exceptions under the APA.

drug's approval denied. By contrast, the NHTSA has no authority to license motor vehicles for safety. If it wants to require any particular level of safety performance, it must do so by rule.

In short, the ability to satisfy all analytic requirements and adopt rules of conduct is critically important to effective implementation of a broad range of policies. Many of our most important health, safety, and environmental statutes contain virtually no self-executing rules of conduct. They simply empower agencies – the EPA, the NHTSA, the OSHA or the CPSC – to adopt rules. Until a rule is formulated through the usual rulemaking process and, in many cases, survives both the OMB and judicial review, there is no law to apply. Agency guidance in the absence of a rule has little, if any, coercive effect outside of markets where strong reputational effects make producers and sellers highly risk averse.

Third, my own qualitative work, with my co-author David Harfst, provides what we believe to be overwhelming evidence that the demands of the legal culture dramatically reshaped the regulatory behavior of the NHTSA.[90] During the first twenty years of the agency's operations these changes included a pronounced shift from the development of new safety performance standards by regulation to the recall of defective vehicles. This shift in regulatory technique was not dictated by the superior protective effects of recalls. Safety performance regulations adopted early in the NHTSA's history have demonstrable effects on the prevention of death and injury from vehicle accidents. Recalling defective vehicles has never been demonstrated to have any. The causes of this change in regulatory technique were straightforward: demonstrating the reasonableness of technology-forcing regulation was extremely difficult; demonstrating that a given automobile had some defect that might relate to automobile safety was easy. The legal de-legitimatization of the agency's rulemaking efforts fed back into the agency's internal organization and processes and into the political process that controlled the agency's funding. Recalls were rewarded with judicial, legislative, and public approval; regulations demanding enhanced safety performance generally were not.

After nearly a decade of virtual inactivity on the rulemaking front, the agency's return to rulemaking was not marked by requiring new technological safety advances. Instead, rules often were demanded by new legislation and required automobile manufacturers to do essentially what they were already doing – or had promised to do shortly. The only legal challenge to these rules has been by consumer groups urging that they are too undemanding.[91]

---

[90] Jerry L. Mashaw and David L. Harfst, Regulation and Legal Culture: The Case of Motor Vehicle Safety, 4 *Yale J. Reg.* 257 (1987); Jerry L. Mashaw and David L. Harfst, Inside the National Highway Traffic Safety Administration: Legal Determinants of Bureaucratic Organization and Performance, 57 *U. Chi. L. Rev.* 443 (1990).

[91] Jerry L. Mashaw and David L. Harfst, The Transformation of Auto Safety Regulation: Bureaucratic Adaptation to Legal Culture, 34 *Yale J. on Reg.* 167 (2017).

There is much more to the NHTSA story, but suffice it to say that the effects that Harfst and I have found at the NHTSA simply cannot be discerned by quantitative analysis. The NHTSA has adopted a substantial number of rules in the past two decades. But without looking at the substance of those rules and what auto manufacturers were already doing, quantitative analysis misses that these rules are not actually requiring much. Adding up the costs and benefits reported for the NHTSA's rules similarly misses the point. These estimates use a methodology that presumes that anything that happens after the effective date of a rule is a result of the rule itself. But if manufacturers were already doing – or planning to do – what the agency demands, the rule has little-to-no marginal cost or benefit. Noting that automobile deaths and injuries per million miles traveled have steadily declined over the life of the agency's regulatory action is equally misleading. By the agency's own estimates, two-thirds of those reductions would have occurred with no safety regulation whatsoever.[92] The remaining reductions are largely attributable to the increased use of lap and shoulder belts that were first introduced into motor vehicles ten years before the Motor Vehicle Safety Act was passed.

Finally, arguing that the agency actually seldom gets sued to test the reasonableness of its rules provides no evidence that the agency's behavior is not shaped by its historic difficulties in demonstrating the reasonableness of its technology-forcing innovations. The agency's rules over the past two decades have not been forcing the technology. Manufacturers can hardly sue to overturn rules as unreasonable when those rules simply require them to do what they are, in large part, already doing.

Authors are, of course, prejudiced in favor of their own findings, and the like findings of others. But, even were we to be misled in describing the NHTSA's experience with motor vehicle safety regulation as one shaped by the demands of legal culture, our findings nevertheless demonstrate that quantitative approaches to agency productivity, without serious contextual interpretation, simply cannot tell us much about whether agencies are performing well in relation to their stated goals. Moreover, even the sort of in-depth case study that Harfst and I conducted cannot answer the deeper and more important question: Has the legal demand for reasoned administration made the NHTSA's regulatory output better than it otherwise would have been? Or have ambitious demands for reasoned administration so clogged the arteries of administrative decision processes that significant welfare-enhancing opportunities are foregone? In short, is reasoned administration as structured in American administrative law worth its costs? We have no standard against which to assess that issue.

However, as just stated, the question may be badly framed. First, even if we assume that there are real welfare losses associated with reasonableness review of rulemaking as structured in the American legal system, those costs may be largely attributable to the timing of review, not its form. Pre-enforcement review of rules

[92] Ibid.

both invites litigation and provides review at a time when reasonableness, judged by standards of technological and economic feasibility, is difficult to evaluate.[93] Courts cannot allow agencies to simply mouth bromides like "necessity is the mother of invention," or "cost curves slant downward over time." Courts demand evidence that, in the absence of efforts at compliance, may be missing. The modesty of the NHTSA's standards may be explained simply as the agency's response to the necessity of having some real-world evidence that the technology the standards demand is "reasonable" and "appropriate," as its statute requires. Demanding broader dispersion of technologies already in widespread use solves the evidentiary problem. Second, and more importantly, the value of reasoned administration lies not just in enhanced information and more informed decision-making, but also in the potentially increased legitimacy of administrative governance – a subject to which we will return in Chapter 7.

---

[93] Jerry L. Mashaw, Improving the Environment of Agency Rulemaking: An Essay on Management, Games and Accountability, 57 *L. & Contemp. Probs.* 185 (1994).

5

Reasons, Reasonableness, and Judicial Review

The discussion up to this point has largely described how administrative reason-giving has been institutionalized as the bedrock requirement for the legality of administrative action and has explored some of this requirement's effects on agency structure and performance. The basic model of "reasoned administration" developed thus far is fairly straightforward: whether deciding cases or making general policies, agencies must explain how their decisions further the goals of the statutory programs that they implement; how the underlying facts, as developed in appropriately structured agency proceedings, support their decisions and fit within the statutory (or other cabining) criteria for agency judgment; and how their decisions are responsive to material issues that outside participants raise. Providing reasons in this form is a necessary condition for demonstrating that agency action is substantively reasonable as well. Or, to put the matter slightly differently, demonstrating through reason-giving that the agency has engaged in an appropriate reasoning process is a means for partially satisfying the Administrative Procedures Act's (APA) requirement that agency action be nonarbitrary.

Why "necessary," but only "partial"? Just this: This model of reason-giving is a model of rationality, but rationality does not exhaust reasonableness. Burning down my house to get rid of mice is instrumentally rational.[1] I want the mice gone and burning down my house will do the trick. I will not have mice, in part, because

---

[1] To avoid confusion, I want to distinguish my use of "instrumental rationality" from Max Weber's well-known typology. Max Weber, 1 *Economy and Society* 24–26 (Guenther Roth and Claus Wittich eds., Ephraim Fischoff et al. trans., 1968) (1922). For Weber, instrumental rationality included weighing the rationality of the ends pursued in the sense of making choices among alternative ends. Which ends are worth pursuing was for Weber a "value rational" choice that might be determined by various ethical, religious, aesthetic, or other commitments. For many administrative actions, the ends or values to be pursued are specified by statute. Where tradeoffs among ends are concerned I am treating the agency choice as involving primarily reasonableness considerations, although the decision calculus may include evaluation of the degree to which an action will achieve one or more appropriate ends, and how those ends should be understood.

I will not have a house. Unless I have some other undisclosed purpose for these pyrotechnics, however, this sort of action is patently unreasonable. Rationality and reasonableness are not coextensive.[2]

Setting mouse traps in my neighbor's house to get rid of my mice is unreasonable as well. But, that action is unreasonable in a different way. My action, putting mouse traps in my neighbor's house, fits poorly with my purpose, getting rid of mice in *my* house. This sort of behavior is irrational because it is predictably ineffective. A reasonable strategy for ridding my house of mice must also entail rational action. Hence, instrumentally rational agency action is a necessary, but partial, condition for satisfying any requirement of substantive reasonableness.

The distinction between rationality and reasonableness has a long history in moral and political philosophy, as well as in economics and decision theory. Without diving too deeply into these troubled waters, I will simply specify that, as I am using these terms, rationality has two components: (i) instrumentality, meaning choosing appropriate means to whatever goal is specified, and (ii) coherence, meaning non-contradiction among or within means, ends, and explanations. Reasonableness is a broader concept that encompasses rationality, but in addition it evaluates the pursuit of particular goals or ends – or pursuing them in a particular fashion – against some standard of normative judgment, all things considered.

Clearly, we want agency action to be both rational and reasonable. But reasonableness is an unruly standard. It is also a standard that raises serious institutional issues in the context of judicial review. Few agency actions will be as patently unreasonable as my house-burning example. Reasonable people can easily disagree about what is reasonable. Is there any means for giving an objective or neutral ground for judgment that agency action is rational, but nevertheless unreasonable?

THE VIRTUES OF REASONABLENESS AS REASON-GIVING

That question haunts judicial review of administrative action, both in the United States and elsewhere. If we believe that agencies have been given statutory responsibility for policy choice and for exercising judgment about the application of legal

---

[2] *See, e.g.,* Allan Gibbard, *Wise Choice, Apt Feelings: A Theory of Normative Judgment* (1990); Alan Gewirth, The Rationality of Reasonableness, 57 *Synthese* 225 (1983) (exploring and defining the concepts of reason and rationality); John Rawls, Kantian Constructivism in Moral Theory, 77 *J. Phil.* 515, 530 (1980)

> The Reasonable presupposes the Rational, because, without conceptions of the good that move members of the group, there is no point to social cooperation nor to notions of right and justice, even though such cooperation realizes values that go beyond what conceptions of the good specify taken alone. The Reasonable subordinates the Rational because its principles limit ... the final ends that can be pursued.

rules to particular fact patterns, then, when reviewing courts declare these exercises of discretion unreasonable they seemingly invade the administrative space of the executive branch. This was the insight of nineteenth-century American judges. Those jurists were skeptical about the constitutionality of giving courts a reviewing function over such executive discretion. But we have long-since moved past that strict institutional vision of separation of powers. Because of that movement, courts have needed to mediate the tension between requirements for judicial reasonableness review and the allocation of vast areas of public policy choice to one or another administrative instrumentality. Reasonableness as reason-giving is a major device for taming reasonableness review.

Indeed, reasonableness as reason-giving has institutional virtues that go beyond the mediation of these tensions. The focus on reason-giving facilitates a form of judicial review that seeks to preserve the appropriate roles of all three branches in articulating and interpreting federal law. The demand that an agency's rationale demonstrate fidelity to all relevant statutory criteria (and avoid consideration of irrelevant ones) recognizes and reinforces Congress' role as decision-maker concerning the general normative standards that should guide administrative action. The demand that agencies be responsive to the comments of rulemaking participants, or to the submissions of parties in adjudicatory proceedings, seeks to ensure that an agency pursuing an instrumentally rational program of statutory implementation has, in fact, attended to the empirical claims and policy alternatives that emerge from administrative proceedings designed to inform agency decision-making. Requirements that agencies give sufficient and adequate notice of the issues to be addressed and provide an adequate factual basis for a proposed action thus protect statutory and constitutional participation rights. While agency decisional legitimacy depends on more than expertise, the expectation that agencies will act on the basis of knowledge is a core feature of acceptable administrative action. The demand that decisions be factually supported also helps to protect against political direction by a chief executive whose constitutional function is to "take Care that the Laws be faithfully executed,"[3] not to make them by administrative fiat.

On the other hand, the judiciary's usual deference to agency agenda setting, enforcement priorities, and interpretation of ambiguous statutory terms is based importantly on a recognition of the President's appropriate oversight role. The President possesses a direct connection to both electoral politics and the legislative process that the courts do not. As suggested in Chapters 2 and 3, holding agencies to this instrumentally rational paradigm through a focus on agency rationales for action helps to insulate reviewing courts from the perception that the judiciary is invading the proper space of the administration. Hence, reviewing courts deploy that form of review, or some procedural variant, in cases where they might otherwise have straightforwardly addressed the issue of substantive reasonableness. This

---

[3]   U.S. Const. art. 2, § 3.

proceduralization of the asserted grounds for judicial judgment "tames" the unruliness of judging an agency action's substantive reasonableness.

Examples could be multiplied, but for illustrative purposes, consider the case of *United States* v. *Nova Scotia Food Products Corp.*,[4] discussed in Chapter 3. At issue was a Food and Drug Administration (FDA) rule that required that smoked fish be heated to a specific temperature and held there for a sufficient length of time to reliably eradicate any trace of botulism-causing bacteria. In this enforcement proceeding, Nova Scotia Food Products, a producer of smoked whitefish, was pursued for failure to follow the FDA rule. There had not been a case of botulism in smoked whitefish for over a decade, and the only prior cases involved vacuum-packed, not smoked, whitefish (a packing process that had since been abandoned).[5] Thus, the FDA could not demonstrate that this producer had violated the general safety standards of the Food Drug and Cosmetic Act itself, which only demands that foods be safe for human consumption. Nova Scotia Food Products had only, and admittedly, violated the FDA's further specification of food safety required in its smoked-fish rule. As a practical, culinary matter, the company justified its breach on the ground that heating whitefish to, and maintaining it at, the FDA's required temperature for the specified period "destroy[ed]" the product.[6] As a legal matter, the petitioner challenged the validity of the rule itself.

Under these circumstances, a substantive claim of unreasonableness would have been straightforward. A judicial judgment that the destruction of the smoked-whitefish industry to solve a nonexistent safety problem violated the APA's non-arbitrariness requirement could easily have been articulated. But that was not how the case was litigated or decided. The court remanded the rule to the FDA and stayed its application to Nova Scotia Food Products on two quite different grounds. First, the court found that the agency had not explained why it declined to provide different standards for different fish species depending upon their relative safety hazards and the necessities of production.[7] Second, the FDA had not revealed in its Notice of Proposed Rulemaking a sufficient underlying scientific basis for the particular heat and salinity requirements that it had adopted in the rule.[8] Because of this latter failing, the court believed that participants like Nova Scotia had no sufficient opportunity to challenge the factual and scientific bases for the FDA's proposal. If the agency wanted to enforce these manufacturing requirements for smoked whitefish, it would need to start over. Because this was an enforcement proceeding, as a formal matter the judicial judgment merely prevented enforcement of the rule against Nova Scotia. The rule otherwise remained in force, but the agency was likely to get the substantive message and rethink its policies.

---

[4]   568 F.2d 240 (2nd Cir. 1977).
[5]   Id., at 250–1.
[6]   Id., at 245.
[7]   Id., at 253.
[8]   Id., at 252.

TROUBLE IN CAMELOT

In the remainder of this chapter, I want to take up three different concerns related to the apparently deferential approach of American courts to administrative decision-making. First, there are generally acknowledged limits to "proceduralism" in the form of review of reason-giving. Whether a reason must be given or is adequate depends on substantive judgments concerning the importance and meaning of various criteria for agency action. Reasonableness is a necessary, but generally inarticulate criterion for determining what must be reasoned about and in how much detail. Second, the uneven deference accorded agency statutory interpretation suggests a judicial conceptualization of the processes of administration as narrowly instrumental. This construct is both unrealistic as a model of human purposive action and anti-democratic in ways more fully developed in Chapter 7. Analysis of statutory ends and administrative means cannot be sharply divided, nor, I will argue, should they be, given the institutional structure of American government. *Chevron* deference gestures at this recognition, but it fails to recognize the deeper sense in which independent judicial interpretation of agency statutes ignores and potentially undermines the democratically deliberative character of administration. These problems raise a third question: Should the current model of reasonableness review be abandoned? A more transparent and candid judicial assessment of agency decisions' substantive reasonableness might, somewhat paradoxically, better implement the separation of powers and democracy-reinforcing norms upon which this deferential judicial review is premised.

Procedure or Substance

The degree to which concerns about reasonableness can be "proceduralized," or ascribed to gaps in an agency's proffered rationale for its actions, varies with context. In *Nova Scotia*, the concern that the FDA had not developed an adequate factual basis for its heat and salinity conclusions could be translated easily into a procedural problem of adequate notice. The agency's failure to explain why it had not taken account of the different traits of different fish species responds to a slightly different, but still procedural, analysis. Because this issue had been raised in the rulemaking proceeding, and was clearly relevant to the policy choice that the agency was making, the FDA's failure to address it might be viewed as a simple procedural failure. Agencies are required to respond to material issues raised in their proceedings, and the agency's reasoning on that issue was missing.

Indeed, the *Nova Scotia* holding on the issue of missing alternatives mimics the Supreme Court's analysis of the National Highway Traffic Safety Administration's (NHTSA) reasoning concerning the rescission of its passive restraints rule in the *State Farm* case,[9] also discussed in Chapter 3. To paraphrase the Supreme Court

---

[9]   *Motor Vehicle Mfrs. Ass'n of the United States v. State Farm Mut. Auto. Ins. Co.*, 463 U.S. 29 (1983).

in *State Farm*, having failed to even address retention of the airbag as an exclusive means of meeting the passive restraints rule, the agency had given no reason for rejecting that alternative. But in both *Nova Scotia* and *State Farm*, finding these gaps in the agencies' reasoning presupposes some criterion for identifying gaps. Failure to respond is in a sense procedural, but agencies need not respond to all comments – only those that raise material issues, a substantive criterion of importance. The Court took a similar approach in *State Farm* to NHTSA's failure to explain why it did not mandate another alternative – continuous spool belts[10] – a technology already installed in some vehicles.

In both of these instances, the Court's findings of gaps in the agencies' reasoning can be explained within an instrumental rationality paradigm. The argument in *State Farm* would go something like this: the statutory goal is motor vehicle safety. Passenger restraints that work without motorists' actions are understood to be an important method of protecting vehicle occupants in crashes. The agency has decided not to use any method of passive passenger restraint, but explained its rejection of only one of the available methods. There is a gap in its means–ends analysis.

State Farm also illustrates the coherence prong of rationality review. In rescinding its passive restraints rule, NHTSA had also reasoned that the automatic belts that manufacturers proposed to use to satisfy the rule would likely provide little advantage over the manual lap and shoulder belts that were already installed in virtually all vehicles then on the road. To ease ingress and egress from the vehicle, these automatic belts came equipped with a release buckle. And the agency reasoned that, once the buckle was released, the automatic belt would become essentially the same as a manual belt.[11] Hence, in the agency's view, the inertia that seemed to explain the low percentage of motorists who used their manual belts would similarly afflict the automatic belts once they were unbuckled.

The Supreme Court majority faulted the agency for this reasoning as well. Obviously, the agency had addressed the issue of the safety advantages of automatic belts. There was no gap here. What, then, was the problem? The majority wondered why inertia operated only in one direction.[12] If the buckle release had not been used and the belt was in automatic mode, why did the agency think that the belt would not remain that way and provide automatic protection? In short, while the agency had addressed the automatic belt issue, it had done so in a way that the Court believed to be inadequate because it was incoherent. Without further explanation of the apparent inconsistency in its treatment of the inertia problem, the agency's decision was arbitrary.

To be sure, once again the agency's fault is articulated as a failure to explain, but, at least as concerns the inertia issue, the problem is not failure to consider a relevant

---

[10] Id., at 55–7.
[11] Federal Motor Vehicle Safety Standards; Occupant Crash Protection, 46 FR 53,419, 53,421–2 (Oct. 29, 1981).
[12] *State Farm*, 463 U.S. at 53–4.

question. The problem is a failure of logic or coherence. The agency explanation is something like: "If motorists are lazy, unbuckled automatic belts will stay unbuckled and operate essentially like manual belts. Motorists are lazy. Ergo, automatic belts will operate no better than manual belts." But that syllogism works just as well substituting the words, "buckled automatic belts will stay buckled and operate automatically." The agency's reasoning suggests that it does not have a coherent theory of how inertia works.

Addressing these *State Farm* issues as a broader question of substantive unreasonableness would clearly have been feasible. After all, the Court might have said simply:

> The agency has estimated that effective passive restraints will save 10,000 lives per year and prevent many more serious injuries. The NHTSA has concerns about the effectiveness of one of several available technologies that might meet its performance standards. Because of those concerns, the NHTSA has rescinded the entire rule rather than revising it to assure the use of an available and effective safety equipment. When implementing a statute that charges the agency with improving the safety of motor vehicles, rescinding this rule is unreasonable and arbitrary within the meaning of the APA. The rescission order is vacated.

In both of the hypothetical substantive decisions that I have concocted for the *Nova Scotia* and *State Farm* courts, the decisions suggested would have gone beyond mere rationality review by weighing the considerations presented to the agency and finding that, "on balance," the agency decision was unreasonable. But, although the APA's judicial review provisions authorize courts to decide whether agencies have committed what reviewing courts often characterize as a "clear error of judgment,"[13] American federal courts almost never straightforwardly address that question. The answer to the obvious question, "Why not?" has already been suggested – the judiciary's longstanding program of attempting to fulfill its reviewing function without impinging excessively on legislatively conferred administrative discretion. "That's a stupid policy," looks a lot like a policy decision.

But this rationale is both suspect and incomplete. Suspect because the techniques of proceduralized rationality review may give a false impression of the degree to which judicial review in practice invades the policy space legitimately delegated to administrators implementing legislative programs. Proceduralism can both obscure the degree to which substantive reasonableness is in play and invite judicial activism on the theory that the court is only identifying an easily correctable procedural error. The rationale is incomplete because proceeding in this fashion may ignore

---

[13] *See, e.g., Judulang v. Holder*, 132 S. Ct. 476, 484 (2011) ("When reviewing an agency action, we must assess, among other matters, 'whether the decision was based on a consideration of the relevant factors and whether there has been a clear error of judgment.'" Quoting *State Farm*, 463 U.S. at 43).

democratic and rule-of-law values that should be weighed against the attempt to walk the fine line between judicial abdication and judicial usurpation. We will consider these matters in turn.

From Procedure to Substance

Whether an administrator has given a reason that addresses a relevant consideration, been responsive to issues raised by participants, or collected a sufficient evidentiary base for reasoned judgment, depends upon how those issues are framed. And a reviewing court's vision of how the agency should have framed the questions for resolution is virtually indistinguishable from a judgment about what is required for substantive reasonableness.

Federal Communications Commission v. *Fox Television Stations, Inc.*[14] provides a good example. The case involved review of a change in Federal Communications Commission (FCC) policy concerning the use of "fleeting expletives" in radio or television broadcasts. Federal law prohibits "utter[ing] any obscene, indecent, or profane language by means of radio communication."[15] In 1975, the FCC first defined indecency as "language that describes, in terms patently offensive as measured by contemporary community standards for the broadcast medium, sexual or excretory activities or organs, at times of the day when there is a reasonable risk that children may be in the audience."[16] This definition was enunciated in an enforcement proceeding concerning George Carlin's "filthy words" monologue, a program that was seemingly designed to test the limits of what could be broadcast over the airwaves. In subsequent years, the FCC broadened its enforcement of the indecency prohibition, but long maintained that "'deliberate and repetitive use ... is a requisite to a finding of indecency' when a complaint focuses solely on the use of nonliteral expletives."[17]

In 2004, the Commission for the first time found that nonliteral, or expletive, use of the f— and s— words were potentially "actionably indecent," even when not repeated.[18] The *Fox* case involved two broadcasts, both of which had used the f— word only once (one of the broadcasts also had a fleeting s— word, for good measure), but which fell under the FCC's ban because, in the Commission's view, that word had an "inherently ... sexual connotation."[19] Under this new policy, lack of repetition would weigh against a finding of indecency, but it would not be a safe harbor from finding a violation of a statute.

[14]   556 U.S. 502 (2009).
[15]   18 U.S.C. § 1464 (2012).
[16]   *Fox Television Stations, Inc.*, 556 U.S. at 506–7 (quoting *In re* Citizens against Pacifica Found. Station WBAI [FM], 56 F.C.C.2d 94, 98 [1975]).
[17]   Id., at 508 (quoting *In re* Pacifica Found., Inc., 2 FCC Rcd. 2,698, 2,699 [1987]).
[18]   Ibid.
[19]   Id., at 511.

The Commission's order explained that its prior strict dichotomy between expletives and literal descriptions of sexual or excretory functions was artificial in light of an expletive's power to offend by its inherent sexual or excretory meaning. It viewed its prior policy as unsound because an automatic exemption for isolated or fleeting expletives forced viewers, including children, to take "'the first blow,' and would allow broadcasters 'to air expletives at all hours of the day as long as they did so one at a time.'"[20] The Second Circuit Court of Appeals found the FCC's reasoning inadequate under the APA, and the case proceeded to the Supreme Court.

In a 5:4 decision, the Supreme Court upheld the FCC determination. The majority opinion described the disagreement between its view and those of the four dissenters as a dispute about whether an agency's change in policy required a more searching review for arbitrariness than would an initial enunciation of that policy.[21] But that was not really the issue, as the dissenters were at pains to point out.[22] The basic issue was whether the FCC's rationalization was adequate under the circumstances. And, in comparing the approach of the majority and the dissenters, it will become clear that the adequacy of the FCC's explanation reasoning depended importantly on how the "circumstances" and the issues they entail are described. Differing descriptions raise different issues. In one description there is a gap in the FCC's reasoning, a delegitimating failure to explain. But what requires explanation depends ultimately on what is required for the decision to be substantively reasonable.

According to the majority, it was clearly reasonable for the FCC to determine that it should no longer distinguish between literal and non-literal uses of offensive words when the offense came from the inherent meaning of the words used. Moreover, as the Commission explained, the old safe-harbor rule was at odds with the Commission's overall enforcement policy, which otherwise always took context into account. And, finally, technological advances had made it much easier than it was in 1975 for broadcasters to bleep out offending words, thus avoiding violating the indecency ban.[23]

Below, the Second Circuit Court of Appeals had found the Commission's action arbitrary and capricious in part because its "first blow" rationale was not supported

[20] Id., at 512 (quoting *In re* Complaints Regarding Various Television Broadcasts Between Feb. 2, 2002 & Mar. 8, 2005, 21 F.C.C. Rcd. 13,299, 13,309 [2006]).

[21] Id., at 514 ("We find no basis in the Administrative Procedure Act or in our opinions for a requirement that all agency change be subjected to more searching review.").

[22] Id., at 550 (Breyer, J., dissenting) ("Contrary to the majority's characterization of this dissent, it would not [and *State Farm* does not] require a "*heightened standard*" of review ... Rather, the law requires application of the *same standard* of review to different circumstances, namely circumstances characterized by the fact that *change* is at issue. It requires the agency to focus upon the fact of change where change is relevant, just as it must focus upon any other relevant circumstance. It requires the agency here to focus upon the reasons that led the agency to adopt the initial policy, and to explain why it now comes to a new judgment.")

[23] Id., at 529.

by any evidence suggesting that fleeting expletives were harmful.[24] The majority rejected this finding on the ground that there was no ethical way to run an experiment subjecting children to fleeting expletives to see how it affected their behavior.[25] The majority also rejected the Second Circuit's finding that the FCC decision was arbitrary for lack of any evidence that the per se exemption of fleeting expletives would lead to increased use of expletives one at a time. But, in the Supreme Court majority's view, the FCC's prediction that immunity from liability for fleeting expletives would lead to their increased use in broadcasts was, even in the absence of evidence, "an exercise in logic rather than clairvoyance."[26]

Justice Breyer and his dissenting colleagues did focus on the fact of a change in FCC policy, but not as the basis for requiring a heightened or more rigorous standard of review. Rather, for them, the fact of change was a circumstance that affected the way in which the relevant issues that the FCC should have addressed should be characterized. Two of the issues emphasized by the dissenting Justices provide particularly apt illustrations of how the question of whether adequate reasons have been given – that is, whether there is a gap in the agency's reasoning – implies a stance concerning what would be substantively reasonable for the agency to reason about.

First, the dissenters noted that the FCC's original safe-harbor policy had been predicated importantly on its understanding of the First Amendment's free speech requirements.[27] But, when justifying its new policy, the FCC discussed the constitutional decision upon which it had based its earlier policy in only two conclusory sentences.[28] In the dissenters' opinion, why the FCC had changed its mind about whether the regulation of fleeting expletives skirted too close to the constitutional line was, in effect, left entirely unexplained.

The majority's approach to this issue was radically different. The majority opinion seems implicitly to characterize the constitutional question as irrelevant. It acknowledges the canon of statutory construction that advises courts to adopt reasonable statutory constructions that avoid serious constitutional questions.[29] But, in the majority's view, arbitrary and capricious review of an administrative agency's determinations provides "no precedent for applying" that canon to "executive action."[30] There may be a question about the constitutionality of the FCC's new policy, but that is a separate issue of constitutional law, not an issue the FCC had to address to avoid reversal for arbitrariness.

Here, the majority and dissenting Justices are like the proverbial ships passing in the night. The dissent's position is not that the FCC should employ the avoidance

---

[24] *Fox Television Stations, Inc.* v. *FCC*, 489 F.3d 444, 458–59 (2nd Cir. 2007).
[25] *Fox Television Stations, Inc.*, 556 U.S. at 519.
[26] Id., at 521.
[27] Id., at 553–55 (Breyer, J., dissenting).
[28] Id., at 555–6.
[29] Id., at 516.
[30] Ibid.

canon. Those Justices simply believed that, as a substantive matter, an FCC rule limiting speech must grapple with the issue of whether its prohibitions violate the First Amendment. Failure to recognize and analyze that question was, for them, a failure to give reasons concerning a relevant issue.

Second, the dissenters took issue with the majority's acceptance of the FCC's technological explanation. The dissenting opinion did not deny the fact of technological change, but noted that broadcasters had informed the FCC that bleeping delay systems could cost $100,000 for installation and annual operation.[31] These costs would put the equipment out of the reach of many small, independent local stations. For the dissenters, this raised the question of the new policy's impact on the local coverage of live events, such as city council meetings, local sports events, community arts productions, and the like.[32] But when looking for the FCC's analysis of those impacts, and an explanation of why they were insufficient to cause the Commission to change its mind, the dissenters found that the FCC said nothing at all.[33]

The dissenting opinion puts the question in terms of reason-giving. But its disagreement with the majority is, again, about what reasonableness demands in this context. Does the FCC have to attend to the special circumstances of local independent stations in its general policy? Or is it free to take these contextual factors into account at the level of enforcement? Or perhaps the agency believes that it need not attend to the consequences for small, independent broadcasters at all?

On these two grounds alone, the dissenters would find that the FCC's explanation for its new policy was inadequate. In standard reason-giving format the agency's failure to discuss these two important aspects of the problem meant that the decision was arbitrary and capricious within the meaning of the APA. But, of course, these matters need discussion only if it would be unreasonable to ignore them. Built into the judgment that they must be discussed is a vision of the goals of, and constraints on, FCC regulatory policy – promoting public service broadcasting and protecting free expression – goals and constraints that the FCC had, in the dissenters' view, treated too cavalierly.

The dissenters were also unimpressed with the FCC's discussion of its "first blow" rationale and the perverse incentive effects of providing a fleeting expletive safe harbor. For them the problem was not that the FCC had failed to run some controlled study to measure the harms of first blows on child listeners. Their concern was that the agency had not provided any discussion of a limited existing literature on this question that had failed to find harmful effects.[34] And given that the safe harbor had been in effect for over two decades, the dissenters thought it incumbent upon

[31] Id., at 558 (Breyer, J., dissenting).
[32] Id., at 558–9.
[33] Id., at 560.
[34] Id., at 564.

the FCC to at least ask whether there was any evidence of an increase in fleeting expletives over that period as a result of the Commission's earlier policy.[35] The FCC had mentioned these issues, but unlike the majority, the dissenters believed that the Commission needed to say more. The majority's assertion that the FCC's action was simply an exercise in logic might be characterized as a belief that incentives equal behaviors. The dissenters seem to believe that human action is not that easily predicted or explained, and in this context needed some further discussion of why it would be reasonable simply to rely on an assumption about incentives rather than looking for some evidence concerning conduct.

Once again, the dissent in *Fox* did not address substantive reasonableness directly by questioning the weight the Commission gave to various considerations. But it does so implicitly by characterizing which questions the FCC needed to address for a reasoned decision to be reasonable. By demanding that the Commission discuss, more than cursorily, the constitutional issues, the local stations problem, and the evidentiary bases for its "first blow" and incentive effects rationales, the dissent is insisting that those issues must have greater weight in the Commission's calculus than its opinion gave them. By rejecting these demands, the majority implicitly affirms that the agency gave enough weight to these matters. And how much weight must be given to various considerations in the agency's decision calculus is a question of substance.

Only one Justice, Justice Stevens, was willing to take a direct substantive approach in *Fox*. Although he joined the Breyer dissenting opinion, he would have found the FCC's assertion that the f— and s— words are inherently descriptive, even when used simply to express an emotion, was simply "absurd."[36] Justice Stevens here invokes the image – or perhaps rather the sound – of a golfer who has just blown an easy approach shot. Apparently in Justice Stevens' experience a golfer shouting "s—" or "f—" is pretty common and far from inherently descriptive. (It is a nice question whether, for a televised golf tournament, the predictable number of such expletives would make "fleeting" a poor descriptor.) Without that finding, in Justice Steven's view, the new policy banning fleeting expletives became almost impossible to justify.

The *Fox* case, like *Nova Scotia*, *State Farm*, and many others that divide reviewing courts on the adequacy of agency reasons, suggests at the very least that unacknowledged issues of substantive reasonableness motivate judges to calibrate the intensity of their search for the adequacy of an agency's rationale. Moreover, a demand that an agency add considerations to its analysis is obviously a means for insisting that greater weight be put on particular issues – issues that tend to cut against the

---

[35] Id., at 565 ("The FCC's initial 'fleeting expletives' policy was in effect for twenty-five years. Had broadcasters during those twenty-five years aired a series of expletives 'one at a time?' If so, it should not be difficult to find evidence of that fact. But the FCC refers to none.").

[36] Id., at 543 (Stevens, J., dissenting).

agency's preferred outcome. Pressed hard enough on these matters, agencies will at least sometimes be forced to modify or even reverse their positions. The difference between substantive and proceduralized rationality review can be vanishingly small.

But that is not always the case. And we must still ask whether this proceduralized approach actually grapples with all the issues that a review for reasonableness should entail. To get at that question, we must ask two others: what do we mean by "reasonable"? And what values might be served by a more forthright approach to reasonableness as a substantive question of whether the agency's decision properly weighed or balanced the competing considerations?

WHAT DO WE MEAN BY REASONABLE?

Standards based on what is reasonable or unreasonable (or close analogues) are ubiquitous in the law.[37] Wherever used these reasonableness standards have a capacity to be troublesome. But they serve different functions in different contexts, and different contexts yield different approaches to the determination of reasonableness. In a host of cases, for example, the ultimate determination of whether a behavior, action, or decision meets a particular reasonableness standard can be relegated to the black box of a jury determination. And, perhaps the most analogous function of judicial reasonableness review in civil or criminal litigation to its function in administrative law is when courts impose constraints on jury determinations of reasonableness. But here, the standard approach is the one that inhabits substantive due process determinations of the arbitrariness of legislative enactments. Questions are not to be taken from a jury, nor is a jury determination to be overturned, unless the judge believes that no reasonable jury could, on the evidence presented, make the findings that are required by a particular cause of action.[38] This standard, like the substantive due process standard, is much more deferential than judicial review for reasonableness of administrative action. As described in Chapter 2, the "rational basis" standard is one that administrative law has long since abandoned.

But, perhaps we can make some progress in disaggregating or deconstructing reasonableness review by asking exactly what question is being asked when litigants request that a reviewing court find agency decisions unreasonable. One possibility, analogizing to private law contexts, is that the court is trying to determine whether the agency has behaved like a reasonable agency. This is to ask, in some sense, a question about conventional behavior, the analogue of determinations of whether individuals or firms have behaved as reasonably prudent actors would have behaved

---

[37] *See generally* Benjamin C. Zipursky, Reasonableness In and Out of Negligence Law, 163 *U. Pa. L. Rev.* 2131 (2015) (exploring concepts of reasonableness in diverse areas of the law).

[38] *Jackson* v. *Virginia*, 443 U.S. 307, 319 (1979) ("[T]he relevant question is whether, after viewing the evidence in the light most favorable to the prosecution, *any* rational trier of fact could have found the essential elements of the crime beyond a reasonable doubt.").

under the circumstances,[39] or whether a product meets the reasonable safety expectations of consumers given the standard safety performance of similar products in the relevant market.[40]

Put in this way reasonableness could be understood as asking the question of whether an agency has engaged in a satisfactory reasoning process – that is, whether the agency: (i) has addressed the criteria made relevant by the statute that it implements; (ii) has engaged in sufficient fact-finding to establish a factual basis for its decision; and (iii) has made a decision that can be explained in terms of the statute's goals and criteria and the facts and arguments that were developed in the relevant agency proceeding. In short, on this view, reasonableness review addresses the procedural, evidentiary and responsiveness questions that inhabit what we have previously called "proceduralized rationality review." Procedure and reason-giving become the focus because they define the expectations for reasonable agency behavior.

But, as we have just seen in the discussion of the *Fox* case, substantive reasonableness implicitly intrudes. Even if courts could commit themselves to examining only whether an agency, in some formal sense, engaged in all the necessary activities of an instrumentally rational reasoner, surely this is too narrow a definition of what reasonableness should mean.

To put the matter starkly, this truncated approach would validate agency action that a court viewed as reasonably arrived at, but clearly erroneous. That sort of approach to reasonableness is found in other areas of law, including the liability of federal government officials in tort. The qualified immunity standard for tort liability of federal administrative officials, for example, is whether the officer could reasonably have believed that the action taken was lawful, even though a court might find that the officer was mistaken.[41] Here, the question is essentially whether the official action is epistemically justifiable, a reasonable mistake under the circumstances.

But this approach to reasonableness seems a poor fit for judicial review of administrative action. The question before a court is whether the agency's decision should be invalidated, not whether the agency is culpable. If the court believes that the agency's decision is arbitrary, then it can hardly allow that decision to stand just because it was an honest and well-considered mistake.

Reasonableness review under the *Chevron* deference doctrine for statutory interpretation suggests another perspective on what reasonableness might mean.[42] Under *Chevron*, a court gives deference to an agency interpretation of a statute if: (1) the

---

[39] See *Vaughan* v. *Menlove*, (1837) 132 Eng. Rep. 490, 493; 3 Bing. (N.C.) 467, 475 ("[W]e ... adhere to the rule which requires in all cases a regard to caution such as a man of ordinary prudence would observe.").

[40] E.g., *Potter* v. *Chi. Pneumatic Tool Co.*, 694 A.2d 1319, 1333 (Conn. 1997) ("[A] product's defectiveness is to be determined by the expectations of an ordinary consumer.").

[41] See, e.g., John C. Jeffries, Jr., What's Wrong with Qualified Immunity?, 62 *Fla. L. Rev.* 851 (2010). However, this qualified immunity standard of course does not have the procedural rationality requirements involved in judicial reasonableness review of agency action.

[42] *Chevron, U.S.A. Inc. v. Nat. Res. Def. Council, Inc.*, 467 U.S. 837 (1984).

statute is ambiguous, and (2) the agency interpretation is reasonable. The court only reaches the second issue after first determining that there is no single "correct" interpretation of the statute.

Abstractly considered, asking only whether an agency decision is reasonable in the context of statutory interpretation seems a bit puzzling. When courts grapple with statutory meaning in civil or criminal litigation, in cases that do not involve an agency interpretation, they simply decide what the statute means, thus giving it an authoritative interpretation. To limit the reviewing court to determining reasonableness seems to imagine that it could not interpret the statute if left to its own devices. But that, of course, is not what reasonableness review is doing in the *Chevron* context.

Because the *Chevron* doctrine is attempting to allocate policy authority between courts and agencies, the question of reasonableness must be articulated in some way that respects the supposed deference due to agency policy choice, but leaves room for judicial invalidation, as the APA requires,[43] on the ground that the agency has misconstrued the statute. The conundrum arises because, as suggested in Chapter 2, there is substantial overlap between interpreting an agency's authorizing statute and choosing agency policy. Many statutory terms obviously confer discretion. Moreover, as the Supreme Court has recognized,[44] changing circumstances may demand that agency policy shift in ways that would be defeated by the notion that statutory terms have one, and only one, proper interpretation. In the context of deference doctrine, the query needs to be something like: "Is the agency's decision within the range of reasonable decisions that might have been made in this context?"

To put the question this way suggests that statutory terms may be sufficiently vague or ambiguous that there is no clearly correct interpretation, but that there may be incorrect ones. Indeed, some statutory terms are so plainly vague or ambiguous that *Chevron's* second, so-called reasonableness prong is the only issue to be addressed. In the Supreme Court's 2014 term, *Michigan v. Environmental Protection Agency* posed just this problem.[45] The Clean Air Act directed the EPA to regulate emissions from power plants if the agency found the regulation "appropriate and necessary."[46] These terms are not rules of conduct for regulated parties, but rather constraints on the statutory policymaking authority delegated to the EPA. Moreover, they are so obviously vague that they necessarily devolve broad policy choice to the agency. And it is that delegation idea that partially undergirds the *Chevron* doctrine's deference to agency interpretation.

While these Clean-Air-Act terms obviously are not self-defining, the EPA provided a definition of "appropriate" and "necessary" in its rule setting emission standards. It

---

[43] 5 U.S.C. § 706 (2012) ("[T]he reviewing court shall decide all relevant questions of law [and] interpret ... statutory provisions").

[44] *Nat'l Cable & Telecomm. Assoc. v. Brand X Internet Servs. Corp.*, 545 U.S. 967 (2005).

[45] *Michigan v. EPA*, 135 S. Ct. 2,699 (2015).

[46] 42 U.S.C. § 7412(n)(1)(A).

determined that regulation of these plants was "appropriate" because: (i) power plant emissions of mercury and other hazardous pollutants posed risks to human health, and (ii) technical controls were available to reduce those emissions.[47] It found regulation "necessary" because the imposition of the Clean Air Act's other requirements had not eliminated these risks.[48] The EPA further concluded that the compliance costs of regulation should not be considered when deciding whether regulation was appropriate and necessary because EPA and state implementing authorities would necessarily consider cost issues at later stages of the regulatory process.[49]

A plurality of the Supreme Court found this latter interpretation unreasonable. (Justice Thomas agreed that the agency's interpretation was wrong, but he would have abandoned *Chevron* deference and determined the interpretive issue de novo.)[50] In the plurality's view, it could not possibly be "appropriate" to regulate these power plants under the statute if the costs of regulation vastly outweighed the public health benefits that regulation might realize.[51] The plurality opinion recognized that the agency could consider costs at other stages of the regulatory process as it decided precisely what regulatory standards to apply to different categories of power plants. But in the view of these justices, these other, more individualized opportunities for addressing cost could not make up for the failure to consider the regulation's global costs and benefits at the time that the initial decision was made that regulation was appropriate and necessary.[52]

On this view, a court should be willing to entertain a broad range of factors as responsive to the congressional direction that the agency consider appropriateness and necessity, but should still retain the discretion to find that the failure to consider certain factors as within that range would be unreasonable. Hence, the plurality in *Michigan* v. *EPA* is not saying that the agency is barred from considering any number of factors (public health effects, technological feasibility, employment effects, distributional effects, energy reliability, and so on) in making a decision about appropriateness or necessity. But leaving cost out of account goes beyond the range of reasonable approaches that the agency might have taken. The four dissenters disagreed with this analysis, of course, but they disagreed because they understood the statutory context differently than the plurality, and thought the agency's view was correct.[53]

Indeed, it might be possible to see the disagreement among the justices in *Michigan* v. *EPA* more clearly by asking the reasonableness question in yet another

---

[47] National Emission Standards for Hazardous Air Pollutants, 77 Fed. Reg. 9,304, 9,310 (Feb. 16, 2012).

[48] Id., at 9,310–11.

[49] Id., at 9,327.

[50] *Michigan*, 135 S. Ct. at 2,712 (Thomas, J., concurring).

[51] Id., at 2,707 ("One would not say that it is even rational, never mind 'appropriate,' to impose billions of dollars in economic costs in return for a few dollars in health or environmental benefits.").

[52] Id., at 2,709.

[53] Id., at 2,717–18 (Kagan, J., dissenting).

form: "Would a reasonable agency make this decision?" To ask the question in this way implicitly introduces a normative element into judgments about reasonableness. Indeed, it is often argued that rationality does not exhaust reasonableness precisely because instrumentally rational pursuit of particular goals leaves out of account whether those goals, all things considered, should be pursued.[54] Instrumentally *rational action* is not necessarily *right action* given countervailing considerations and competing values. Reasonableness, on this view, involves weighing and balancing instrumentally rational action against alternative courses that accommodate competing values and respect alternative viewpoints.

To return to *Michigan* v. *EPA*, the plurality opinion could be understood as asking rather straightforwardly: "Would a reasonable agency charged with determining whether a particular form of regulation was appropriate ignore the burden that might be placed on regulated parties, and perhaps society as a whole, by the costs of compliance?" Given that there is always a possibility that the costs will dwarf the benefits, a decision to ignore costs is simply unreasonable. No reasonable agency would proceed in this way, absent some clear statutory instruction to ignore costs. Here "unreasonable" has the sense of "excessive" or "unbalanced." In the plurality's view, the agency is pursuing a public health mission heedless of alternative and competing considerations. This failure to weigh the costs of action against the benefits ignores the full range of interests that must be taken into account in order to engage in "right action."

It is important to understand that the disagreement between the plurality and the dissenters was not about whether this very general issue of the rightness of the agency's action is the proper way to frame the reasonableness question. The dissenters did not disagree that agency action heedless of costs would be excessive, unbalanced, and unreasonable. They simply believed that the structure of the regulatory regime permitted the agency to engage with these questions fully at other stages of the regulatory process. The plurality, by contrast, believed that constraints in the statutory scheme would necessarily prevent the agency from fully engaging with the balance of costs and benefits of its regulation at later stages.[55] That was the nub of the disagreement about reasonableness.

As we shall discuss shortly, *Michigan* v. *EPA* also raises a somewhat different question that is highlighted by the disagreement between the majority and dissenting Justices. The question of how to take costs into account, and at what stage of the implementation process to do so, is a policy question that blends means and ends analysis in ways that give a different orientation to reasonableness analysis. The EPA position seems to be that how implementing costs are to be assessed and whether

---

[54] *See* sources cited *supra* note 1.

[55] Justice Scalia argues the point with his characteristic verve. Id., at 2,709 ("By EPA's logic, someone could decide whether it is 'appropriate' to buy a Ferrari without thinking about cost, because he plans to think about cost later when deciding whether to upgrade the sound system.").

they are reasonable – or, in the statute's terms, "appropriate" – depends on the differing situations of regulated parties that can only be evaluated in the context of concrete implementing directives. Pursuit of the statutory goal of protecting the environment from damaging power plant emissions might be pursued in different ways, using differing technologies, on different timetables, and with differing environmental consequences across different geographic areas and production processes. What is appropriate will, in the agency's view, take on differing meanings and be subject to differing considerations in different contexts. In short, the meaning of whether such regulation is appropriate, including an analysis of whether particular environmental benefits justify the imposition of the associated compliance costs, cannot be divorced from the process of implementing that regulation. The reasonableness of means and ends are not separate issues, and the understanding of ends is discovered in the process of developing and applying means. I will suggest below that this proposition has implications for our understanding not only of the proper role of judicial review, but also for administrative governance's democratic pedigree in a system of reasoned administration.

Michigan v. *EPA* notwithstanding, reviewing courts can generally avoid finding that agency interpretations are unreasonable.[56] If a court finds a statute ambiguous, that determination almost always signals that the court will find the agency's interpretation reasonable. For, if the agency interpretation does not look reasonable in the light of a complaining party's alternative interpretation, the court is unlikely to find the statute ambiguous. *Michigan* v. *EPA* is one of those relatively rare cases where the terms at issue are so obviously vague that finding a single definitive answer to what Congress meant is facially implausible. Whether the agency's interpretation was reasonable was the only reasonable question to ask.[57]

Job Well Done?

An optimistic view of this discussion of ways to frame reasonableness review would suggest that American courts have done a reasonably good job of taming the unruliness that inheres in that activity. They have developed a rational paradigm of reviewing administrative decision-making that, in a wide range of cases, can police the reasonableness of agency action without directly addressing the thorny substantive question of reasonableness. Most cases can be, and are, resolved on a basis that

---

[56] This point seems true notwithstanding the plausible suggestion that *Chevron*'s Step 1 analysis – is the statute ambiguous? – may be properly viewed as a special case of the Step 2 reasonableness inquiry. For that argument, see Matthew C. Stephenson and Adrian Vermeule, Chevron Has Only One Step, 95 Va. L. Rev. 597 (2009).

[57] The problem of deference in cases of judicial review of agency statutory interpretation tends to lie instead in the assessment of whether a statute is ambiguous. Because courts and agencies approach the interpretive task from different institutional perspectives, judicial determinations of "ambiguity" may be inherently non-deferential. Jerry L. Mashaw, Between Facts and Norms: Agency Statutory Interpretation as an Autonomous Enterprise, 55 U. Tor. L. J. 497 (2005).

speaks instead to the reasonableness of the agency reasoning processes. If those processes are found wanting, the outcome is a remand to the agency to do better, or perhaps do differently. As was argued earlier, this form of review is inherently deferential while maintaining the requirement that agencies legitimate their action by reasoned analysis, not by hunch, intuition, or political preference.

That underlying concerns about substantive reasonableness may motivate, and modulate, the intensity of this rationality review can be viewed as a feature of this system, not a bug. Calibrating the "hardness" of "hard look" review in terms of "danger signals"[58] that may have caused an agency to go off the rails is a practical approach to retaining agency discretion while ensuring sober second looks. Holding in reserve possible straightforward substantive review is necessary if review for arbitrariness or abuse of discretion is not to become a validation of decisions that are technically competent, but substantively obtuse. But using that substantive review sparingly helps to mediate ultimately unresolvable questions concerning the constitutionally appropriate division between executive and judicial authority.

Not So Fast

Two problems cloud this rosy picture of an appropriately tamed judicial review focusing on the adequacy of agency reason-giving. The first was suggested in Chapter 4: even where judicial review is highly deferential in this form, it may have significant systemic effects that implicate both the substance of policies and the way in which administrators formulate them. My earlier and ongoing work with David Harfst on NHTSA rulemaking[59] provides significant, and we believe persuasive, evidence that judicial review, or its prospect, has shifted both the techniques of agency regulation (from rules to recalls to information provision) and the substance of agency rulemaking (from new technology-forcing to existing technology diffusion). Judicial review is clearly not the only causative element in shaping NHTSA policymaking,

---

[58] *See Boston Television Corp.* v. *FCC,* 444 F.2d 841, 851 (D.C. Cir. 1970)

> The function of the court is to assure that the agency has given reasoned consideration to all the material facts and issues. This calls for insistence that the agency articulate with reasonable clarity its reasons for decision, and identify the significance of the crucial facts, a course that tends to assure that the agency's policies effectuate general standards, applied without unreasonable discrimination... Its supervisory function calls on the court to intervene not merely in case of procedural inadequacies, or bypassing of the mandate in the legislative charter, but more broadly if the court becomes aware, especially from a combination of danger signals, that the agency has not really taken a 'hard look' at the salient problems, and has not genuinely engaged in reasoned decision-making. (internal citations omitted).

[59] Jerry L. Mashaw and David L. Harfst, *The Struggle for Auto Safety* (1990); From Command and Control to Collaboration and Deference: The Transformation of Auto Safety Regulation, 34 *Yale J. On Reg.* 167 (2017).

but it has had a crucial impact. NHTSA's shift in regulatory techniques might, of course, be justified on other grounds. The point here is merely to remember that deference is not always operationally deferential.

Similarly, the restrained approach of the *Nova Scotia Food Products* opinion – faulting the agency's notice of proposed rulemaking rather than its ultimate conclusion – made law in ways that have rippled through other domains of regulatory action. That an agency must have a sufficiently clear view of its ultimate policy such that it can reveal, at the notice of the *proposed* rulemaking stage, the underlying facts and scientific methodology on which it proposes to rely, has significant implications for public participation in rulemaking processes. But, the broader consequences are not necessarily the ones that the *Nova Scotia* court had in mind. The sort of detailed notice necessary to such disclosure suggests that agencies should do very substantial work on rulemaking proposals before inviting public participation and comment. As noted in Chapter 7, some observers believe that this frontloading of pre-comment agency effort has a deleterious effect on early public participation in agency processes. The direction of agency policymaking becomes more difficult to alter substantially after the agency has expended significant effort to develop a well-specified and factually-substantiated proposal.

These systemic effects suggest a serious issue: might direct engagement with the substantive reasonableness of agency policymaking be more appropriately deferential than American courts' focus on analyzing the adequacy of reasons? It is at least conceivable that substantive review would have two reinforcing effects. First, a simple determination that a particular policy is unreasonable makes essentially no doctrinal contribution. That sort of ruling contains some information, but it does not necessarily suggest any new criteria, either substantive or procedural, with which agencies must subsequently comply. Second, the transparent determination that courts are overturning agency judgments on substantive grounds of unreasonableness may make courts more directly and transparently responsible for intervening in administrative policy processes. And that responsibility, in turn, may encourage courts to be even more careful in substituting their judgments about reasonableness for those of responsible agencies.

These claims are, of course, mere speculation, and it may well be that courts, at least in the American context, would have difficulty justifying this transparent substitution of substantive judgments in ways acceptable in our constitutional culture. We will return to that question in the final sub-part of this chapter when we analyze judicial review of administrative action based on proportionality analysis and compare it with American-style review for the adequacy of agency reason-giving.

The second major problem with the rosy picture of the deference doctrine has to do with statutory interpretation. Remember from Chapter 4 the radical indeterminacy of Supreme Court deference to agency statutory interpretations. In the

Eskridge and Baer study,[60] the Court not only deployed multiple deference doctrines, but more than half the time, it ignored all of them. And without providing any criteria for identifying when this wild card might be played, the Court has said that deference is not appropriate whenever the question of interpretation raises major issues of social or economic policy. But it is not just this radical uncertainty that should stimulate our interest. The problem is more fundamental. Judicial construction of agency statutes may undermine ongoing processes of developing public meaning that are vastly more democratic than judicial reasoning divorced, as it generally is, from political and institutional context. Indeed, I want to suggest that the failure to take the democratic underpinnings of *Chevron* seriously misunderstands the role of administrative agencies in an ongoing project of democratic governance. I will make this argument by looking back at three of the major cases that were discussed in Chapter 3.

DEFERENCE, DEMOCRACY, AND STATUTORY INTERPRETATION

We should begin with *Chevron* itself. In one sense, it is difficult to take the case seriously. As Thomas Merrill has shown, the decision is in many ways an "accidental precedent."[61] Neither the litigants nor the Court viewed the case as preeminently about deference doctrine as applied to statutory interpretation until after the decision was issued.[62] The Supreme Court also often ignores *Chevron*, and where and when it applies befuddles both lower courts and commentators. Moreover, it is based on a transparent legal fiction, that the delegation of lawmaking authority to administrative agencies entails a simultaneous delegation of interpretive authority concerning the statute that has been put in their charge.

Nevertheless, I believe that the considerations underpinning that legal fiction – agency expertise and the greater political accountability of the administrative state relative to reviewing courts – deserve to be taken seriously. Indeed, more seriously than the Supreme Court has taken them. Why? Because both of these considerations point toward an understanding of agency implementation of statutes that is both realistic about the connection between administrative and political processes and democracy-reinforcing in its interpretive approach. In terms of political accountability, implementation is not a technical process of finding facts and drawing logical conclusions from those facts based on statutorily pre-determined ends or values. Nor is it an acontextual process of interpreting language based on some abstract notion of its meaning.

---

[60] William N. Eskridge, Jr. and Lauren E. Baer, The Continuum of Defense: Supreme Court Treatment of Agency Statutory Interpretations from Chevron to Hamdan, 96 *Geo. L.J.* 1083 (2008).

[61] Thomas W. Merrill, The Story of Chevron: The Making of an Accidental Precedent, in *Administrative Law Stories* 398 (Peter L. Strauss ed., 2006).

[62] Id., at 402.

The matters delegated to administrative agencies are indeed often technical and demand expertise. But that expertise is not merely technocratic. As suggested by the discussion of *Michigan* v. *EPA*, it is rather an expertise gained by immersion in implementation and in the often-unanticipated problems concerning both the facts of the matter and how program goals ought to be understood. It is in the ongoing project of meaning-making under a statute that administrative processes' connection to political institutions becomes important. For, if democracy means "rule by the people" rather than "rule by administrators," an ongoing dialogue between administrators, political institutions, and interested publics is crucial to maintain democratic legitimacy. We will have much more to say about this issue of democratic legitimacy in Chapter 7.[63] For now I want to illustrate the connections of administrative implementation to processes of democratic governance by reconsidering the *Overton Park*,[64] *Massachusetts* v. *EPA*,[65] and *Benzene* cases.[66] While the *Chevron* opinion gestures at democratic connections through the medium of executive oversight, those connections are much more diverse and important than that opinion or its progeny suggest. These three cases all involve independent judicial interpretation of regulatory goals that, in differing ways, ignore those connections.

The *Overton Park* case is a particularly striking example of the use of statutory interpretation to force an agency into a narrowly instrumental form of reasoning. In important ways this result falsified the basic political presuppositions of the program that was being implemented and overrode years of public engagement with the question of the appropriate location of I-40 as it passed through Memphis Tennessee. The Interstate Highway Program involves three levels of government: the federal government that provides a substantial portion of highway funding; state governments that do some of the funding and virtually all of the planning, engineering, and construction; and local governments that do land use planning, including transportation planning, for their jurisdictions. The process of highway building is, in fact, a fluid process of planning and negotiation among all three levels of government.

The statutory provisions at issue in *Overton Park* recognize this intergovernmental process. Congress instructs the Department of Transportation not to approve location decisions by state departments of highways that use park land of local significance where "feasible and prudent alternative[s]"[67] exist to that location. Where parkland was nevertheless to be used, the design of the highway was to "include all possible planning" to reduce the impact on the park.[68] Other sections of the statute demanded that location and construction decisions be generally consistent with local land use planning.

[63] For a similar argument anchored in a complex theory of democratic legitimacy *see*, Henry Richardson: *Democratic Autonomy: Public Reasoning about the Ends of Policy* (Oxford, 2002).
[64] 401 U.S. 402 (1971).
[65] 549 U.S. 497 (2007).
[66] *Indus. Union Dep't v. Am. Petroleum Inst.* (*The Benzene Case*), 448 U.S. 607 (1980).
[67] 23 U.S.C. § 138(a) (2012).
[68] Ibid.

As Peter Strauss has shown in detail,[69] the routing of Interstate I-40 through Memphis was a significant public issue in Memphis for a number of years. Planning for the highway involved intense negotiations among all levels of government. The routing decision and project design went through multiple public hearings and were, indeed, a major issue in state and local politics.[70] The planning for the roadway included a number of features to lessen the highway's potential impact on the aesthetics and utilization of the park.[71]

In short, the I-40 route through Memphis had taken account of a broad range of values and perspectives. As anyone who has ever been involved in the land use planning exercise will recognize, the values at stake are an enormously complex set of economic, social, cultural, aesthetic, and environmental considerations whose relative importance varies from project to project and, indeed, from person to person involved in the process.

The Supreme Court's intervention in *Overton Park* to interpret the word "prudent" as meaning "uniquely difficult" exalted the protection of park land over virtually all other values at stake in the highway planning process.[72] It recasts the location question in narrowly instrumental terms: "Can you find a route that will avoid the park, be feasible in engineering terms, and otherwise not uniquely destructive to other relevant values?" This characterizes an otherwise complex intergovernmental process of planning, negotiation, and deliberation – and, in this case, elective politics – as a top-down, federal, bureaucratic process of instrumental rationality with park land protection as the preeminent goal. It also gives veto power (or at least near veto power) to any local citizen group whose primary interest is preservation of a particular park.

I think this result is quite unlikely to have been what Congress had in mind when it made the protection of park land an explicit statutory criterion for highway planning. But quite apart from whether the Supreme Court incorrectly interpreted congressional purposes, the Court's approach seems to misunderstand the basic process of goal-oriented reasoning that is necessary to administrative implementation of legislative programs. Implementation is not the simple deployment of technological expertise, nor is it a process of if–then deductions from fixed principles to logical results based on determinate facts. Goals and principles take on meaning in light of facts found and uncertainties uncovered. Deliberation within an agency and with outside parties fuels new understandings, accommodations, and compromises that cannot be tied up in neat if–then bundles of reasoned argument.

Moreover, as the *Overton Park* case puts in stark relief, implementation is a micro-political process involving not just intergovernmental institutional cooperation, but

---

[69] Peter L. Strauss, Revisiting Overton Park: Political and Judicial Controls Over Administrative Actions Affecting the Community, 39 *UCLA L. Rev.* 1251 (1992).

[70] Id., at 1290–311.

[71] Id., at 1311–12.

[72] *Overton Park*, 401 U.S. at 416.

public deliberation through various processes of consultation, participation, and contestation. As I will argue more directly in Chapter 7, reasoned administration is a deliberatively democratic process. To narrow the focus of administrators to demonstrating decisional fidelity to singular statutory ends as judicially interpreted hence jeopardizes democratic values.

The democratic values at stake in narrowing an administrator's implementing discretion are particularly prominent in an intergovernmental program like the building of interstate highways. The peculiar facts of the *Overton Park* dispute featured multiple opportunities for public discussion and local electoral competition. But the stakes are there in other contexts as well. *Massachusetts* v. *EPA* is another instance in which the Court demanded that the agency focus on technocratic or scientific considerations and left aside the broad policy concerns that the EPA had articulated for its decision not to regulate greenhouse gas emissions from new motor vehicles. I am, of course, perfectly content with the majority's position that the agency needed to give reasons for abandoning its preliminary proposal to regulate greenhouse gas emissions from automobiles under the Clean Air Act. So far as one can tell, the dissenters agreed with that decision as well. The issue was what sorts of reasons can be given for not making a particular judgment – that is, that greenhouse gasses are air pollutants, that would then actuate EPA's statutory duty to regulate.

As I understand the underlying situation in *Massachusetts* v. *EPA*, at the agency level this controversy was really a question of regulatory priorities. So far as I know, virtually no one in the environmental community with deep understanding of both climate change and the Clean Air Act believes that the latter is a good instrument for combatting the former. But, it is also apparently the case that EPA could take certain regulatory initiatives under the statute that would have some effect on greenhouse gas emissions. Whether to act is a question of policy priorities. Those priorities will differ across different administrations, as evidenced by the simple facts that the George W. Bush Administration avoided acting, the Barack Obama administration energetically pursued climate change initiatives, and the Donald Trump administration is on course to reverse the Obama initiatives.[73] All of these positions were politically motivated, in at least the unobjectionable sense of being policy-driven and legally contestable. Our question is how a court should understand the role of administrative policymaking in those legal contests.

As I read the majority opinion in *Massachusetts* v. *EPA*, I see the court saying essentially:

> You, EPA, are an expert agency charged with making scientific judgments about the effects of putting particular substances into the air. In particular, you are to determine whether those emissions affect public health and welfare. You may only

---

[73] For a brief description see Jerry L. Mashaw and David Berke, Presidential Administration in a Regime of Separated Powers: An Analysis of Recent American Practice, 35 *Yale J. on Reg.* 549 (2018).

make that sort of decision using your scientific expertise, and you can justify a failure to make such a decision only by demonstrating that your scientific expertise has run out – that is, the scientific situation is so uncertain that you cannot make a judgment.

This intervention, once again, prevents the agency from reaching a reasoned decision on the basis that other values are at stake. The agency thought it had an uncertain mandate to pursue climate change regulation under a statute enacted when that problem was not recognized as a major issue. Congress had subsequently mandated further research on that matter,[74] and there were strategic considerations concerning how independent United States action might jeopardize international climate negotiations.[75] When those concerns were weighed against the agency's belief that its tools under the statute were likely to have little, if any, impact on the climate problem, the EPA thought the wiser course was to desist.

I have little doubt that the Bush administration's climate skepticism and Republican ideological aversion to costly environmental regulation influenced, if not wholly dictated, the EPA's conclusion. But it is, in part, precisely that connection to the political process that the *Chevron* Court thought justified judicial deference to reasonable agency statutory interpretations.

My point here, however, is that judicial deference to agency statutory interpretation based on an assessment of policy priorities can be given a different grounding. Being reasonable does not mean just being instrumentally rational. Judicial interpretations that confine agencies to narrowly instrumental, technocratic, and scientific grounds for decision-making promote rationality at the expense of reasonableness. They also make it difficult for the administrative process to be a site of democratic deliberation, which of necessity must include an orientation toward value questions, toward the practical ends of public action and toward the wisdom of acting or not – and in what way – all things considered.

Even where the Court uses statutory interpretation apparently to broaden the considerations necessary for reasoned administration, the effect may be to reinforce technocratic rationality at the expense of a more values- or ends-oriented approach. Consider the so-called *Benzene* case, *Industrial Union Department* v. *American Petroleum Institute*.[76] There, as previously described, the Supreme Court decided that a definitional section of the Occupational Safety and Health Act, § 3(8)'s definition of a health and safety standard as one that is "reasonably necessary or appropriate to provide safe or healthful ... places of employment,"[77] imposed an additional findings requirement on the Occupational Safety and Health Administration (OSHA)

---

[74] *Massachusetts* v. *EPA*, 549 U.S. 497, 511–12 (2007).

[75] Id., at 533.

[76] 448 U.S. 607 (1980).

[77] Occupational Safety and Health Act of 1970, Pub. L. No. 91–596, § 3(8), 84 Stat. 1590, 1591 (codified at § 29 U.S.C. § 652(8)).

when it regulated exposure to toxic substances under § 6(b)(5) of the statute. That latter section provides:

> The Secretary, in promulgating standards dealing with toxic materials or harmful physical agents under this subsection, shall set the standard which most adequately assures, to the extent feasible, on the basis of the best available evidence, that no employee will suffer material impairment of health or functional capacity even if such employee has regular exposure to the hazard dealt with by such standard over the period of his working life.[78]

In the Supreme Court's view, even when rulemaking under § 6(b)(5)'s highly worker-protective framework for action, the OSHA was required to first, under § 3(8), determine that the regulated hazard posed a "significant risk."[79] Otherwise, the Court reasoned, how could the agency determine that a standard was, per § 3(8)'s language, reasonably necessary or that a workplace was unsafe?[80]

The Supreme Court's concern, as elaborated elsewhere in the opinion, was that "[i]n light of the fact that there are literally thousands of substances used in the workplace that have been identified as carcinogens or suspect carcinogens, the Government's theory would give the OSHA power to impose enormous costs that might produce little, if any, discernible benefit."[81] As a consequence, the Court ruled that the statute required "that the risk from a toxic substance be quantified sufficiently to enable the Secretary to characterize it as significant in an understandable way."[82] The Court went on to suggest:

> Some risks are plainly acceptable and others are plainly unacceptable. If, for example, the odds are one in a billion that a person will die from cancer by taking a drink of chlorinated water, the risk clearly could not be considered significant. On the other hand, if the odds are one in a thousand that regular inhalation of gasoline vapors that are 2 percent benzene will be fatal, a reasonable person might well consider the risk significant and take appropriate steps to decrease or eliminate it.[83]

---

[78] Id., at § 6(b)(5), 84 Stat. at 1594.

[79] *The Benzene Case*, 448 U.S at 639–40.

> [I]t is clear that § 3(8) ... requires the Secretary, before issuing any standard, to determine that it is reasonably necessary and appropriate to remedy a *significant risk* of material health impairment. Only after the Secretary has made the threshold determination that such a risk exists ... would it be necessary to decide whether § 6(b)(5) requires him to select the most protective standard he can consistent with economic and technological feasibility." (emphasis added).

[80] Id., at 642–3.

[81] Id., at 645.

[82] Id., at 646.

[83] Id., at 655.

Let us assume, for the moment, that the Court was correct in taking the somewhat unusual step of using a statute's definitional section to impose a fact-finding obligation not contained in the statute's operational sections. Indeed, it is hardly obvious that the Court needed to rely on the definitional provisions of the statute to find that the agency needed to explain the health risk that it was seeking to combat (which, arguably it had done). Solving non-problems is unreasonable. The issue that I want to highlight is the Court's conception of what was entailed in analyzing whether a standard was "reasonably necessary" to combat a safety or health problem in the workplace.[84] What the Court had in mind is what has come to be called quantitative risk assessment. Indeed, the Court specifically seemed to contemplate largely that element of a quantitative risk assessment that focuses on the probability or likelihood that exposure to a hazard will lead to a given health result. But, the Court didn't seem to understand what that sort of analysis entailed. The Court's chlorinated drinking water and gasoline vapor examples should have led to the opposite conclusion than the one that the Court suggested. Because of the vastly larger exposure of the population to chlorinated water than to gasoline vapors – a one-in-a-billion chance of dying of cancer from drinking water produces more cancer deaths per year than the one-in-a-thousand probability of the same result from benzene exposure. Viewed as a purely technical matter of quantitative risk assessment, chlorine in drinking water is the more serious problem.

But, put even that aside. The real problem, as I see it, is that the Court demands a narrowly technocratic approach to the issue of reasonableness. Such an approach is foreshadowed nowhere in the statute. Neither "risk" nor "significant risk" is a term used in the OSHA, nor is quantitative analysis of risk the only, or necessarily even the best, way to think about whether hazards or risks are unreasonable. We know that people find risks acceptable or unacceptable for a host of reasons that have nothing to do with the probability of harm. The United States focuses staggering resources on the prevention of terrorist attacks, even though the probabilities of being killed or injured by a terrorist are vanishingly small.[85] Voluntarily assumed risks with high probabilities of harm are often viewed as acceptable, as determined by either opinion polls or behavioral observation, while involuntarily assumed risks with much lower probabilities are often viewed as unacceptable.[86] Risks to vulnerable populations, such as children or the aged, may have higher priority than

---

[84] Occupational Safety and Health Act of 1970, § 3(8).

[85] Andrew Shaver, You're More Likely to Be Fatally Crushed by Furniture than Killed by a Terrorist, Wash. Post (Nov. 23, 2015), available at: www.washingtonpost.com/news/monkey-cage/wp/2015/11/23/youre-more-likely-to-be-fatally-crushed-by-furniture-than-killed-by-a-terrorist/ (Last accessed May 25, 2018) ("In the United States, an individual's likelihood of being hurt or killed by a terrorist ... is negligible. Consider, for instance, that since the attacks of Sept. 11, 2001, Americans have been no more likely to die at the hands of terrorists than ... crushed to death by unstable televisions and furniture.").

[86] *See, e.g.*, Cass R. Sunstein, A Note on "Voluntary" Versus "Involuntary" Risks, 8 *Duke Envtl. L. & Pol'y F.* 173 (1997)

quantitatively higher risks to other parts of the population, perhaps because differential distribution of certain risks implicates other highly salient public values, such as systemic bias or powerlessness.[87]

In short, I have no quarrel with the *Benzene* Court's concern that the OSHA's coercive powers conferred under § 6(b)(5) of the OSHA might, if read for all they are worth, confer unreasonable powers on the agency. But the Court's increasing of the agency's burden, through the Court's creative, significant-risk criterion, suggests a narrowly technocratic approach to consideration of the proper statutory ends. That approach forecloses a broader approach to what "reasonably necessary or appropriate" should be taken to mean in this regulatory context. The Court intervenes via statutory interpretation to insist on consideration of what exactly the agency is meant to do, but in a fashion that precludes a broader discussion of what social values might be relevant to reasonableness in work-safety regulation. "Tell us what you mean by reasonable" invites a values-based deliberation at the agency level that can be informed by participants in the agency's rulemaking process. "Give us a quantitative risk assessment" invites a technocratic analysis that excludes such deliberation and limits meaningful participation to the technically sophisticated.

In summary, the *Chevron* opinion's insistence on deference to agency statutory interpretations was on to something important. And its reference to an agency's political connections to the executive are at least a gesture in the direction of linking administrative implementation to one form of democratic processes. But, it would seem that the Court's other ground for presuming a congressional delegation of interpretative authority to agencies, agency expertise, has been too narrowly understood. Expertise exists in the form of scientific and technological competence, but it also exists in the form of contextual understanding derived from the practical difficulties of implementing broad goals in heterogeneous contexts and in consultation with diverse interested parties and institutions. That practical understanding, what might be called "craft expertise," informs the way that goals (and not just instrumental means) need to be understood to develop acceptable public policies. Administrative implementation is a normative as well as an instrumental process. And, as I shall argue in later chapters, this implementation is not just connected to electoral politics as the *Chevron* opinion suggests. It is also connected to a deliberative democratic process that is equally important to the legitimacy of administrative governance. For the Supreme Court's model of judicial deference based on proceduralized rationality review to be both properly deferential and appropriately demanding, the Court needs to broaden the questions for which deference is due. It also needs to allow a broader, rather than a narrower, set of reasons for agency action – reasons that engage with values and ends, not just with means.

---

[87] For further elaboration of this point in the context of risk regulation *see* Richardson supra at 231–41.

OTHER PATHWAYS TO REASONABLENESS
REVIEW: PROPORTIONALITY ANALYSIS

To summarize the foregoing concerns: relentless focus on the rational rather than the reasonable has costs as well as benefits. Emphasis on procedural, evidentiary, or reason-giving issues can facilitate interventionist judicial review, perhaps motivated by political predispositions, while maintaining a facade of deference to administrative discretion. Deciding cases by remand for rethinking may have far greater negative impacts on the administrative state's capacity to carry out important functions than reviewing judges imagine.[88] And a focus on the reasoning process may obscure and misdirect analysis that would be better performed if questions of substantive values and the weighing of competing considerations were done in a more open and straightforward fashion. Is there a superior approach?

It has not escaped the notice of American lawyers that a quite different system of reasonableness review is prominent in a number of developed democracies outside the United States and the British Commonwealth. In those jurisdictions, reasonableness review proceeds under a general doctrine of proportionality that addresses, in a staged but explicit fashion, the substantive reasonableness of administrative action. We should not leave this discussion of reasonableness without looking at the proportionality alternative.

According to Justice Aharon Barak,[89] former President of the Supreme Court of Israel and a prominent practitioner and theorist of proportionality analysis, the inquiry into whether an administrator or legislature has adopted a proportional means for achieving a particular legal end involves three inquiries. First, is there a sufficient rational connection between an appropriate goal pursued and the means utilized by the law to achieve that goal? Second, can the goal be achieved by other means that are less restrictive concerning the interests of those that the government action adversely affects? Third, is there a proportionate balance between the social benefits of realizing the appropriate goal and the harm caused to those adversely affected?[90]

This approach can be illustrated by one of Justice Barak's well-known opinions, *Beit Sourik Village Council* v. *Government of Israel*.[91] The case involved an order by the Commander of Israeli defense forces in Judea and Samaria to take possession of land for the purpose of building a separation fence to protect Israeli residents against

---

[88] *See, e.g.,* Jerry L. Mashaw and David L. Harfst, Inside the National Highway Traffic Safety Administration: Legal Determinants of Bureaucratic Organization and Performance, 57 *U. Chi. L. Rev.* 443 (1990).

[89] Aharon Barak, Proportionality and Principled Balancing, 4 *L. & Ethics of Hum. Rts.* 1 (2010).

[90] Id., at 6. Justice Barak also notes the "threshold requirement" that the legal end be "appropriate" in itself. Ibid.

[91] HCJ 2056/04, [2004] IsrLR 264.

terrorist threats from Palestinian extremist groups. The plaintiffs represented villagers whose lives would be severely complicated by the fence. It would cut off their access to lands that they farmed, destroy many hectares of olive groves, and impede their travel outside the village. The plaintiffs raised a host of issues, but their substantive claims were basically two: They argued that the fence was not constructed for a proper defensive purpose, but as a device to annex territory to the State of Israel. In addition, even if the fence were constructed for an appropriate purpose, the lost protection that the State of Israel would suffer from building the fence elsewhere was modest in relation to the serious detrimental effects of building the fence as planned. In short, the adverse effects on the villagers were disproportionate to the projected benefits that Israel would gain by constructing the fence on the lands that the military commander was seizing.

In much of his opinion for the Court ruling in favor of the villagers, Justice Barak seemed quite deferential to the military authorities.[92] The opinion viewed a separation fence with check points for ingress and egress as a perfectly rational approach to protect against terrorist attacks. And the Court found that the plaintiffs had failed to carry the heavy burden of demonstrating that this defensive measure was in essence a smoke screen for annexation of Palestinian territory.[93] Moreover, although there were submissions in the case by retired military and defense officials arguing that the fence could be further from the village with no loss of its defensive capabilities, the Court felt compelled to accept the argument of the responsible defense force officials who claimed that locations further from the village would not provide equivalent protection.[94] On questions one and two of the proportionality analysis, the court upheld the Defense Forces' location decision.

But, on the final question of substance, the villagers prevailed. After outlining the many inconveniences and difficulties that would be the necessary result of the separation fence in its proposed location, the Court concluded:

> The real question is whether the security benefit reaped by the acceptance of the military commander's position ... is proportionate to the additional injury resulting from his position ... Our answer to this question is that the military commander's choice of the route of the separation fence is disproportionate. The gap between the security provided by the military commander's approach and the security provided by the alternate route is minute, as compared to the large difference between a fence that separates the local inhabitants from their lands, and a fence which does not separate the two (or which creates a separation which is smaller and possible to live with).[95]

[92] Id., at 303–4.
[93] Id., at 287.
[94] Id., at 309.
[95] Id., at 311.

Recognizing the delicacy of the Court's position, the *Beit Sourik* opinion contains an epilogue. It reads in part:

> Our task is difficult. We are members of Israeli society. Although we are sometimes in an ivory tower, that tower is in the heart of Jerusalem, which is not infrequently hit by ruthless terror. We are aware of the killing and destruction wrought by the terror against the state and its citizens. As any other Israelis, we too recognize the need to defend the country and its citizens against the wounds inflicted by terror. We are aware that in the short term this judgment will not make the state struggle against those rising up against it easier. But we are judges. When we sit in judgment, we are subject to judgment. We act according to our best conscience and understanding. Regarding the state's struggle against the terror that rises up against it, we are convinced that at the end of the day, a struggle according to the law will strengthen her power and her spirit ...
>
> Only a separation fence built on a base of law will grant security to the state and its citizens. Only a separation route based on the path of law, will lead the state to the security so yearned for.[96]

Earlier in the opinion, the Court had also been at pains to point out that the proportionality test was a general principal both of international law and of Israeli administrative law.[97] And the Court distinguished its judgment from the judgments exercised by the military commanders. In considering whether the route was proportionate the Court said:

> The standard for this question is not the subjective standard of the military commander. The question is not whether the military commander believed, in good faith, that the injury is proportionate. The standard is objective. The question is whether, by legal standards, the route of the separation fence passes the test of proportionality. This is a legal question the expertise for which is held by the Court.[98]

Immediately following that statement, Justice Barak cited to his opinion in an earlier case that also involved military activity. In the cited language, Justice Barak made a similar distinction:

> The fact that the activity is necessary on the military plane, does not mean that it is lawful on the legal plane. Indeed, we do not substitute our discretion for that of the military commander's, as far as it concerns military considerations. That is his expertise. We examine the results on the plane of the humanitarian law. That is our expertise.[99]

---

[96] Id., at 323.
[97] Id., at 292–3.
[98] Id., at 303–4.
[99] Id., at 304 (quoting HCJ 4764/04 *Physicians for Human Rights* v. *IDF Commander in Gaza* 58(5) PD 385 [2004]).

Yet, despite these heroic efforts to distinguish the question of military policy from the question of legality, Justice Barak's arguments are less than wholly persuasive. The distinction between the military commander's position and that of the reviewing court is of course perfectly correct. The commander weighs the security benefits of the fence against the disruption of the villagers' lives from the perspective of an official responsible for protecting Israel and its citizens. The Court weighs this balance from the perspective of an institution charged with protecting individual rights and assuring the rule of law. But that does not answer the question of what makes the military commander's weighing of these considerations subjective, while the Court's weighing is objective.

To be sure, the military commander engages in this balancing from the standpoint of one responsible for public safety. He or she may therefore strike a balance that is biased toward security over rights protection. Yet the Court has responsibilities as well. Those responsibilities are to protect individual rights and maintain the rule of law. The Court obviously has no official responsibility for national defense. This position insulates the court from a particular form of policy bias. Yet, the Court's peculiar institutional position and responsibilities could cause it to discount military necessities when balanced against the values that it is institutionally charged with protecting. Nor does the expertise of the military authorities that was recognized in considering the first two proportionality inquiries suddenly evaporate when the question becomes one of balancing state security needs against the villagers' loss of freedom.

The *Beit Sourik* opinion might be understood as teaching two lessons. First, proportionality analysis directly addresses the substantive reasonableness of administrative action. It puts the judge in the position of weighing and balancing the considerations for and against the administrative action and making a transparent decision concerning whether the official got the balance right. And, judged by Justice Barak's opinions, that posture pushes the court to be cautious and reflective concerning its mandate and to address directly the questions of the legitimate jurisdiction of administrative and judicial authorities. But, second, this approach leaves courts open to the obvious claim that they are substituting their judgment for that of administrative officials on policy questions that are only in a formal sense questions of law. The final decision on proportionality is made by a legal institution operating under review standards that make the ultimate balance of competing considerations a question of law. But that is no answer to those who would complain that it is proportionality analysis itself, as the accepted approach to judicial review of administrative action, that puts the judge in the position of substituting his or her judgment for that of the reviewed public authority. Proportionality analysis was not decreed by God; it is, at least in Israel, a judicial creation.

Cases like *Beit Sourik* look doubly strange to American administrative lawyers. Balancing tests are hardly unknown in American administrative law, but they do not tend to be applied to substantive decisions of administrative policy without a large measure of deference – a presumption of regularity like those that the *Beit Sourik* Court employed with respect to the first two proportionality questions. The double strangeness arises from the nature of the decisions at issue in the *Beit Sourik* case. Decisions of American military authorities in a theater of war or in occupied territory are not reviewable at all pursuant to the American APA.[100]

But this peculiarity of proportionality analysis in cases like *Beit Sourik* is hardly an argument for the undesirability of the proportionality approach. Concerns about judicial second-guessing might be evaluated from two quite different perspectives. The first would be an internal defense of the practice that seeks to shore up the "objectivity" of this form of judicial review. From this perspective a judge declaring an administrative decision to be disproportionate is not merely second-guessing a policy question that has been entrusted in the first instance to an administrative official. The second approach looks at proportionality analysis comparatively. The argument here would be that, although proportionality analysis may involve some degree of second-guessing, any analysis that involves weighing competing values has that feature, and proportionality analysis has other virtues that make it a superior approach to the proceduralized rationality review that we have discussed.

To be sure, the concern that proportionality analysis in the end is just a substitution of one subjective judgment for another does not always have bite. The *Nova Scotia Food Products* case is perhaps an example of a clear case. Destroying an industry to solve a non-problem is a disproportionate regulatory response. It looks a bit like my example of burning down my house to get rid of mice. But this class of cases is not particularly interesting. Administrative judgments rarely exhibit this sort of imbalance. Balancing judgments that make their way to reviewing courts generally pose more difficult problems of evaluation.

For one, unless the competing values can be reliably reduced to a common medium – such as money, as is done in statistical cost-benefit analysis – the balancer runs up against the problem that Justice Scalia once described as determining "whether a particular line is longer than a particular rock is heavy."[101] That certainly looks like the problem in *Beit Sourik*, when Israel's defense needs had to be weighed against the interference with the lives of affected Palestinians. When Justice Barak and his colleagues found that the military's choice was disproportionate, they had little to say about why, beyond the institutional argument that they are judges and must decide. But this statement is about constitutional allocation of authority, not objectivity. Without more, that statement begs the question of the appropriateness of the allocation of authority that the proportionality test instantiates.

---

[100] Under 5 U.S.C. § 701(b)(1)(G), an agency subject to judicial review under the APA does not include "military authority exercised in the field in time of war or in occupied territory."

[101] *Bendix Autolite Corp.* v. *Midwesco Enters.*, 486 U.S. 888, 897 (1988) (Scalia, J., concurring in judgment).

To be sure, there is, abstractly considered, a way to objectify the mental process of balancing. Perhaps the most prominent proponent of balancing analysis is Robert Alexy, who developed the "weight formula" as a means of demonstrating that balancing is a rational process.[102] But while Alexy's formula demonstrates that one can take a reasoned approach to balancing, it does not demonstrate that the balancing process will have any determinate outcome. The weight formula requires that cardinal numbers be assigned to the competing values. If the values are like those at issue in *Beit Sourik* and many, many other cases, there is no way to assign those cardinal numbers.

Other approaches have suggested that balancing need not have cardinal values attached to the competing interests, so long as there is some way to compare the degree to which some proposed administrative action affects the two values at issue.[103] Hence, the comparison is not between the weight of a stone and the length of a line, but an analysis of whether a particular action adds proportionately more length to the line than it decreases the weight of the stone. Arguably, that is what Justice Barak was doing in *Beit Sourik*. His discussion suggests that he thinks that the separation fence's proposed placement adds much less to the military value of the fence than it detracts from the ability of the affected villagers to live their lives in a reasonably acceptable way.

The problem, of course, is that Justice Barak cannot tell us how he knows this. He certainly has not attempted to argue, for example, that placing the barrier fence where it was proposed would add only 10 percent to its military effectiveness while subtracting 20 percent from the villagers' reasonable enjoyment of life. At best, he asks us to believe with him that the security loss is small, while the disruption effects of the fence location are large. Perhaps he is right. But even if he is, the balancing analysis must also contend with the problem that any attempt to determine relative effects also presumes that the two interests or values have equal normative weight. The degree to which they are affected would be an appropriate basis for comparison only if that equality holds.

And, indeed, in other writing,[104] Justice Barak recognizes clearly that the balancing approach entailed at the third level of proportionality analysis is much more complex. Not only must the judge assess the relative normative weights of the two competing values, and the degree to which the proposed action enhances one and detracts from the other, but also the relative likelihood that the proposed action will accomplish its objectives as well as the likelihood that the negative effects on

[102] Robert Alexy, The Construction of Constitutional Rights, 4 *L. & Ethics of Hum. Rts.* 20, 28–32 (2010).

[103] Niels Petersen, How to Compare the Length of Lines to the Weight of Stones: Balancing and the Resolution of Value Conflicts in Constitutional Law, 14 *German L.J.* 1387, 1390–1 (2013).

[104] Aahron Barak, *Proportionality: Constitutional Rights and Their Limits* 362–5 (2012).

the competing value will be realized. This is a formidable analytical challenge that Justice Barak also concedes cannot totally eliminate subjective elements.[105]

That balancing in the form of the proportionality approach does not lead to determinate outcomes is not necessarily an argument against its use in judicial review of administrative action. There may be an institutional argument for judges or courts as the best institutions to balance competing interests and values. This claim seems to lie at the base of the justifications for judicial balancing in constitutional review of legislative or administrative action where particular interests are likely to be slighted in legislative or administrative processes.[106] And much of the academic discussion of proportionality analysis has been around its use in constitutional adjudication, particularly the protection of individual constitutional rights, rather than in judicial review of administrative action.[107] This institutional argument for the superiority of courts as "neutral" balancers could easily have application in cases like *Beit Sourik*. It is certainly plausible to believe that the commander of the Israeli defense forces in occupied territory may be prone to discount the interests of Palestinian villagers, some of whom may harbor – or even be – the very terrorists against which the separation fence is meant to provide protection.

But this institutional argument has limited reach with respect to run-of-the-mill judicial review of administrative action. The interests and values at stake are things like the protection of the environment as against promoting economic development, the potential health and welfare effects of risk regulation as against the costs to consumers or producers, and so on. The basic question is whether approaching these sorts of balancing issues in the straightforward substantive fashion that proportionality analysis entails is superior to other means of attempting to assure that agency action is not unreasonable in the sense of being disproportionate. After all, American courts were able to deal with potentially disproportionate administrative action in cases like *Nova Scotia Food Products*, the *Benzene* case or *State Farm*, by using the tools of proceduralized rationality review while maintaining, at least rhetorically, a respectful distance from making policy judgments that Congress had delegated to the relevant administrators. Since proceduralized review has managed to handle such cases, one has to ask whether there are other values to the proportionality approach that would recommend it.

As previously noted, Justice Barak is not only a practitioner of proportionality analysis as a jurist, but, as an academic, is a proponent and theorist of how proportionality analysis should be deployed and justified. In his academic writings, Justice Barak makes clear that he believes that the weighing at the third stage of proportionality analysis is indeed a weighing of the marginal effects of the proposed action on

---

[105] Id., at 478.
[106] *See* Jud Mathews and Alec Stone Sweet, All Things in Proportion? American Rights Review and the Problem of Balancing, 60 *Emory L.J.* 797 (2011).
[107] Alec Stone Sweet and Jud Mathews, Proportionality Balancing and Global Constitutionalism, 47 *Colum J. Transnat'l L.* 72 (2008).

the two competing values or interests at stake. He is equally clear that there is no possibility of arriving at determinate solutions that absolve the judge from exercising judgment in weighing the balance. He is under no illusion that the scale metaphor of balancing analysis accurately portrays the certainty with which a judge can determine that the marginal adverse effects on one interest are disproportionate to the marginal benefits for another. Justice Barak nevertheless believes the advantages of proportionality analysis are considerable. In his words: "It stresses the need to always justify limitation on human rights; it structures the mind of the balancer; it is transparent; it creates a proper dialog[ue] between the political branches and the judiciary; and it adds to the objectivity of judicial discretion."[108] We should look at these proposed advantages in turn.

Justice Barak's emphasis on the way in which proportionality stresses the need to justify limitations on human rights suggests that he is thinking here only of proportionality in its constitutional role. But his view of human rights is broader than constitutional guarantees, as the *Beit Sourik* opinion itself demonstrates. The interests of the villagers were human rights protected, not by the Israeli constitution, but by international human rights norms that apply to military authorities in occupied territory. I think Justice Barak's suggestion is correct, but the feature that virtually any legitimate interest can be fit into the balancing equation is not necessarily an argument in favor of proportionality as against American courts' stress on reason-giving. In the American system the demand for a reason is almost universal. It stresses the need for justification for any administrative action and many administrative failures to act, whether or not some particular human right can be asserted as hanging in the balance. The rights-protecting advantage displayed in *Beit Sourik* is that the action is reviewable at all under Israeli law, whereas it would be exempt from review under the American APA. That is a function of reviewability doctrine, not the proportionality methodology.

Moreover, the requirement that administrators respond with reasons to issues raised by participants in administrative processes may have a rights-respecting value of its own. It articulates a vision of responsiveness and justification that reinforces the idea of participants as independent moral agents entitled to reasons. By contrast, proportionality analysis asks its questions in substantive terms that do not necessarily suggest any particular structure for the underlying administrative processes. The question is whether the action can be justified to the court as proportionate, not whether the administrator has exercised judgment in a fashion that is responsive to the issues that the affected parties raised. The American proceduralized rationality approach presses administrators to build dialogue and justification into the administrative process itself.

But we should not make too much of these procedural considerations. Told to rethink the location of the fence, the military commander would surely be foolish to

---

[108] Barak, *supra* note 89 at 14–15 (internal citations omitted).

do so without thorough consultation with the affected parties who might haul him back into court. And the prospect of judicial review, combined with independent consultation requirements under Israeli law, had generated a dialogue with the *Beit Sourik* villagers long before the question ended up in litigation.[109] Indeed, Justice Barak urges the capacity of proportionality analysis to promote transparent reason-giving and dialogue as one of the important virtues of that form of analysis. Here he is thinking of a judicial–legislative dialogue, but there is no reason to believe that transposed to the administrative context the same virtues might not obtain. An agency subject to the structured form of proportionality review suggested by Justice Barak would be imprudent, to say the least, not to structure both its requests for comments and its ultimate rationale for action in ways that would elicit public input on these issues and explain its action in terms of proportionality review's demands.

Moreover, there may be something to be said for the lack of precedential effect of any particular ultimate judgment on proportionality. When the *Nova Scotia* court dodged substantive reasonableness analysis by focusing on the adequacy of the agency's notice, it sent a message that had broad legal consequences. If agencies must provide detailed notice of their scientific findings and scientific methodology in order to properly request comments on their proposals, they may feel it necessary to prepare a defensible, and therefore close-to-final, position before any dialogue with affected parties begins. Real dialogue may be stifled. Or, alternatively, the agency may feel compelled to engage in a lengthy, iterative, and increasingly detailed notice and comment process that insures early consultation with affected parties, so no one can claim surprise when the final decision emerges.[110] This is, of course, the sort of resource-intensive process that critics claim empowers adversaries who benefit from delay whatever the final outcome. That proceduralized rationality review is likely to inform agency processes is not a benefit without costs.

How should we think about Justice Barak's plausible claim that proportionality analysis structures the mind of the balancer? Here, Justice Barak seems to be think-ing specifically of the mind of the judge. Fair enough. But so does the approach of American courts seeking to determine whether an agency has given sufficient rea-sons for its policy choice or adjudication. The search for reasoning adequacy is struc-tured necessarily by the statute that sets out criteria for administrative judgment and by the record of the proceeding that develops the issues that must be addressed in the administrative rationale. This approach structures the mind of the administrator as well. The demand that the administrator attend to relevant statutory criteria, avoid the use of irrelevant ones, and be responsive to issues raised by the parties, structures administrative balancing well before (and even in the absence of) judicial review.

---

[109] HCJ 2056/04, [2004] IsrLR 264, 277 [2004].

[110] *See* Jack M. Beermann and Gary Lawson, *Reprocessing Vermont Yankee*, 75 *Geo. Wash. L. Rev.* 856, 899 (2007) (noting the "strong incentive to overproceduralize rulemaking by issuing, as we see today, highly detailed proposed rules with voluminous supporting material, and by conducting additional comment periods whenever a significant change is warranted by the comments.").

Moreover, a proceduralized version of proportionality analysis is arguably already built into American administrative law's reason-giving requirements.[111] Remember that under existing Executive Orders agencies adopting major rules must do a cost-effectiveness analysis that addresses whether the agencies' goals could be achieved via rules imposing less cost on affected parties – part two of the proportionality inquiry outlined by Justice Barak in *Beit Sourik*. The Regulatory Flexibility Act also demands an analysis of whether major rules impose unwarranted costs on small entities. More importantly, judicial demands for responsiveness to objections in the record of agency proceedings – rulemaking or otherwise – embed a requirement for considering the potential disproportionate impact of a proposed agency decision on participating parties whenever that issue is raised. And to the extent that courts review the adequacy of those considerations based on the weight that the court believes the agency should have given the issue, that is, its substantive importance, the differences between reason-giving requirements and proportionality review become very thin indeed.

On the question of transparency, proportionality analysis may have a real advantage over American practice. The judge who finds an agency action disproportionate is perfectly clear about what he or she is doing. And, as we have seen, American courts may be avoiding a finding of substantive unreasonableness that is almost certainly motivating the intensity of their review of administrative reasons. Transparency has consequences. The court finding that an administrative action is disproportionate takes responsibility for thwarting government action. That responsibility obviously weighed heavily on the Supreme Court of Israel in the *Beit Sourik* case. The Court went out of its way to explain that it understood what was at stake and to argue that its decision promoted security, although it thwarted the immediate plans of the Israeli Defense Force. It is quite possible, as well, that this transparency, and the responsibility that comes with it, reinforces an appropriate judicial deference to the judgments of administrative authorities. It may be all too easy for American judges to remand decisions to administrative authorities for further rationalization while believing that they have not had serious effects on administrators' capacity to carry out public programs. The widespread evidence of the "ossification" of the United States agency rulemaking processes suggests otherwise.[112]

Finally, I find Justice Barak's claim that proportionality analysis adds to the objectivity of judicial discretion somewhat puzzling. Beyond structuring the mind of the balancer, I'm not sure what this approach adds to objectivity. The question is objectivity as compared to what alternative method of judging agency reasonableness. Perhaps, once again, the idea is that taking ultimate responsibility for the final

---

[111] The European Court of Justice seems to be doing something like proceduralized proportionality review. See Joined Cases C-92/09 and C-93/09 of November 2010 (*Schecke and Eifert*).

[112] *E.g.*, Richard J. Pierce, Jr., Rulemaking Ossification is Real: A Response to Testing the Ossification Thesis, 80 *Geo. Wash. L. Rev.* 1493 (2012).

balance of interests gives the judge the appropriate mindset – one that promotes careful and thoughtful balancing, which is as close to objectivity as the judge, or anyone else, can get.

CONCLUSION

The transparency advantages of the proportionality approach are substantial. Moreover, a straightforward finding that an agency's decision is unreasonable as disproportionate mitigates real risks that the avoidance of substance for process will impose unanticipated burdens on all similar administrative actions when the real problem is just the unreasonableness of the particular litigated decision. Moreover, it seems entirely plausible that the proceduralized approach of American courts might cause judges not only to impose unanticipated burdens, but also to fail to take institutional responsibility for procedural decisions motivated by substantive concerns. Deciding that an agency has engaged in a clear error of judgment, as the United States jurisprudence often puts it, is a heavy responsibility, and it should be.

A full-scale adoption of the proportionality approach is, of course, not necessary to achieve the benefits of facing substantive reasonableness questions on judicial review. There are real advantages, as well, to the consistent demands for reasoned explanation that populate much of the American judicial review jurisprudence. A considerable degree of transparency can be achieved by simply admitting, or making clear, that judicial rejection of an agency's analysis is motivated by the court's sense that the agency's response to a perceived problem is disproportionate to the problem identified, or that less burdensome alternatives are apparently available. The *State Farm* opinion comes very close to saying just that. The precedential effect of technical or procedural grounds for remand or reversal can be limited by appropriate language that contemplates the all-too-real possibility that the vagaries of decision-making in adversary litigation might have led the court to misunderstand either the factual situation or the good sense of an agency's explanation. American reviewing courts have tamed reasonableness review in the interests of preserving appropriate institutional responsibilities. They could further that project by more transparently revealing when they do so.

The "rights-protecting" focus of proportionality analysis also leaves a potential blind spot that other doctrines would have to fill. Proportionality is focused on administrative overreach – the imposition of costs that are disproportionate to the benefits achieved. Cases like *State Farm* feature what might be called "underreach," the failure, for no persuasive reasons, to achieve benefits that are worth their costs, perhaps many times over.[113] To be sure, the doctrine of proportionality could be

---

[113] *See* Jud Mathews, Agency Discretion, Judicial Review and 'Proportionality' in US Administrative Law, *in The Judge and the Proportionate Use of Discretion: A Comparative Study* 160, 177 (Sofia Ranchordás and Boudewijn de Waard eds., 2015).

deployed creatively to reach these sorts of cases. Rescission, rather than revision, might be viewed as a disproportionate response to the problem presented by the automakers' choice of technology for compliance with NHTSA's passive restraints rule. But a judicial decision based on that premise seems to carry with it a demand that the NHTSA amend and reissue the rule. Thus, proportionality results here in a much stronger judicial incursion into the agency's policy space than a remand for better reasons.

Finally, it's worth noting that a number of the analytic requirements that have been previously described, such as requirements for cost–benefit analysis, analysis of environmental impacts, analysis of regulatory effects on small entities or the analysis of paperwork burdens, can be understood as instructions to agencies to behave reasonably as well as instrumentally rationally. These anti-tunnel-vision statutes and executive orders tell agencies that they should question whether an instrumentally rational pursuit of their particular statutory missions is reasonable, or could be more reasonably pursued, when taking into account economic costs, environmental impacts, and the differential effects on particular groups or constituencies. This is not the place for a full-scale evaluation of these analytic regimes. Nevertheless, as was described in Chapter 4, these requirements have effects on the internal organization of agencies and bring broader perspectives to bear on inquiries that may be otherwise narrowly technocratic, and that as a result may impose disproportionate costs related to values that lie outside an agency's particular mission. Moreover, the availability of these analyses for review by hierarchical superiors in the executive branch, congressional overseers, and affected publics helps to make agencies accountable for reasonableness beyond the narrow confines of judicial review. In these alternative fora, concerns about the appropriateness of judicial second-guessing disappear. For these are fora in which policy analysis and political reason support democratic values in ways that are unavailable to the judiciary.

My preliminary conclusion is that American courts' approach to reasonableness review can be modified in ways that provide many, if not all, of the advantages of proportionality analysis. These modifications can be made while retaining the emphasis on reason-giving that fits better with American traditions of separation of powers and that, if properly deployed, has participatory and democracy-reinforcing characteristics as well. But as we will see in Chapters 7 and 8, reasoned administration's core legitimating characteristics require some significant reinforcement themselves to achieve a fully functioning model of administrative government that is understood as an acceptable vision of democratic self-rule. Perhaps most importantly, courts need to reimagine administrative reason-giving as the output of an implementation process that generates meaning, as well as technical means of implementation and as a part of a process of democratic deliberation that completes, at least provisionally, the generation of policies that serve the will of the people. But before engaging in that critical and reconstructive institutional analysis, we need to spend a bit more time grappling with the competition between reason and politics in administration.

6

Reasons, Administration, and Politics

POLITICS IN ADMINISTRATION

The founding generation that drafted the United States Constitution virtually ignored political parties, save for a decided antipathy toward them.[1] And widespread involvement of ordinary Americans in politics was viewed with alarm.[2] Indeed, for most of the early years of the Republic, "democracy" was largely an epithet conjuring up visions of "mobocracy."[3]

Andrew Jackson, by contrast, believed not only in broadening the electorate and the number of elected officers, but also that peopling the federal bureaucracy with partisan office holders was critical to wresting governmental control from the social and political elites favored for office in both the Federalist and Jeffersonian periods.[4] The triumph of Jackson's political party, "The Democrats," in the 1830s made "democracy" almost synonymous with partisan control of administration. Politics

---

[1] E.g., President George Washington, Farewell Address, (1796), available at: http://avalon.law.yale .edu/18th_century/washing.asp (Last accessed May 25, 2018) (warning against "the danger of parties in the State" and "the baneful effects of the spirit of party generally"); Benjamin Franklin, Address to the Constitutional Convention (June 2, 1787), available at: http://avalon.law.yale.edu/18th_century/ debates_602.asp (Last accessed May 25, 2018) (warning against factional politics, which in Britain were "perpetually dividing the Nation, distracting its Councils, hurrying sometimes into fruitless & mischievous wars, and often compelling a submission to dishonorable terms of peace").

[2] E.g., James Madison, Address to the Constitutional Convention (May 30, 1787), available at: http:// avalon.law.yale.edu/18th_century/yates.asp (Last accessed May 25, 2018) (arguing for longer, six-year senate terms "as to protect the minority of the opulent against the majority").

[3] E.g., John Jay, writing to federal judge and fellow former revolutionary Richard Peters, mused that "*pure* democracy, like *pure* rum, easily produces intoxication, and with it a thousand mad pranks and fooleries. Ebriety, whether moral or physical, is difficult to cure; and the more so, as such patients cannot easily be convinced of the value and the necessity of temperance and regimen." The Life of John Jay: Vol. II 315 (William Jay, ed., 1833).

[4] See generally Jerry L. Mashaw, *Creating the Administrative Constitution: The Lost 100 Years of American Administrative Law* 175–86 (2012).

and administration were conjoined.[5] The Jacksonian era's enduring political legacy was to change the image of democracy to one of government by the people.

Jackson's vice president and successor Martin Van Buren gave theoretical support to the Jacksonian program by writing a cogent democratic defense of the "spoils system."[6] On Van Buren's account, political parties were essential to the functioning of electoral politics. Financial (and other) support for those parties could be maintained only by assuring the enthusiasm of large numbers of citizens for each party's electoral goals. That energetic and loyal support could be purchased only with the parties' most coveted benefit – opportunities for office for those who supported the party. For democracy to work, to the victor must go the spoils.

Van Buren believed that partisan office-holding did more than solidify a party apparatus capable of waging effective election campaigns. It also provided a vehicle by which otherwise ordinary citizens could be intimately involved in the administration of public policy. Van Buren had a lively sense of administrative implementation's important role in the carrying out of public policies. If citizens were to have an influence on government beyond episodic electoral voting, the best way to organize that influence was to include party loyalists in the day-to-day work of governance. For Van Buren, partisan administration gave concrete effect to the victorious parties' enacted policies, and the knowledge that party loyalists gained in that administration helped to set the agenda for further policy innovation by revealing problems and opportunities to those politically attuned, grassroots administrators.

Like any institutional arrangement designed to promote a vision of democracy, the spoils system had the defects of its virtues. Party loyalty turned out to be a rather poor proxy for competence, and the advantages of multiplying party loyalists by multiplying offices were hardly lost on reelection-oriented politicians. The spoils system had a tendency to create administration which was incompetent, bloated, and corrupt,[7] but that system persisted for over a half-century.

Late nineteenth-century reformers, a rather diverse group lumped together as the Progressive Movement, had an administrative objective in common – the desire to

---

5   See Martin Van Buren, *Inquiry Into the Origin and Course of Political Parties in the United States* (1867).

6   Important general studies include Donald B. Cole, *Martin Van Buren and The American Political System* (1984); Richard Hofstadter, *The Idea of a Party System: The Rise of Legitimate Opposition in the United States 1780–1840* (1969); Richard P. McCormick, *The Second American Party System: Party Formation in the Jacksonian Era* (1966); and Robert V. Remini, *Martin Van Buren and the Making of the Democratic Party* (1959).

7   See, e.g., Matthew A. Crenson, *The Federal Machine: Beginnings of Bureaucracy in Jacksonian America* (1975); see also Carl Russell Fish, *The Civil Service and the Patronage* 105–57 (describing the spoils system in the Jacksonian era) (1905); Leonard D. White, *The Jacksonians: A Study in Administrative History 1829–1861* (1954).

divorce partisan politics from administration.[8] By contrast with the spoils system that the Progressives aimed to replace, the Progressive agenda included merit selection for public office; administrative bureaus organized as "independent commissions" not dominated by any political party; city manager forms of local government that took much day-to-day local administration out of the hands of elected politicians; and administrative decisions based on knowledge or expertise in the particular subject matter relevant to public action. Theoretical writings that began to build a "science of administration" reinforced this practical, and often successful, program of reform. The apotheosis of this Progressive campaign was perhaps the election of Woodrow Wilson as president. Wilson was not only a Progressive politician; he was the intellectual godfather of public administration conceived of as a scientific, managerial enterprise divorced from partisan politics.[9] Progressives did not necessarily believe that administration was a value-free enterprise. Their interest was in protecting the pursuit of public ends from partisanship, incompetence, and corruption.

Remnants of the Progressive reform movement are not difficult to identify in twenty-first-century American government. Civil service employees numerically dominate public employment in the federal government. They are selected based on examinations or other merit criteria and are protected from political dismissal by the requirement that removal can be made only to promote "the efficiency of the [federal] service."[10] Nonpartisan, independent commissions, and the protection of certain other office holders by "for cause" dismissal requirements remain prominent features of federal administrative organization. And administrative government has become complexly organized around specialized bureaus that attempt to bring relevant knowledge and expertise to bear on the implementation of government programs. The governing presumption that administrators should legitimate their actions by providing instrumentally rational explanations in some sense presupposes an organization of government bureaus that, by and large, fits the Progressive administrative template.

But the notion that administration could be divorced from politics is a cartoon of the Progressive vision. Indeed, as a description of the organization of public administration, it is not normatively attractive. Administration in the American constitutional scheme has no independent constitutional basis. Administration is an artifact of – and subservient to – the political actors in Congress, who create and fund it,

---

[8]   The standard history is Paul P. Van Riper, *History of the United States Civil Service* (1958). For other general histories, see Ari Hoogenboom, *Outlawing the Spoils: A History of the Civil Service Reform Movement 1865–1883* (1961); and U.S. Office of Pers. Mgmt., U.S. Civil Serv. Comm., Biography of an Ideal: A History of the Federal Civil Service (2003).

[9]   Woodrow Wilson, The Study of Administration, 2 *Pol. Sci. Q.* 197, 210 (1887) (arguing that administration should "lie outside the proper sphere of *politics*" and "is a part of political life ... only as machinery is part of the manufactured product"); *see* John Milton Cooper, Jr., *Woodrow Wilson: A Biography* 59 (2009) (noting that Wilson "pioneered the new field of political science that later came to be called public administration.").

[10]   5 U.S.C. § 7513(a) (2012).

and the President who appoints high-level personnel and has the constitutional duty to oversee implementation. Administration's connection to politics promotes a particular vision of political accountability, and is a necessary condition, if perhaps not a sufficient one, for administrators' constitutional legitimacy.

The Progressives were correct that American government, as then administered, could be made decidedly more scientific, expert, and competent than the spoils system. But the idea that administration can be reduced to only scientific principles and technocratic know-how is divorced from the reality of administrative implementation (see Chapter 5). The implementing discretion given to almost all federal administrators necessarily implicates normative questions that are the very stuff of politics. The Federal Trade Commission cannot protect the economy from "unfair methods of competition" in a normative vacuum,[11] nor can the National Highway Traffic Safety Administration decide how to "meet the need for automobile safety"[12] by protecting the public from "unreasonable risks" without some normative criteria of reasonableness. These questions are not "political" simply because they involve policy. They involve contested issues of policy about which the adherents of different political parties often have opposing views – as our prior discussions of the *State Farm* and *Massachusetts* v. *EPA* cases aptly illustrate.

Hence, in the real world of administration, high-level policymaking officials continue to be appointed, at least in part, because of their basic agreement with the sitting president's political principles and policy vision. Those appointments may be hotly contested in congresses in which a majority of the Senate is not of the President's party. But where government is unified, as it was at the beginning of the Trump Administration, Presidents may appoint agency heads whose primary agenda is dismantling the policies of the preceding administration. Congressional oversight and funding of agencies is hardly independent of the majority party's view of whether the agency's administrative approach is politically acceptable. Nonpartisan commissions may be formally bipartisan in composition, but their agendas and actions rarely are in practice. In the past two decades, bare, politically-aligned majorities have supported many "independent" commissions' most momentous decisions.[13]

[11] 15 U.S.C. § 45(a)(1).

[12] 49 U.S.C. § 30111.

[13] Recent experience at the SEC illustrates this point well. *E.g.*, Andrew Ackerman and Joann S. Lublin, *SEC Proposes Disclosure Rules on Pay Versus Performance*, Wall St. J. (Apr. 29, 2015, 7:55 PM), available at: www.wsj.com/articles/sec-votes-3-2-to-propose-executive-compensation-rules-1430327372 (Last accessed May 25, 2018) (describing the SEC's party-line 3:2 vote on pay disclosure rules, with sharp Republican dissent); Ed Beeson, *SEC Passes Dodd-Frank Securitization, Credit Rating Rules*, Law 360.com (Aug. 27, 2014, 1:17 PM), available at: www.law360.com/articles/571599/sec-passes-dodd-frank-securitization-credit-rating-rules (Last accessed May 25, 2018) (describing SEC's party-line 3:2 vote on major Dodd-Frank rules); Jessica Holzer, *SEC, in Split Vote, Backs Bonus Curbs on Brokers, Hedge Funds*, Wall St. J (Mar. 3, 2011, 12:01 AM), available at: www.wsj.com/articles/SB10001424052748703559604576176320753985628 (Last accessed May 25, 2018) (describing another party-line vote on financial firm pay regulations, which the dissenting Republican commissioners called "wholly unnecessary"). The FCC is also illustrative. *E.g.*, Clarece Polke, *FCC Approves Proposal To Boost*

Cooperative bipartisanship has often broken down. And as we have seen, presidents have increasingly tried to bring administration under presidential control and direction by executive order, Office of Management and Budget (OMB) monitoring, and the creation of White House policy czars. These high-level officials with coordinating and monitoring responsibilities seek to bring multiple administrators in particular policy domains into line with the President's program.[14]

Politics and administration remain deeply intertwined, which raises two important questions for the American vision of reasoned administration. The first is to what extent standard administrative law doctrines of reasonableness and reason-giving permit or prohibit political control of administration. The second is what place political reason should have in reasoned administration. There remains an undeniable tension between visions of legitimate administration premised on instrumentally rational implementation of statutory mandates and administrative accountability to the current office-holders in the political branches.

POLITICS AND JUDICIAL REVIEW

Illicit Incursions of Politics

As our prior discussions of judicial review have revealed, political influence may invalidate agency decisions of either an adjudicatory or rulemaking sort, but for quite different reasons. Persons entitled to an adjudicatory hearing involving their private rights, privileges, or immunities are entitled under the APA, and as a more general matter of due process, to a hearing before an unbiased decider. Like civil or criminal judges, administrative adjudicators may be disqualified because of personal or financial conflicts of interest that could prejudice their decisions, or by a demonstration that the adjudicator has prejudged the facts or outcome of a case prior to the presentation of evidence and argument. The connection of prejudgment to politics is just this: prejudgment may result from political pressures, such as congressional oversight hearings,[15] which press an agency head or other adjudicative official to take positions on a case that is currently before his or her agency. Prejudgment

---

TV Set-Top Box Competition, Reuters (Feb. 18, 2016), available at: www.reuters.com/article/us-fcc-tv-regulations-idUSKCN0VR0GU (Last accessed May 25, 2018) (describing FCC's party-line 3:2 vote on major cable television initiative); Rebecca R. Ruiz and Steve Lohr, *F.C.C. Approves Net Neutrality Rules, Classifying Broadband Internet Service as a Utility*, N.Y. Times (Feb. 26, 2015), available at: www.nytimes.com/2015/02/27/technology/net-neutrality-fcc-vote-internet-utility.html (Last accessed May 25, 2018) (describing FCC's party-line 3:2 vote on seminal net neutrality decision).

[14] Justin S. Vaughn and José D. Villalobos, *Czars in the White House: The Rise of Policy Czars as Presidential Management Tools* 22 (2015) ("[P]residents have turned to czars for help in coordinating policy action on important issues where strong presidential performance is key.").

[15] *See Pillsbury Co. v. FTC*, 354 F.2d 952 (5th Cir. 1966); *see also Am. Pub. Gas Ass'n v. FPC*, 567 F.2d 1016, 1069 (D.C. Cir. 1977) ("Congressional intervention which occurs during the still-pending decisional process of an agency endangers, and may undermine, the integrity of the ensuing decision, which Congress has required be made by an impartial agency charged with responsibility for resolving controversies within its jurisdiction.").

might also be found on the basis of positions that the adjudicator takes when acting in a political role, such as spokesperson for his or her agency, or as legislative staff, prior to taking the position as a commissioner or agency head with adjudicatory responsibilities.[16]

Simply holding policy views that are contrary to a particular litigant's position is not in itself disqualifying.[17] Administrators with no policy views on the laws in their charge are probably not professionally qualified for their posts. Disinterestedness is a virtue, but complete policy neutrality has an uncomfortable correlation with ignorance. Prejudgment is disqualifying for administrators and judges only to the extent that it concerns the facts of a particular case or its specific outcome.

Participants in rulemaking processes are not entitled to a neutral decider, at least in the sense of being "policy neutral."[18] Rulemaking is about making policy. It often involves scientific or technical facts, to be sure, but also the policies and purposes embodied in the relevant legislation. Administrators, if competent, are expected to have preexisting views about both. While an administrator involved in deciding whether to adopt a rule might, in one circuit court's opinion, be disqualified if he or she has "an unalterably closed mind,"[19] there seems to be no case in which that strict standard has been met. Facts and arguments put forward in the rulemaking process are meant to matter, but they are not required to be put before administrators with no preexisting views concerning an appropriate outcome.

On the other hand, political considerations may invalidate a rule if those considerations caused the administrator to deviate from the criteria appropriate to his or her particular decision. We have already discussed the Three Sisters Bridge case in which the Secretary of Transportation's delicate compromise with Representative William Natcher – that is, trading a particular highway project for funding for the Washington D. C. Metro System – caused the court to remand the decision to the Secretary.[20] In the court's view, the politics of Metro funding were simply not relevant to the consideration of the highway project's location.

---

[16] *See Am. Cyanamid Co.* v. *FTC*, 363 F.2d 757 (6th Cir. 1966) (vacating FTC order because the participating FTC chairman previously served as chief counsel to a Senate subcommittee that investigated the same parties).

[17] *United States* v. *Morgan*, 313 U.S. 409 (1941) (noting that an administrative adjudicator may permissibly "have an underlying philosophy in approaching a specific case.").

[18] Bias in the sense of financial interest may be a different matter. Although the Supreme Court held that Amtrak was, at least in certain respects, a public entity to which Congress might delegate regulatory authority, *Dep't of Transp.* v. *Ass'n of Am. R.R.*, 135 S. Ct. 1225 (2015), the D.C. Circuit, on remand, held that Amtrak's financial interest in maintaining its preferential position in the use of shared tracks disqualified it, on due process grounds, from adopting regulations that affected the operations of private freight railroads. *Am. Ass'n of R.R.* v. *Dep't. of Transp.*, 821 F.3d 19, 34 (D.C. Cir. 2016) ("Amtrak is required both to 'maximize its revenues' and to develop new performance metrics, a set of responsibilities that, if adhered to, will inevitably boost Amtrak's profitability at the expense of its competitors.").

[19] *Ass'n of Nat'l Advertisers, Inc.* v. *FTC*, 627 F.2d 1151, 1170 (1979), *cert. denied*, 447 U.S. 921 (1980).

[20] *D.C. Fed'n of Civic Ass'ns* v. *Volpe*, 459 F.2d 1231, 1236 (D.C. Cir. 1971).

A similar situation arose with respect to the Food and Drug Administration's fraught policymaking concerning the so-called "Plan B" or "morning after" contraceptive pill. After the Food and Drug Administration (FDA) Commissioner, on the advice of both FDA staff and an advisory committee, approved the pharmaceutical for over-the-counter sale to young women, her immediate superior, the Secretary of Health and Human Services, intervened to reverse that decision.[21] There was some question whether the Secretary had the statutory authority to take a position different from the Commissioner's, but on judicial review, the court was more focused on the problem of political intervention.[22] While there was no direct evidence that the decision had been made on political grounds, the reasons that the Secretary gave for reversing the Commissioner were transparently contrary to the evidence of record and well-established FDA policy.[23] From this, the reviewing court deduced that the decision must have been made on political grounds rather than on the grounds made relevant by the Food, Drug and Cosmetic Act.[24] The Secretary's political reasons, whatever they might have been, were not relevant reasons at all. Political preferences or considerations beyond the criteria that the statute and existing policy or practice provide simply do not count as validating reasons.

Where political considerations are insufficient to disqualify an adjudicator or cause a deviation from statutory criteria for judgment, the legal situation becomes somewhat murkier. As a doctrinal matter, that administrators have meetings with or make reports to political actors in the course of arriving at a decision, is not invalidating, at least where those contacts are not in connection with decision-making in a formal adjudicatory context. Such contacts might be invalidating in formal adjudication because adjudicators are not meant to receive evidence or argument that supports one party's position in the absence of an opportunity for the opposing party to hear that evidence or argument and contest it. A fair hearing in adjudication generally excludes all so-called ex parte contacts.

But rulemaking proceedings are not so constrained. Over the course of a major and controversial rulemaking, which may take years or even decades, it would be rare for administrators to avoid contact with both Congress and the Executive Office of the President, if not the President himself. Litigants who oppose an agency's final

---

[21] For a short timeline of these events, see Alexandra Sifferlin, *Timeline: The Battle for Plan B*, Time (June 11, 2013), available at: http://healthland.time.com/2013/06/11/timeline-the-battle-for-plan-b/ (Last accessed May 25, 2018).

[22] For an extensive discussion of the legal and political history of the controversy over Plan B contraception pills, see Lisa Heinzerling, The FDA's Plan B Fiasco: Lessons for Administrative Law, 102 *Geo. L.J.* 927 (2014).

[23] *Tummino v. Hamburg*, 936 F. Supp. 2d 162, 170–71 (E.D.N.Y. 2013) ("Thus, three distinguished scientists, including the Editor-in-Chief of the New England Journal of Medicine, wrote: 'In our opinion, the [HHS] Secretary's decision to retain behind-the-counter status for Plan B One-Step was based on politics rather than science.'" [quoting The Politics of Emergency Contraception, 366 *New Eng. J. Med.* 101, 102 (2012)]).

[24] *Id.*, at 171 ("[T]he reasons she [the Secretary] provided are so unpersuasive as to call into question her good faith.").

rule may believe that its true basis lies in some form of political influence rather than in the analysis that the agency provided to justify its decision. Courts have, however, resisted attempts to make these political contacts invalidating, or to require that their content always be revealed in the rulemaking record.

The leading case is *Sierra Club* v. *Costle*,[25] a review proceeding involving the Environmental Protection Agency's (EPA) rule concerning permissible emissions of sulfur dioxide from power plants. Environmental groups challenging the EPA's adoption of the rule argued that nine separate meetings between EPA staff and members of Congress, the President, and their respective staffs were held after the rulemaking docket had been closed for comment.[26] The EPA had failed to note two of these meetings in the rulemaking docket. The circuit court, in an opinion by Judge Patricia Wald, in effect told the complaining parties "welcome to Washington."

This was a rulemaking proceeding, not an adjudicatory one, and hence ex parte contacts were not prohibited either in general or by the particular statute under which the EPA was acting.[27] The EPA's explanation for its final rule relied not at all on any data or arguments presented in these meetings. Unlike the Three Sisters Bridge case or the Plan B contraception case, there was no evidence that political considerations caused the agency to act on irrelevant criteria.

To be sure, the agency's rule would not be upheld unless its contemporaneous justification passed the APA's reasonableness test, but that was not a problem for the *Costle* court on the evidence of record and the agency's explanation. Moreover, the reviewing court viewed the political contacts that went on around this rulemaking process as presupposed by the constitutional structure of American government.[28] With respect to the President's intervention, the court noted both the President's responsibility to see that the laws are faithfully executed and the constitutionally-based doctrine of executive privilege that gives legal protection to confidential conversations within the Executive Branch.[29] Failure to reveal the extent or content of presidential consultations simply could not, by themselves, invalidate an agency's policy choice. With respect to congressional intervention, the court was unsympathetic to complaints about the people's representatives making their views known to an administrative agency engaged in high-stakes policymaking, absent something like Representative Natcher's hostage-taking tactics in the Three Sisters Bridge case.[30]

---

[25] 657 F.2 298 (D.C. Cir. 1981).
[26] *See* id., at 387–91.
[27] Id., at 400 ("[W]here agency action involves informal rulemaking of a policymaking sort, the concept of ex parte contacts is of more questionable utility.").
[28] Id., at 404–8.
[29] Ibid.
[30] Id., at 408–10.

Policing Politics through Reason-Giving

Judge Wald, an experienced Washington practitioner prior to taking the bench, clearly did not believe that the participation of political actors could or should be banished from the administrative rulemaking process. On the other hand, reviewing courts have not been willing to take political reasons as themselves sufficient for administrative rulemaking. Many cases suggest that reviewing courts see political pressure or political commitments by an administration as one of the "danger signals" that suggest that the court should take a close or hard look at the agency's justifications for its decisions.

The *State Farm* case is a poster child for this position. The Supreme Court in that case made clear that a change of administration was an insufficient ground for Department of Transportation (DOT)'s change of mind concerning its passive restraints rule. The suspicion that the Reagan Administration's often repeated promises to provide regulatory relief to the motor vehicle industry had strongly influenced the NHTSA, seemingly motivated the intensity of the Court's review. In partial dissent, Justice Rehnquist went out of his way to make clear his belief that a change of administration could certainly provoke a new look at an existing policy. He would have accepted two of the three explanations that the majority of the Court found inadequate to justify rescission of the rule. The majority's concern that political pressure had seriously contaminated the rulemaking process almost certainly influenced its more jaundiced view of those explanations.

This danger-signals rationale seems to lurk beneath other prominent reason-giving cases discussed in prior chapters. For example, suspicion that a Bush Administration antipathy toward climate change regulation motivated the EPA's refusal to use its Clean Air Act jurisdiction to combat greenhouse gases in the form of carbon dioxide lay just beneath the surface of the majority opinion in *Massachusetts* v. *EPA*. Academic commentators have interpreted that case as a triumph of expertise over politics.[31] *Gonzalez* v. *Oregon* is another case in point.[32] The challenge there was to Attorney General John Ashcroft's determination that physician-assisted suicide under Oregon's death with dignity statute did not involve a "legitimate medical purpose."[33] That finding provided a potential predicate to disqualify any suicide-assisting Oregon physician from prescribing federally controlled pharmaceuticals. Because drugs used in physician-assisted suicide have multiple other common uses, a federal prescription ban would devastate many physicians' capacity to practice medicine.

---

[31] Jody Freeman and Adrian Vermeule, *Massachusetts* v. *EPA: From Politics to Expertise*, 2007 *Sup. Ct. Rev.* 51. There are anecdotal stories, perhaps apocryphal, that EPA staff held champagne parties to celebrate the government's loss in the Supreme Court.

[32] 546 U.S. 243 (2006).

[33] Id., at 255 (quoting Dispensing of Controlled Substances to Assist Suicide, 66 Fed. Reg. 56,607, 56,608 [Nov. 9, 2001]).

The Court was hardly unaware that this was the same Attorney General Ashcroft who, as *Senator* Ashcroft, unsuccessfully pressured the prior administration's Justice Department to take this same action.[34] The Attorney General's pre-commitment to his position seemed pretty evident. But, rather than find that Ashcroft was disqualified from deciding (a difficult finding, since this interpretive rule was not an adjudicatory proceeding) or that he had invoked irrelevant criteria as the basis for his decision (he had not), the Court found that the Attorney General lacked authority to make the decision at all.

The underlying statute[35] and related regulation[36] were ambiguous and might well have warranted deference to the Attorney General's interpretation. Indeed, because, in substance, the Attorney General's interpretive rule was really an interpretation of an existing regulation that the Department itself had issued, substantial deference might have been expected.[37] The Court, however, found it unlikely that Congress would delegate this sort of professional *medical* judgment to the government's chief *law enforcement* officer, who had no particular expertise in medical practice.[38] Moreover, regulation of medical practice has long been virtually the exclusive domain of the several states. Invoking considerations of relevant technical expertise and federalism are not necessarily doctrinally problematic moves. Yet again, they seem motivated by a concern that political ideology was trumping the law enforcement purposes of the statute. Implicit in the opinion is the idea that the Attorney General's enforcement authority over controlled substances could legitimately be used to prevent doctors from becoming drug dealers, but not to enforce the A. G.'s moral objections to Oregon's public policies.

It seems fair to say, in summary, that on judicial review, courts have been vigilant to protect certain structural constitutional values. They have been loath to allow litigants' interest in political transparency to undermine the constitutional structure of political accountability of administrative agencies to the President and Congress. Yet the courts have also been alert to protect the integrity of the administrative process. In adjudicatory contexts, that has meant protecting due process rights to a neutral decider and to an opportunity to contest any facts or arguments that opposing parties make. Similarly, political considerations have not been allowed, at least where evident on the face of the record or implied by surrounding circumstances, to alleviate administrative agencies' responsibility to provide reasoned and statutorily relevant arguments for their policy choices in rulemaking proceedings and when issuing interpretive rules.

---

[34] Id., at 253.

[35] 21 U.S.C. § 824(a)(4) (2012).

[36] 21 C.F.R. § 1306.04(a) (as amended 2005).

[37] *Auer* v. *Robbins*, 519 U.S. 452 (1997), holds that courts should defer to agency interpretations of their own regulations unless "plainly erroneous or inconsistent with the regulation." Id., at 461.

[38] *Oregon*, 546 U.S. at 266 ("The structure of the [Controlled Substances Act], then, conveys unwillingness to cede medical judgments to an executive official who lacks medical expertise.").

Yet, notwithstanding this "balanced" judicial posture, a nagging question remains: If agencies in rulemaking are engaged in an essentially legislative policymaking activity, why don't political reasons count? To put the question more concretely, let us return to the passive restraints rule at issue in the *State Farm* case. After rehearsing the agency's current uncertainty about how motorists would respond to the industry's proposed passive belts system, what if the NHTSA administrator had said this:

> There has been an election since this rule was promulgated. The Carter Administration thought passive restraints were a good idea; we do not. This disagreement reflects a fundamental difference in political ideology. When in doubt, the Carter Administration chose to pursue protection of the public safety, notwithstanding substantial economic costs and the intrusions on individual choice that such protection entailed. Faced with these competing considerations, and acting pursuant to a statute that empowers us to protect the public only from *unreasonable* risks from motor vehicles, we make the contrary choice.

Should not such a transparent revelation of an underlying political rationale be sufficient to justify a rulemaking decision?

THE PLACE OF POLITICAL REASONS

When, where, and what type of political reasons might be used to justify administrative decision-making is a question of no small importance. For one thing, that political considerations influence administrative judgments is simply too plain to be denied. Consider, for example, what transpired after the remand of the passive restraints rule to the DOT in the *State Farm* case.[39] One might have thought that the agency would come back with a rule that could be satisfied by either continuous spool belts or air bags, or that it would have provided further explanation for why either, or both, of those technologies were unlikely to provide safety benefits that were commensurate with their costs. The agency did neither of those things. Instead, it adopted a passive restraints rule that incentivized the use of air bags, while permitting compliance using any available technology that met its performance standards. But in a surprising bit of fence-straddling, the rule provided that if states representing two-thirds of the population of the United States adopted acceptable mandatory seatbelt-use laws, the passive restraints rule would lapse.

The political compromise here is rather obvious. The agency had amassed significant evidence over the course of a nearly twenty-year rulemaking process that passive restraints were likely to have very substantial public health benefits. But the Reagan Administration was skeptical of federal regulation in general and a proponent of devolution of authority to states and localities. Hence, DOT went forward

---

[39] See the discussion in Jerry L. Mashaw, et al., *Administrative Law: The American Public Law System* 641–3 (7th edn. 2014).

with the passive restraints rule, but gave the people, acting through their state legislatures, a means for rescinding it. The new rule was, of course, not justified in these
political terms. Instead, the agency adduced evidence that manual lap and shoulder
belts were, if used, as effective as passive technologies. Evidence from other jurisdictions that had pioneered mandatory use laws suggested that such statutes, if properly
crafted, could substantially increase the use of the manual lap and shoulder belts
already available in all American vehicles. Further, because the administration was
still concerned about the costs of air bags and the possible public reaction to continuous spool belts – the latter could, after all, be disabled with a pair of scissors –
substituting mandatory use laws for passive restraints was arguably the superior
policy. If people buckled up, the safety benefits would be, unlike any passive technology, immediate – and at essentially no cost. But, the agency had no authority
to institute a federal mandatory seatbelt requirement under its governing statute.
Hence the decision to incentivize the states to implement mandatory seatbelt-use
laws by holding out the prospect of eliminating the passive restraints rule, which
many citizens opposed.

DOT's rule was politically motivated in the sense that it was crafted with concern
for the Reagan Administration's commitment to reduce federal regulatory burdens
and return power to states and localities. But it was also arguably both reasoned and
reasonable from the standpoint of existing knowledge about automobile safety and
the available technologies to promote it. Indeed, the rule was not just politically
motivated; it implemented a particular vision of appropriate political organization.
It linked the decision about manual versus passive restraints to the joint actions of
the federal bureaucracy and the legislative processes of the several states. Politics
being unpredictable, American motorists ended up, not with a choice between
these technologies, but with both. Most states adopted mandatory use laws fairly
promptly, but because of astute lobbying by safety partisans, many of those state laws
purposely failed to meet the criteria set out in the DOT rule for a qualifying mandatory use law. Thus, the passive restraints rule remained in effect.

The denouement of this passive restraints episode is perhaps an extreme example
of the interaction of technical and political reason to produce a result difficult to
imagine based on either operating alone. But it underscores the ubiquity of political
considerations in administrative decision-making and the importance of the question of what role politics should play. Policy choice is about values, the very stuff of
political contest, not just about technical or scientific facts or the predicted efficacy
of various policy instruments. When the NHTSA is told to "meet the need" for vehicle safety and to protect the public against "unreasonable" risks, there is no technical answer to exactly what that "need" is or what risks are "unreasonable." A legal
approach to administrative reason-giving that addresses the role of politics in administration only when policing against its extreme forms, thus, seems out of touch with
reality. And indirect judicial policing for suspected improper political influence, as
by independent judicial interpretation of agency mandates in cases like *Gonzalez* v.

Oregon, may, if generalized to less politically fraught circumstances, be a cure that is worse than the disease. As I argued in Chapter 5, taking the values or ends question out of the hands of administrators via independent judicial interpretation of the relevant statutory goals ignores the extent to which statutory ends take on meaning in the context of implementation.

Second, current administrative law doctrine tells us that political reasons may be legitimate without telling us how those considerations should be figured into reasoned administration. Justice Rehnquist suggested as much in his partial dissent in the *State Farm* case when he opined that a change of administration was a perfectly reasonable ground upon to which to premise a reconsideration of regulatory policy. But when reconsideration results in a new policy, it would seem that prudent administrators would be better off on judicial review describing any political considerations as bearing on the more technical issues confronting the agency. Secretary Dole, for example, in adopting the trap door rule, was faulted for not simply requiring non-detachable belts, airbags, or both. When dealing with these issues, the Secretary's rationale might have been that to do so was likely to create a political backlash like the one that undid the agency's earlier passive restraints rule that required ignition interlocks to compel seatbelt use.[40] Instead, she tied "public acceptance" to regulatory efficacy by pointing to surveys showing that motorists were likely to defeat the non-detachable belt technology, and that the public both feared airbag malfunctioning and was unlikely to replace airbags once deployed because of expense.[41]

Justice Scalia's opinion for the plurality in the *FCC v. Fox Television Stations, Inc.*,[42] case seems to go further. The plurality accepts congressional pressure as supporting the FCC's decision to change its rule concerning the acceptability of "fleeting expletives" in radio or television broadcasts.[43] Scalia's position did not go uncontested. In his dissent in that case, Justice Breyer pointedly rejects the idea that political pressure can be a valid basis for agency policy.[44] And he and Justice Scalia simply disagreed about whether the FCC had given an otherwise acceptable explanation for its change of position. But neither he nor Justice Scalia told us anything about what sorts of pressure, from whom, in what circumstances, and related to which sorts of decisions, make political reasons appropriate or inappropriate as justifications for agency action. After all, "congressional pressure" may simply be a proxy for popular political sentiment. In a value-laden decision like the one at issue in *Fox*, involving a determination of how to implement the statutory policy to

---

[40] *See* Jerry L. Mashaw and David L. Harfst, *The Struggle for Auto Safety* 131–40 (1990).

[41] *See State Farm Mut. Auto. Ins. Co. v. Dole*, 802 F.2d 474, 487–89 (D.C. Cir. 1986).

[42] 556 U.S. 502 (2009).

[43] Id., at 523–24 ("Indeed, the precise policy change at issue here was spurred by significant political pressure from Congress.").

[44] Id., at 546 (Breyer, J., dissenting) (arguing the FCC cannot "make policy choices for purely political reasons.").

prohibit "indecent" broadcasts, what would be wrong, or right, with agency action on the basis of public sentiment channeled through the medium of the people's representatives? Neither Justice gives us a cogent answer.

Third, it strikes many commentators as strange for agencies to avoid, and courts to be skeptical of, political reason-giving in a polity that views administrative accountability to the political branches as a cornerstone of administrative legitimacy.[45] Some would go so far as to say that presidential control of administration is the basic underpinning for the administrative state's legitimacy, and that this vision of administration has supplanted Progressive and New Deal notions that the expertise that administrators bring to bear on the pursuit of public purposes justifies agency lawmaking.[46] These latter "presidentialist" commentators almost surely overstate the case, for they tend to ignore Congress and the more-than-two centuries of competition between presidents and congresses over control of administration. "The President made me do it" is not a reason that any court would accept as an independent and controlling explanation for agency action outside of: (i) military and foreign affairs, much of which is excepted from judicial review in any case, or (ii) when an agency exercises authority delegated to the President by statute. Yet in justifying its deference to agency interpretations of their own statutes, the Supreme Court has grounded that deference in a combination of the agencies' expertise in the statutory domain for which they have been delegated policy-making authority *and* agencies' political accountability within the Executive Branch.[47] The problem of the appropriate role of political reasons thus might appear, at base, to be a problem of managing the tension between two rather distinct grounds for the legitimacy of administrative lawmaking – agencies' accountability to political controllers and agencies' capacity to exercise statutorily delegated power on the basis of knowledge.

But my view is that this traditional tension between politics and expertise does not put the question in quite the right way. As Glen Staszewski has pointed out,[48] and as will be further developed in Chapter 7, these two justifications appeal to distinct aspects of democratic theory. Political accountability as a legitimating feature of administrative governance is premised on majoritarian politics. In short form, from this perspective, administrative decisions are democratically legitimate because administrators are under the political control of the people's representatives. Deliberative democratic theory takes a different approach. For deliberative democrats, coercive government action is justified in impinging on individual

---

[45] *See* Kathryn A. Watts, Proposing a Place for Politics in Arbitrary and Capricious Review, 119 *Yale L.J.* 2 (2009).

[46] Id., at 33–9.

[47] *Chevron, U.S.A., Inc. v. Nat. Res. Def. Council, Inc.*, 467 U.S. 837 (1984). The court combined these two reasons for deference in a succinct sentence: "Judges are not experts in the field, and are not part of either political branch of the government." Id., at 865.

[48] *See* Glen Staszewski, Political Reasons, Deliberative Democracy and Administrative Law, 97 *Iowa L. Rev.* 849 (2012).

liberty to the extent that government can give public-regarding reasons that all citizens might accept.[49] All deliberative democrats emphasize reason-giving as critical to democratic legitimacy. For them, administrative policymaking, like all government action, is legitimate just to the extent that it can be justified by reasons. We should, therefore, forgo any attempt at a final resolution of the appropriate reason-giving role of political justifications until we have looked more carefully at these twin, democratic grounds for administrative legitimacy. Nevertheless, there are some fairly straightforward propositions concerning the appropriateness of political reason-giving that do not require a deep dive into democratic theory.

Let us return, therefore, to the hypothetical political justification for rescission of the *State Farm* passive restraints rule. Charitably interpreted, the administration is saying:

> We have a political rationale for regulatory tiebreaking when we are (1) uncertain about the safety benefits that a regulation may generate and (2) certain that regulation will impose substantial costs on market actors. Where these considerations are fairly balanced, we simply weigh economic costs and intrusions on individual liberty as more important than possible public safety benefits. That is a political judgment, but we got elected to make political judgments. And we revealed clearly in the election campaign our commitment to implement *this particular* political approach.

At one level, this is a perfectly appropriate and reasoned justification. The rationale offered invokes public values, the cost to consumers and intrusions on consumer choice, not some rationale related to partisan political advantage. The explanation does not say, for example, that this rescission rewards the automobile industry for its substantial contributions to our election campaign. No one believes that such a political rationale would pass muster. Indeed, that crass political rationale would surely fall outside any criteria that Congress intended the administrator to consider when making a decision about automobile safety regulation. Administrators must surely give "public regarding" reasons, that is, reasons calling on some understandable vision of the public welfare or public purposes. And those public purposes must be those embodied in the statutory scheme being implemented.

On the other hand, cost and incursions on individual liberty fit quite happily within a statutory scheme that requires the agency to adopt rules that are "reasonable," practicable," "appropriate," and that "meet the need" to protect the motoring public against "unreasonable" risks. And where those broad policy issues leave a realm of uncertainty about what should be done, political reasons or political judgments seem to me to provide appropriate decision rules. For by "political reason"

---

[49] Id., at 886 ("[P]ublic officials and citizens are expected to provide reasoned explanations for their positions that could reasonably be accepted by free and equal citizens with fundamentally competing perspectives, and to explain how a proposed course of action would promote the public good.").

I mean broad considerations about the appropriate political organization of the state, such as, the appropriate role of national and state or local governments, the proper balance between individual and collective responsibility, the ubiquitous tradeoffs between liberty and security, and so on. These are background ideological values against which all other public value choices tend to be made. Bringing them into the conversation about administrative policy choice is both realistic concerning how public policy choices are made and democratically empowering in ways that will be argued for in Chapter 7.

Given even a moderately skeptical court, the administrator would doubtless need to say more than my hypothetical rationale has described. The agency would have to say more in particular about the uncertainties that beset this decision. Here, the administrator would be back in the standard business of demonstrating that the agency had made a competent technical analysis of the certainties and uncertainties involved in its proposed action. The *State Farm* Court was seemingly concerned that the NHTSA's invocation of uncertainty masked an unwillingness to look carefully at the facts before the agency (or to investigate further). To put the matter slightly differently, other than candor about motivation, there is really nothing new here. Political reasons need to be connected to the relevant statutory criteria for judgment or some other legitimate source of public values, such as the Constitution or generally applicable framework statutes, and those reasons must be justified by reference to the factual record. Assuming those requirements are met, there seems no reason that political reasons should not be acceptable grounds for administrative action.

On political accountability grounds, this transparent thumb-on-the-scale may be preferable to an attempt to make the more technical analysis seem more persuasive than it is. And on deliberative democracy grounds, forcing the policymaking conversation into a technocratic mold may short-circuit meaningful conversation and debate about policy choices that are necessarily value-laden. For I agree with Henry Richardson that deliberation about the meaning and reasonableness of statutory ends or purposes at the agency level is crucial to maintaining what he terms "democratic autonomy" in the modern administrative state.[50]

There is also a large class of cases in which no statutory criteria for judgment exist. This void is particularly common for agency agenda-setting, that is, determining regulatory, enforcement, or other policy priorities. To be sure, some statutes set time limits on the adoption of particular policies[51] or make particular policy outcomes mandatory on a particular factual finding or state of the world. But in the mine–run of cases, administrative agencies have broad jurisdictions, multiple possible policy or enforcement initiatives, and limited resources. These sorts of determinations are

[50] Henry Richardson, *Democratic Autonomy: Public Reasoning about the Ends of Policy* (Oxford, 2002).
[51] For instance, the Dodd-Frank financial reform bill was replete with rulemaking deadlines. *See, e.g.,* *Dodd Frank Progress Report: Third Quarter 2015,* Davis Polk & Wardwell LLP 2 (2015), available at: www.davispolk.com/sites/default/files/Q32015_Dodd.Frank_.Progress.Report.pdf (Last accessed May 25, 2018).

often viewed as either unreviewable in court or subject to an extremely lenient or deferential form of judicial oversight. They are understood to involve political discretion and often entail no requirement of reason-giving.

But this seems too broad a recognition of political reason's potential role. As Justice Thurgood Marshall pointed out in his concurrence in *Heckler* v. *Chaney*, the leading case on the presumptive non-reviewability of enforcement discretion, the FDA had given broad public policy reasons for its decision not to pursue sanctions for off-label prescription drug use in executions by lethal injection.[52] The Court could just as easily review those broad reasons for reasonableness and, in Justice Marshall's view, reach the same result in favor of the FDA's exercise of enforcement discretion.[53] It is surely valuable to determine that an agency has public-regarding reasons for its exercise of discretionary authority, even if statutory guidelines do not closely cabin that authority.

Where reasons are required, as in the rejection of a petition for rulemaking pursuant to the APA,[54] one would think that political rationales of a policy-oriented nature, though not necessarily invoking considerations that the relevant statute contemplated, should be perfectly appropriate. Congress has, by omitting any action-forcing mechanism, left the choice of regulatory targets or policy initiatives to the agency's discretion. And here, consistency with the administration's general program, the need to coordinate with other agencies and respect their jurisdictions, consideration of a proper role for state or local governments as against the federal government, the normative weight given to other possible courses of action, and a host of other possible concerns, do and should play a role in an agency's determination of its policy priorities.

When a majority of the Court in *Massachusetts* v. *EPA* declared the EPA's broad political considerations irrelevant to its decisions under the Clean Air Act, it did so on the assumption that the agency was exercising discretion under the statute and subject to the criteria that the statute made relevant. That was the nub of the disagreement between the majority and the dissenters. The latter believed that the agency was not making a judgment about whether climate change endangered the public health and welfare or whether automobile emissions contributed to climate change. In the dissenters' view, the agency was really addressing the question of whether it should take up the climate change issue pursuant to a particular provision of the Clean Air Act. On that priority setting question the dissenters believed it was appropriate to take account of the administration's other actions related to climate change, the jurisdiction of other federal agencies, and the possible impacts of agency regulation on the President's bargaining position in global negotiations. Without taking sides in that particular dispute, if all an agency is doing is explaining

---

[52] 470 U.S. 821, 841–2 (1985) (Marshall, J., concurring in judgment).
[53] Ibid.
[54] 5 U.S.C. § 553(e) (2012).

why it declines to take up a matter in response to a petition for rulemaking, these sorts of broad political concerns should be an acceptable ground for inaction. If anything, an agency's failure to take these broad considerations into account would seem unreasonable.

Indeed, political reasons in the sense that I am using that term may be the only reasons available in circumstances where agencies must make decisions that Adrian Vermeule has characterized as "rationally arbitrary."[55] These are situations in which factual or predictive uncertainty makes it impossible to justify a decision based on reliable evidence. Moreover, a statutory deadline may foreclose a decision not to decide until further evidence is available. Such decisions may also be beset by excessive costs from delay or by uncertainty about whether the marginal contribution of more evidence justifies the costs of pursuing it. Where the statutory scheme provides no rules-of-thumb about how to skew errors under uncertainty, some decision rule that permits closure is demanded.

In these circumstances, Vermeule argues, agencies will only be able to give "second-order reasons," that is, reasons about why the agency chose a particular decision rule to resolve uncertainties that could not be resolved, or resolved only at excessive cost, by giving first-order reasons that speak directly to why the decision is substantively justified.[56] He argues further that, on a credible showing that first-order reasons are unavailable, second-order reasons should be legally acceptable notwithstanding the fact that they are rationally arbitrary in the decision-theoretic sense that they do not provide substantive arguments for the decision that has been made.[57]

To take Vermeule's argument in a slightly different direction, I believe that political reasons are a particularly important subcategory of second-order reasons. They nevertheless pose a problem for reviewing courts. Absent a finding that the uncertainties that an agency proffers are resolvable (as the Court believed in *State Farm*) or pretextual (as the majority seemed to believe in *Massachusetts* v. *EPA*), courts would almost always have to accept any set of public-regarding reasons as justificatory. Fear of this "rubber-stamp" posture in part drives findings of non-reviewability in the context of agency inaction or priority setting. If serious review is unavailable, courts seem to believe that perfunctory judicial approval – the illusion of legal accountability – is more destructive to political accountability than the frank admission that courts will not be involved. Responsibility then transparently lies with the administrative actors and their political overseers.

As previously noted, I believe that this posture is an overreaction. Demanding reasons has democratic value, even if courts will almost always find the reasons adequate. To return to the problem of agency inaction, political reason-giving in this context tends to unify the deliberative democracy and electoral democracy bases for

55 Adrian Vermeule, Rationally Arbitrary Decisions in Administrative Law, 94 J. *Legal Stud.* 475 (2015).
56 Id., at 483.
57 Id., at 486.

legitimate administrative action. Saying that a particular type of action does not fit the priorities of the current administration, or is undesirable on other grounds not found within the four corners of the statute, is just another way of saying something like: "We are attempting to implement the statute in a reasonable fashion all things considered, including our interpretation of why the voters elected us." That reason not only invokes political accountability, it gives a reason – a political one – that a deliberative democrat should accept. National elections are, after all, characteristically fought out importantly on questions of principles and priorities. And political ideologies embody political principles. Some voters will not agree with any current administration or its interpretation of its mandate, but if they believe in majoritarian democracy, they have been given a reason that they should be able to accept as legitimate. In this context, political reason-giving might be understood to implement rather than to thwart or avoid the project of reasoned administration.

7

Reasoned Administration and Democratic Legitimacy

FROM LEGALITY TO LEGITIMACY

American administrative law has a particularly strong attachment to reason-giving as the touchstone of administrative legality. As we have seen, requirements for reasoned administration emanate from a host of sources. Constitutional due process requires that reasons be given for administrative adjudications whenever private parties have rights to some form of adjudicatory hearing.[1] The Administrative Procedure Act,[2] and other more specific statutes, demand reason-giving in connection with a host of agency functions including virtually any agency action that has either individual or general legal effect.[3] Many of these requirements are premised on the need to facilitate appropriate judicial review in a system of separated powers and to protect individual rights of participation in agency proceedings.[4] On judicial review, agencies may not rely on facts or arguments not previously ventilated in the administrative record.[5] Agency processes must give adequate notice of the issues to be decided, and

---

[1] The basic requirements for administrative due process are elaborated in *Goldberg* v. *Kelly*, 397 U.S. 254 (1970).

[2] The Federal Administrative Procedure Act is at 5 U.S.C. §551 et. seq.

[3] For example, §553 of the Administrative Procedure Act requires that agencies making general rules shall "give interested persons an opportunity to participate in the rulemaking through submission of written data, views, or arguments ... After consideration of the relevant matter presented, the agency shall incorporate in the rules adopted a concise general statement of their basis and purpose." And §555e requires that the denial of any written application, petition or other request by an interested person in connection with any agency proceeding be "accompanied by a brief statement of a grounds for denial." Judicial interpretation of these provisions has vastly expanded their reason-giving mandates. *See, e.g., Massachusetts* v. *Environmental Protection Agency*, 549 U.S. 497 (2007); and *Motor Vehicle Manufacturer's Association of U.S., Inc.* v. *State Farm Mutual Automobile Insurance Co.*, 463 U.S. 29 (1983).

[4] For a description of this development in the United States and the European Union see Jerry L. Mashaw, Reasoned Administration: The European Union, the United States and the Project of Democratic Governance, 76 *Geo. W. L. Rev.* 99 (2007).

[5] *Securities and Exchange Commission* v. *Chenery Corp.* 332 U.S. 194 (1947).

their decisions[6] must explain their consideration, and acceptance or rejection of, the facts and arguments offered by participants in their proceedings. In rulemaking proceedings any interested person may participate, and agencies must respond to petitions for the adoption, amendment, or rescission of a rule.

Further legal obligations, for example, to consider environmental effects, cost effectiveness, the balance of costs and benefits, effects on small entities and vulnerable populations, the distributional effects of government action, or effects on the balance of authority between state and federal governments, broaden the range of topics that mission-specific agencies must reason about and, simultaneously, the individual and group interests that they must take into account.[7] In some broad sense these requirements are focused on making administrative action that might be instrumentally rational from the perspective of an agency's particular mission more substantively reasonable when viewed from the broader perspective of competing public goals and values. To be sure, this description paints with a broad brush and we will not here pursue further the details of these legal demands for agency reason-giving and attention to the claims, evidence, and arguments of outside parties that have been developed in prior chapters. But, taken together, administrative law's contemporary reasonableness demands aspire to construct a system of administrative governance that is well-informed, highly participatory, complexly interconnected with political and legal monitors, and insulated against (although surely not immune from) the seizure of public power for private or partisan advantage.[8]

On this description, the legal structure of the American administrative state might well be a source of pride, even celebration. Yet, that is rarely the case. "Bureaucrat" is not a congratulatory label. And it is often combined with adjectives like "pointy-headed" or "unelected." Indeed, those two adjectives describe two of the most common complaints against administrative governance. "Pointy-headed" seems to imagine an elite cadre of decision-makers sharply focused on bureaucratic imperatives that yield decisions that are technocratically and legally defensible, but nevertheless deeply unsatisfying. "Unelected" raises an issue of democratic legitimacy that has deep roots in American political history. This chapter will consider that latter complaint, administrative government's alleged democratic deficit. It will argue, perhaps surprisingly, that American federal administrative governance has at least as strong a claim to democratic legitimacy as does congressional legislation with which

---

[6] *See, e.g., United States v. Nova Scotia Food Products Corp.* 568 F.2d 240 (2nd Cir. 1977).

[7] These requirements are embodied in a number of statutes and executive orders. *See, e.g.,* The National Environmental Policy Act, Pub. L. No. 91–190, 83 Stat. 852 (1970) (codified at 42 U.S.C. §§ 4321 et. seq.); The Regulatory Flexibility Act, Pub. L. No. 96–354, 94 Stat. 1164 (1980) (codified, as amended at 5 U.S.C. § 601 et. seq.); and Executive Order No. 13,563, Improving Regulation and Regulatory Review, 76 Fed. Reg. 3, 821 (2011).

[8] On the complex accountability regime applicable to American administrative agencies, *see generally* Jerry L. Mashaw, Structuring a Dense Complexity: Accountability and the Project of Administrative Law, 6 Issues in Legal Scholarship, Article 4 (March, 2005), available at: www.bepress.com/ils/iss6/art4 (Last accessed May 25, 2018).

administrative agencies' exercises of policy-making authority are often unfavorably compared.

Democracy may have as many variants as there are democratic theorists.[9] We will here be concerned with two basic models of democracy that seem to have the strongest claim on the contemporary democratic imagination. Ultimately our question will be how reasoned administration – as described in prior chapters and summarized in the preceding paragraphs – responds to or fails to respond to one or both of these visions of democratic governance.

As the "unelected bureaucrats" epithet suggests, one of those models is a model of electoral democracy, sometimes called aggregative democracy. The basic idea, of course, is that governance is democratic to the extent that the voters voted for the policies adopted, or in its representative democracy form, for the representatives who voted for those policies. The answer, then, to the question "why is this law legitimate?" is straightforward. It is legitimate because we voted for it or because we voted for those who voted for it. There are, of course, a host of other conditions that may be necessary to make either model work reasonably well. These include: free and fair elections or referenda, a free press, freedom of speech and association, reasonable transparency of governmental processes, and majority rule to ensure that each vote has an equal weight.[10] Other conditions could be added, such as, protections for minority rights and institutional checks and balances to ensure against the tyranny of the majority, limitations on the use of superior economic resources to skew results, and so on.

So long as the vision of administration is that administrators simply carry out the relatively specific instructions provided in legislation, and legislation is viewed as democratically legitimate, the so-called "transmission belt" theory of administration, administrative implementation poses no particular problems for electoral or aggregative democratic theory. The same may be thought true of "responsible government" in the Westminster parliamentary tradition in which ministers are also elected representatives subject to party discipline and accountability to the parliament as a whole. But, as early as Martin Van Buren's mid-nineteenth-century democratic defense of the spoils system[11] (administrative appointment on the basis of party affiliation), Americans recognized that who administered the laws made a difference both to policy and to agenda-setting for the future. And, the later Progressive vision of separating politics from administration, by delegating broad authority to

---

[9] *See generally* Ian Shapiro, *The State of Democratic Theory* (Princeton University Press, 2003).
[10] *See, e.g.,* Robert A. Dahl, *A Preface to Democratic Theory* (University of Chicago Press, 1956).
[11] Martin Van Buren, *Inquiry into the Origin and Course of Political Parties in the United States* (Hurd and Houghton, 1867).

expert commissions or administrators, seemed to exalt undemocratic governance by promoting institutional designs that broke the connection between the electorate and administrative governance.

Jacksonian Democrats and Progressive reformers both had an answer for the democratic deficit that they perceived in existing arrangements, or that their approach to administration seemed to entail. For Jacksonians the problem was the early American practice of elite administration by officers appointed for reputation or character. Their answer was partisan political appointment to assure that the laws were administered by members of the political party that won the election and therefore spoke for the people. The Progressive's basic claim was that abolishing the spoils in favor of independent and expert administration was actually a move toward greater democratic responsiveness. They argued that opinion polls revealed that what Americans really wanted from government was policies that furthered the public good and administration of those policies that was effective, efficient, and non-corrupt. Independent and expert administrators could be counted on to pursue the public good rather than partisan advantage and to do so on the basis of practical knowledge rather than political ideology. Hence, to give citizens the government that they wanted, elected representatives should delegate authority to expert administrators.[12] This, not the spoils, was real democracy.

The Jacksonian approach to democratic administration, which degenerated into corrupt and incompetent administration, proved unsatisfactory, to say the least. The people got what benefitted the party in power, not necessarily what the people wanted. And, a moment's reflection reveals that the Progressive argument was subject to serious objections. Opinion polls are not elections and they are notoriously subject to variation depending upon when, what, and how questions are asked. The real arguments for the Progressive vision were its predicted results – non-corrupt and effective government delivered by a caste of informed and public-spirited administrators. But their vision of Platonic Guardian administrators was from the perspective of electoral democracy as elitist as the administrative theories of the Federalists and Jeffersonian Republicans that the Jacksonians replaced. Theirs was just an elitism of competence rather than of character or reputation. Squaring competent administrative government with electoral democracy has always been a problem for American constitutional theory – a problem that the outpouring of new agencies during the New Deal exacerbated.

The reality that Americans elect congresses and presidents, but are mostly governed by administrators, has hardly lessened since the New Deal era. The creation of new and powerful administrative agencies in the "Great Society" period may well have eclipsed the New Deal's orgy of institutional innovation. And while recent federal statutes, such as, the Affordable Care Act ("Obamacare") and the Dodd-Frank

---

[12] See the discussion of progressive political science in Jerry L. Mashaw, *Greed, Chaos and Governance: Using Public Choice to Improve Public Law* 6–10 (Yale University Press, 1997).

legislative response to the 2008 financial crisis, may run on for hundreds, even thousands, of pages, they still delegate enormous policy discretion to the administrators whose hundreds of rules are necessary to make those statutes operational. As a legal–constitutional matter, federal courts are willing to invalidate such delegations of authority as an improper transfer of the legislative power reserved to Congress and the President only if the statute contains no "intelligible principle" by which administration might be guided.[13] Only three statutes in American history have failed to pass this test.

It is, of course, arguable that congressional oversight, and presidential monitoring and direction, re-established the electoral connection between administrators and elected officials, which is the litmus test for an electoral or aggregative democracy in good working order. And, indeed, there is much to this claim. But, without investigating the details of that claim's validity, for the moment let us put it aside and examine a competitive democratic vision – deliberative democracy.

Deliberative democracy is again a family of views that situates the legitimacy of political decision-making not in elections, but in the process of public deliberation between free and equal citizens.[14] Deliberative democratic theory is to some degree parasitic on what might be called the "public reason tradition", a tradition in political and moral philosophy that attempts to give an answer to the question of how the authority of the state can be legitimated while simultaneously: (1) accepting the social fact of value pluralism, and (2) respecting the liberty of those subjected to the state's commands.[15] These theories of public reason are motivated in part by the perceived inadequacy of theories of legitimacy based either on consent or on truth.

The consent of the governed is certainly consistent with their liberty, but requiring real consent, not just majority rule, in pluralistic democracies yields anarchism as the appropriate form of governance. This position is philosophically respectable, but operationally untenable. And, because we no longer believe that anyone has direct access to the true principles of moral conduct or political organization, truth is also a non-starter. Public reason theories and deliberative-democracy approaches try to tread a middle ground between these positions while borrowing a bit from both.

---

[13] A unanimous court affirmed this lax standard in *Whitman v. American Trucking Assoc., Inc.* 531 U.S. 457 (2001), with two concurring Justices urging the Court to candidly admit that there was no constitutional prohibition against transferring the legislative power to administrators, so long as the transfer was made with a sufficiently intelligible principle to guide administrative action.

[14] *See generally*, James Bohman, The Coming of Age of Deliberative Democracy, 6 *Journal of Political Philosophy* 400 (1998) and authorities therein cited.

[15] J. Quong, Public Reason, *The Stanford Encyclopedia of Philosophy* (Summer 2013 Edition), Edward N. Zalta (ed.), available at: http://plato.stanford.edu/archives/sum2013/entries/public-reason (Last accessed May 25, 2018). J. Waldron, Theoretical Foundations of Liberalism, (1987) *The Philosophical Quarterly* 37; T. Nagel, Moral Conflict and Political Legitimacy' (1987) *Philosophy and Public Affairs* 26; J. Quong, *Liberalism Without Perfectionism* (Oxford University Press, 2011); G. Gaus, *The Order of Public Reason*, (Cambridge University Press, Cambridge, 2011); and K. Vallier and R. D'Agostino Public Justification (2013) in the Stanford Encyclopedia *Online* available at: http://plato.stanford .edu/entries/justification-public/ (Last accessed May 25, 2018).

In general, public reason demands that moral or political principles be justifiable to – or reasonably acceptable to – all persons to whom the principles are meant to apply. This includes constitutional arrangements, institutional architectures, rules of conduct, and so on. To put the matter succinctly, all public reason theories are directed at reconciling liberty and equality with authority by insisting that authority be justified by reasons that all could accept. Decision-making in theories of deliberative democracy is justified in much the same way.

Some public reason approaches, such as those associated with John Rawls,[16] are more concerned with the types of reasons that can be given. Rawls excludes, for example, arguments or reasons that reflect comprehensive world views, such as religious reasons, that not all could possibly accept. Others are more concerned, as was Jürgen Habermas,[17] with creating idealized speech situations such that the process of deliberation washes out reasons that privilege certain groups or views. In general, one might say that deliberative democracy demands substantively that citizens justify their political assertions with reference to common goods and values, not private interests or idiosyncratic belief systems. Procedurally, public deliberators must proceed with fair-mindedness and civility in their deliberations – rather vague terms that might describe a variety of possible deliberative duties or process features.

Described in this way deliberative democracy and reasoned administration seem to have much in common. Most fundamentally they are approaches that rely on reason rather than on will as the legitimating characteristic of public decisions. Here legitimacy flows from a capacity to give public-regarding reasons that all might accept, even those who disagree about where reason should lead. In some sense, the general processes and constraints on administrative rulemaking under the Federal Administrative Procedure Act might be thought to implement a deliberative democratic vision. Any interested party or group can participate in the process on the basis of at least formal equality. The administrative decision-maker must, to survive judicial review, consider all relevant and material issues, questions, or disagreements raised by the participants. And in coming to a final decision the administrator must give reasons which explain why certain participants' views were accepted or rejected, while also explaining why the decision ultimately reached furthers the public purposes of the statutory scheme being implemented.

There are well-known objections to public reason or deliberative-democracy-based theories of the legitimacy of state action.[18] The heterogeneity of the population in

[16] John Rawls, *Political Liberalism* (Columbia University Press, 1993).
[17] Arie Brand, *The Force of Reason: An Introduction to Habermas' Theory of Communicative Action* (Allen Unwin, 1990); David Ingram, *Habermas and the Dialectic of Reason* (Yale University Press, 1987); and Stephen K. White, *The Recent Work of Jurgen Habermas: Reason, Justice and Modernity* (Cambridge University Press, Cambridge, 1988).
[18] David Enoch, Against Public Reason, in *Oxford Studies in Political Philosophy*, Vol. 1, edited by David Sobel, Peter Vallentyne, and Steven Wall (Oxford University Press, 2015).

large nation states, and the value pluralism that tends to attend that fact, ensures that not every person will find any political principle justified. To deal with this problem public-reason theorists have had to relax the justification or acceptability requirement for reasons in some fashion. Broadly speaking these compromises are of two types. One is substantive. The relevant constituency to whom justification must be given is restricted to those who are "reasonable," that is, those susceptible to persuasion by the type of justifications that count as rational or appropriate in a particular version of public-reason theory. To the extent that these restrictions exclude the values or political beliefs of some parts of the populace, effective participation by some persons is excluded. A similar, but more procedural move, involves imagining that everyone or almost everyone would accept justifications for particular principles if they deliberated long enough, hard enough, and under appropriate procedural rules. In short, a process of legitimation that is meant to treat all persons as free and equal members of the polity seems to be required either to exclude certain persons from concern or to treat them as hypothetical persons who would reason differently than they actually do.

Administrative decision-making in practice often avoids the theoretical problems with public-reason approaches. Administrative agencies are not constructing broad constitutional principles or structures, nor are they legislating on a blank slate. Administrators operate within constrained jurisdictions, focusing on particular types of public policy problems pursuant to statutes requiring them to take certain statutory criteria or considerations into account. The forms of arguments and types of reasons relevant to decision-makers have been specified by statute. Statutory boundaries may exclude certain types of argument, but the exclusion is not a feature of the administrative process; it is a feature of a statute that calls that process into being. The statute itself, of course, may have been enacted under conditions which fail to satisfy any notion of deliberative-democratic legitimacy. But, if so, the problem is with legislative, not administrative policymaking. Moreover, the legislature can always appeal to standard notions of electoral or representative democracy. Elections and legislative outcomes may in some way fail to capture the will of the people, but they have the legitimating arguments for aggregative democracy to fall back on. Administrators operating within those statutory restrictions can make the same appeal. Administrative policy-making is a hybrid. Administrator's jurisdictions, goals and constraints are provided by statutes tethered to the electoral process. But, in addition, administrative officers can offer a deliberative democracy basis for their exercises of power. Their policy choices are required to be both participatory and reasoned.

At this point it would seem that if one is a deliberative democrat the legitimacy of administrative policymaking is relatively non-problematic, at least under the conditions that attend that decision-making in contemporary American administrative law. Indeed, for the deliberative democrat it may have a greater legitimacy than the legislative process, a process rife with procedural power plays, crass political vote trading, partisan obstructionism, and a host of other non-deliberative mechanisms that may simultaneously block the expression of majoritarian sentiment.

On the other hand, if one is committed to electoral democracy as the only legitimating approach to lawmaking, administrative policymaking remains troublesome. No one elected these people, and statutes granting them broad policy discretion are ubiquitous. Moreover, as I argued in Chapter 5, to imagine that administration is an exercise in purely instrumental rationality is a mistake. Statutory goals and the values to which they are attached take on meaning and weight in the process of implementation. Administration is a value or meaning creating process put in the charge of unelected officials.

We should not forget, however, that administrators are further attached to the electoral process by presidential appointment and senatorial approval of high-level officials and by both executive and congressional oversight. As these words are being written, Americans are witnessing the strong connection between presidential elections and administrative policymaking as Trump administration appointees roll back Obama Administration policies on a host of fronts.[19] Indeed, as the Supreme Court recognized in its *Chevron* decision, agencies' relatively greater accountability to electoral processes provides a reason to prefer their understanding of their statutes' proper interpretation to those of the much more insulated federal judiciary. But being relatively more democratic than life-tenured federal judges is hardly an answer to those who view the administrative state as fundamentally undemocratic. To evaluate how seriously to take this complaint we need to take a more nuanced approach to both the strengths and weaknesses of our two approaches to democracy and a closer look at how the model of reasoned administration described here responds to both.

IDEAL THEORY MEETS INSTITUTIONAL REALITY

If the transmission belt idea that legislative action transmits the majority will into administrative practice is confounded by the reality of agency discretion, the notion that electoral politics transmits majority will into legislative action is almost as unrealistic. The American constitutional structure was designed to create a republic, not a democracy. Many subsequent developments have made the original constitutional scheme more democratic: senators are now elected by the populace, not state legislatures; the franchise has been enormously broadened; modern communications make the electorate's access to information about public issues significantly easier; and so on. Nevertheless, we retain an electoral college system that can elect a President who does not garner a majority of votes. Montana's senators have equal weight with California's, notwithstanding the obvious fact that California's

---

[19] See, e.g., Jerry L. Mashaw and David Berke, Presidential Administration in a Regime of Separated Powers: An Analysis of Recent American Experience, 35 *Yale J. on Reg.* 549 (2018).

population exceeds Montana's by a factor of 50. State legislative apportionment of congressional districts makes the vast majority of congressional elections non-competitive. Legislative procedures radically empower minority views by creating a plethora of "veto-gates" that can derail legislation having majority support. The power of single-issue interest groups can keep legislation with broad popular support (think the National Rifle Association and gun control regulation) off the legislative agenda. And, obviously, when voters vote for representatives they have little idea what issues will actually be on the agenda in future legislative sessions. The weak linkages between voter sentiments and legislative outcomes have given rise to whole schools of political theory and analysis that seek to explain institutional arrangements and policy outcomes in terms of the preferences of dominant economic or class interests.[20]

A number of these democratic deficits are clearly cause for concern. Gerrymandering, the power of money in politics, single-issue group influence, and the like, undermine the electoral democratic pedigree of legislative policy-making. Others – the necessity for bicameral agreement to legislation, ponderous legislative procedures, and the requirement of presidential approval for legislative action, while throwing sand in the gears of a straightforward electoral democracy – nevertheless may point in the direction of its deliberative competitor. That a Senate, a House of Representatives and a President, all elected by different constituencies, must agree on legislation may help to assure respectful attention to a wide range of differing viewpoints. Requirements for subcommittee and committee deliberation and reporting, the required harmonization of House and Senate versions of legislation, and even the much criticized filibuster rules in the Senate, can contribute to an assurance that a wide spectrum of views are canvassed and that legislation is well-considered. To have a republic with separated powers and robust checks and balances within legislative institutions can be understood as a compromise between electoral and deliberative models of democracy, notwithstanding the many ways these structural features can be abused for personal or partisan gain.

Moreover, while presidential power to appoint administrators and to some considerable degree direct their exercise of administrative discretion, connects administration to electoral politics, "presidentialism" has the vices of its virtues. Voters should not be understood to have ratified all of a president's pet projects. And, unless constrained to go through the deliberative processes required to make administrative rules, executive policymaking can escape the many checks and balances built into legislative policymaking. "Democracy" should mean more than that we elect our dictators.[21]

A compromise between electoral and deliberative democracy seems eminently sensible. Both have attractive characteristics and well-known theoretical

---

[20] *See generally*, Mashaw, Greed, Chaos and Governance.
[21] Peter M. Shane, *Madison's Nightmare: How Executive Power Threatens American Democracy* (2009).

and practical difficulties. The deeply compromised nature of American electoral democracy has already been sufficiently canvassed. Indeed these deficiencies are the stuff of constant political commentary. The downside of deliberative democracy may be less obvious.

On the theoretical side, the exclusion by many public-reason theorists of all arguments based on self-interest, including deeply held religious or other values, seems problematic.[22] Not only does a limitation of this sort exclude the participation of presumably free and equal citizens, it excludes from the conversation considerations that many not holding those views might nevertheless see as valuable additions to the dialogue about policy or institutions. After all, in many cases, accommodations can be made for those having interests or values that make a proposed action unacceptable to them. But, those reasons for accommodation will not be on the table if arguments originating in what Rawls calls "comprehensive world views" cannot serve as a basis for argument.

Deliberative-democratic theory also has theoretical difficulties with issues of truth.[23] In general terms, dialogue about policy or institutional arrangements raises questions about how it might be best for the polity to proceed. But, there is no reason to think that deliberation will produce the best outcome for the relevant community. A deliberative approach may have that tendency, indeed if it did not deliberative democracy would lose much of its attractiveness, but there are no guarantees of success. There is an empirical and/or predictive dimension to all decision-making and theoretical approaches to getting correct answers, such as the well-known Condorcet jury theorem,[24] do not rely on deliberation for getting things right. Indeed, by promoting compromise among the views of participants in a decision pool of voters, deliberation could undermine accuracy. Prediction markets that aggregate independent estimates of probabilities often outperform expert consensus.

From a practical perspective deliberative democracy is also difficult to institutionalize. Deliberation is an incomplete system for decision-making. Theoretically it is hard to get going. Well-structured processes for deliberation seem to be a requisite for deliberation about what processes deliberators should use in order for their deliberative outcomes to be democratically legitimate from a deliberatively democratic perspective. And, once started, deliberation may be difficult to end. Deliberation may better frame the issues for resolution and better inform decision-makers concerning the dimensions of the problem than they would be likely to come to if

---

[22] *See generally*, Jane Mansbridge, et al., The Place of Self-Interest and the Role of Power in Deliberative Democracy, 18 *Journal of Political Philosophy* 64 (2010).

[23] *See generally* Joshua Cohen, Truth and Public Reason, 37 *Philosophy in Public Affairs* 2 (2009).

[24] For a discussion, *see* David Austen-Smith and Jeffrey S. Banks, Information Aggregation, Rationality, and the Condorcet Jury Theorem, 90 *American Political Science Review* 34 (1996).

considering the issue independently.[25] But consensus is unlikely. As a practical matter, decisiveness must come from some other source – such as voting.

Finally, a dialogue of all free and equal citizens about policy or institutions is an ideal that cannot be realized in modern nation states. Judging whether a policy or institutional design is justified in deliberative democratic terms really asks a hypothetical question about whether reasons can be given for the decision that all reasonable people would accept. But, reality is almost always more complex than we can imagine. What sorts of reasons and considerations might have emerged from a real dialogue engaging the enormous range of perspectives involved in a large polity is virtually impossible to predict.

Of course actual administrative proceedings engage only a small set of citizens who are most directly affected or interested in a particular policy or adjudicatory outcomes, and who have the information and other resources necessary to participate. But this suggests that administrative action is similar to a peculiar variant of partially democratic political organization that Robert Dahl called "polyarchy".[26]

Yet, if I am correct that America's republican form of government is a hybrid, a combination of aggregative and deliberative democratic ideals, then it would seem that the model of reasoned administration that has been built up in the modern American administrative state responds reasonably well to this peculiar vision. On the electoral democracy side, American administrative law has always demanded that administrators be responsive to the statutes that authorize their actions. Even in the constrained judicial review world of the nineteenth-century, lack of authority was a ground for invalidation. And as judicial review for legality expanded to encompass all issues of law, and then to focus importantly on the rationale for administrative action, legality came to include not just authority or jurisdiction, but a demonstration that the administrator had considered all the criteria made relevant by the governing statute and excluded irrelevant considerations. Administrative legality is thus tethered tightly to legislation passed by the people's representatives. As a 2010 book title insists, America is indeed a "republic of statutes."[27]

Complaints that broad delegations of authority to administrators break this electoral connection seem misdirected. Administrative discretion comes from the statute. The people's representatives have delegated the discretion by majority vote. America's particular institutionalization of electoral democracy may imperfectly represent the popular will, but delegation of authority to administrators by the people's representatives does not sever the electoral connection.

---

[25] For an argument that this sort of compromise system is indeed the best system for arriving at the best possible decisions, *see* Helene Landemore, *Democratic Reason: Politics, Intelligence, and the Rule of the Many* (Harvard University Press, 2012).

[26] *See generally*, Robert Dahl, *Polyarchy: Participation and Opposition*, (Yale University Press, 1971).

[27] William N. Eskridge, Jr. and John Ferejohn, *A Republic of Statutes: The New American Constitution* (Yale University Press, 2010).

It might be argued, of course, that the people's representatives did not choose the policy in question, the administrators did. But, conferring discretion on a delegate to make choices on the basis of specified criteria, however broad, and on the basis of facts that are currently unavailable and circumstances that are unpredictable, is a policy choice. Critics of broad delegations fear that these sorts of provisions permit an irresponsible Congress to avoid hard questions and paper over ambivalence and lack of agreement. Perhaps. But if a majority of the legislature has decided that in the face of uncertainty, ambivalence, or disagreement that it is better to authorize action consistent with broad criteria for judgment than to do nothing, perhaps indefinitely, where is the democratic deficit?

All of these considerations, of course, relate to the relationship between administration and congressional legislation. Defenders of what has come to be called "presidential administration"[28] suggest that whatever democratic deficit results from broad congressional delegations can be cured by presidential oversight and direction. The President is, the Electoral College aside, elected by all the people. And because of the vagaries of the legislative process, its internal procedures and checks and balances, statutes may persist long after the times that gave rise to them have changed and the majorities that supported them have moved on. Presidential administration by reorienting priorities toward more contemporary electoral mandates can increase the democratic responsiveness of administration. Indeed, from this perspective, broad statutory delegations have a distinct electoral advantage. They allow different administrations to shift policy priorities within formally static statutory regimes. Administrative responsiveness to the electorate is presumably enhanced.[29]

This optimistic vision can only be pushed so far. Presidents and congresses may be of different political parties, and even if not, congressional preferences may remain fairly constant, even in the face of national elections. Presidents and congresses also are elected on different time schedules and from differently structured constituencies. Who has the right to claim to be the true voice of the people when presidents and congresses disagree? Ambivalence or uncertainty about this question is built into the American form of government. Federal administrators have two political principals, both with legitimate claims on their loyalty, and both connected to electoral politics.

The awkward position of administrators in such a system is obvious. Ministers in a Westminster-style parliamentary system know to whom they are responsible – Parliament. American agency heads must somehow balance the demands of dual principals who may be at loggerheads. American administrative law has struggled to deal with this ambiguity in the notion of legitimate political control of administration. And, broadly speaking, the model of reasoned administration under law that we have been describing has made reasonable accommodations given the tension built

---

[28] *See generally* Elena Kagan, Presidential Administration 114 *Harv. L. Rev.* 2245 (2001).

[29] *See, e.g.,* Jerry L. Mashaw, Pro-Delegation: Why Administrators Should Make Political Decisions, 1 *Journal of Law Economics and Organization* 81 (1985).

into the American constitutional structure. On the one hand, Congress may not under-mine presidential direction of administration by encroaching too far on the President's appointment or removal authority.[30] But, legislation can structure those exercises of presidential authority in ways that promote legislative policies of administrative com-petence and partisan political independence.[31] Presidents may direct agency action or forbearance, but only within the statutory limits set by governing legislation. For a civilian agency, "the President ordered me to do it" is not an independent legal justi-fication for administrative decision.[32] On the other hand, absent some action-forcing or agenda-setting provisions of governing legislation, "we are taking this up as a part of the President's general program to do x" is hardly an undemocratic approach to the setting of agency priorities. Presidential candidates espouse programs and principles that, if they keep their promises, will often have to be pursued by administrative means.

There are well-known complaints about the paucity and vagueness of adminis-trative law or constitutional doctrine concerning presidential directive authority or the limits on congressional interference with the President's constitutional powers of appointments and removal.[33] But the uncertainty of separation of powers doctrine with respect to political control of administration simply reflects a constitutional tension that is baked into the American governmental structure. That courts have difficulty with the job of referee in a power struggle over political control of admin-istration tends to reinforce, not negate, the idea that administrative policymaking is intimately connected to the ongoing process of electoral competition.

Administration is thus embedded in electoral politics. And the affinity of rea-soned administration with theories of deliberative democracy is apparent. Indeed, not only does reasoned administration as an approach to administrative policymak-ing privilege reason over will as the legitimating basis for administrative action, the way in which administrative decision-making is structured tends to mitigate some of the common problems facing deliberative democratic theory. For example, value pluralism is a problem for deliberative democrats to the extent that free and equal citizens disagree about which values are relevant to political decision-making. If I firmly believe that religious convictions are an important source of policy guidance and you are an atheist, we may have great difficulty finding a common ground for discussion in which each of us believes that the reasons provided by the other are

---

[30] *See e.g., Buckley* v. *Valeo*, 424 U.S. 1 (1976) and *Bowsher* v. *Synar*, 478 U.S. 714 (1986).

[31] *See e.g., Humphrey's Executor* v. *United States*, 295 U.S. 602 (1935).

[32] *See e.g., Kendall* v. *United States ex rel Stokes*, 37 U.S. (12 Pet.) 524 (1838).

[33] Maybe the most famous may be Justice Jackson lament in his concurring opinion in *Youngstown Sheet and Tube Co.* v. *Sawyer*, 343 U.S. 579, 636 (1952)

> A judge, like an executive advisor, may be surprised at the poverty of really useful and unambiguous authority applicable to concrete problems of executive power as they actually present themselves. Just what our forefathers did envision, or would have envisioned had they foreseen modern conditions, must be divined from materials almost as enigmatic as the dreams Joseph was called upon to interpret for the Pharaoh.

relevant to the policy or institutional problem that engages us. And, because democratic deliberation might range across an almost infinite number of topics or issues, the chances that these conflicting world views will create difficulties are substantial.

By contrast, most policy choice at the administrative level is directed at issues which do not implicate nonnegotiable fundamental values. When weighing in on an Environmental Protection Agency (EPA) climate change regulation, we may disagree across a whole range of factual and predictive issues, or on the way the values of cautionary regulation versus current economic consequences should figure into the resolution of factual or predictive uncertainties. As an additional complication, the way that we perceive the factual, predictive, or value-questions issues could well be motivated by underlying world views that relate to fundamentally contrasting orientations.[34] But, I am unlikely to attempt to argue that the facts do not matter, that the uncertainty of predicted outcomes is not a problem, or that either current economic costs, or the protection of future generations should not be a consideration as we attempt to decide what to do. That we ultimately disagree about what is to be done does not prevent us from giving each other reasons and arguments about what should be done that we both take to be relevant to a sensible decision.

Alas, limiting the policy space does not always exclude the problem of incommensurate and deeply-held values, or of the necessity for value choice in the weight to be given to competing ends. If, for example, we are instead discussing the question of the degree to which rules by the Department of Health and Human Services concerning the coverage of contraceptive or other family planning services ought to be mandated as a part of acceptable health insurance coverage under the Affordable Care Act, contrasting and incommensurate world views may intrude. But even here, as was suggested earlier, the solution of practical policy problems may involve accommodations, exceptions or waivers that can harmonize general policies with contrary deeply-held beliefs.[35]

Indeed, at the level of crafting administrative policy there is no reason that a simple assertion that a proposed policy is contrary to some participants' economic interests should be ruled out of order. At one level, of course, such private interest claims can usually be translated into some public regarding vernacular. My economic interest is easily articulated as a concern about national productivity or the loss of employment opportunities in my particular sector of the economy. But without making that all-too-familiar translation of private into public interest, there seems no reason that the simple claim that I will be suffering concentrated economic costs should be irrelevant to policy choice. Distributional consequences are in general a relevant concern that public policies might be designed to mitigate, if not eliminate. Rawls

---

[34] *See, e.g.*, Dan M. Kahan, The Cognitively Illiberal State, 60 *Stan. L. Rev.* 115 (2007).

[35] For example, in *Zubik* v. *Burwell*, 136 Sup. Ct. 1557 (2016), the Supreme Court dealt with a challenge to just such an accommodation by sending the parties back to the bargaining table to iron out their differences.

might be perfectly correct that when deciding on basic institutions for governance we should do so behind a veil of ignorance concerning our own economic interests. Arriving at a just overall structure for allocating benefits and burdens may require that sort of objectivity. But at the level of specific policy choice, that argument does not have the same force. In that context just distribution of benefits and burdens may necessitate an understanding of precisely whose interests are benefitted or burdened. The Regulatory Flexibility Act, for example, instructs agencies to consider the possibly differential burdens that their decisions might have for small entities.

Finally, reasoned administrative decision-making does not necessarily privilege process over truth. That there is no process-independent standard for judging whether the administrative process has arrived at the best policy for pursuing appropriately understood public ends is merely a feature that reasoned administration shares with all value-laden decision-making. And as a practical matter, arguments in this realm are often directed to empirics and predictive uncertainties. To give a reason in the administrative policymaking domain is generally to give a reason based in fact. When administrators are told by reviewing courts that their reasons are not good enough it is often because those reasons are not sufficiently supported by the evidence before them.

Finally, reason-giving is critical to treating individuals as free moral agents subject to legitimate coercion only to the extent that appropriate reasons can be given for restricting their freedom of action. From the perspective of public reason or deliberative democracy, administrative decision-making as it is currently structured in American administrative law is more respectful of this interest in individual autonomy than the potential institutional alternatives of legislative or judicial judgment. Neither of those forms of institutional law-making derive their legal validity or their political legitimacy from reason-giving in nearly as focused a way as do the decisions of contemporary administrative agencies. Americans live in a compromised world in which neither electoral nor deliberative democracy is normatively attractive or practically realizable in its pure form, and in a constitutional system that contains elements of both visions of democratic governance. From this perspective, positioned in a government that is a contingent and peculiar electoral/deliberative, democratic hybrid, the process that I have labeled "reasoned administration" may be the most democratic form of collective decision-making in American national political life.

It is tempting to make a stronger claim. Because administrative policies having the force of law must, by law, partake of both electoral and deliberative strands of democratic theory, those policies may have a more vigorous democratic pedigree than congressional legislation. Not only is legislation free from any obligation of reason-giving, and subject to a virtually nonexistent constitutional requirement of reasonableness, there need be no deliberation at all concerning highly consequential public policies that Congress adopts. To be sure, the conventional view of legislation involves initial proposals, committee deliberations leading to a committee proposal, debates on the floor of the House and Senate, voting in each House on both the committee proposals and amendments offered and debated on the floor, conference committee deliberation and compromise between Senate and House versions of bills passed in differing forms in each chamber, and final consideration of the conference committee report in each House. But this highly deliberative process can be short circuited any time a majority in each House chooses to do so. There is no "due process of legislation" that tracks the deliberative processes of agency rulemaking or formal adjudication.[36]

To illustrate let me quote the full text of a statute revoking a rule adopted by the Consumer Financial Protection Bureau concerning the use of mandatory arbitration clauses in contracts related to consumer financial products and services. "That Congress disapproves the rule submitted by the Bureau of Consumer Financial Protection [CFPB] relating to Arbitration Agreements (82 Fed. Reg. 33210 [July 19, 2017]), and such rule shall have no force or effect." That statute was enacted pursuant to the Congressional Review Act.[37] Under that statute such a joint resolution, may, but need not, have committee consideration in both Houses; may be adopted without debate in the House and with a maximum of ten hours debate in the Senate; has priority on the legislative calendar; and is not subject to points of order on the floor of either House. The effect of the joint resolution, adopted without any accompanying committee reports or explanations, is not only to revoke the rule, but to prevent the adoption of any substantially similar rule in the future. By contrast the CFPB rulemaking process lasted more than five years; involved four separate formal occasions, not counting public hearings and advisory committee meetings, to comment on the Bureau's studies, findings, and proposals; generated 110,000 public comments in its rulemaking proceedings, and is explained by a document occupying 224 pages in the Federal Register.[38] In addition to commentators whose interests and affiliations were not clearly identified, participants in the process included consumers and their representatives, consumer financial products and services firms and their representatives, state and local governments, individual Representatives and Senators, Indian tribes, and other federal agencies. The Bureau's explanatory "Preamble" to its rule details its reasoning concerning the interpretation of its statutory mandate, its choices concerning its research methodology when studying the problem, the facts found and the remaining uncertainties concerning the functions and effects of mandatory arbitration clauses, the estimated costs and benefits of pursuing its proposed course of action, and how it reacted to issues raised by participants on material issues related to its studies, findings, and conclusions.

---

[36] Hans A. Linde, Due Process of Lawmaking, 55 *Neb. L. Rev.* 197 (1976).

[37] Pub. L. 104–121, title II, §251, Mar. 29, 1996, 110 Stat. 874, 5 U.S.C. 801–8.

[38] Bureau of Consumer Financial Protection, Arbitration Agreements, 82 Fed. Reg. 3321 (July 19, 2017).

I leave readers to draw their own conclusions concerning whether the adoption or the revocation of this rule was more "democratic". Perhaps that question is unresolvable. But I am hard pressed to conclude that administrative lawmaking in the American national government is "undemocratic" when the legal requirements for and practices of administrative policymaking are compared with realistic alternative modes of action.

8

Reason and Regret

I believe that the developments described in the preceding chapters are, in general, to be celebrated. Environmental regulations should not be based on myth, hunch, or ideology; public benefits should not be awarded on the basis of inarticulate cultural premises. The vast discretion of modern administrators and administrative agencies should not be used as a mask for rule by decree. As has been noted, however, the contemporary emphasis on reason-giving and reasonableness as the touchstones of administrative legitimacy has its downsides.

Even so, the contemporary demand for, and structure of, reasoned administration represents a triumph of legitimate, liberal administrative governance in a world full of dangerous alternatives. Yet this success has not yielded broad popular satisfaction. Since the 1980s, "reform" in much of the developed world has been in the direction of deregulation, devolution, market mechanisms, and contracted-out public services. "Bureaucrat" is generally not a term of approbation; "big government" is out of favor. Given the outcome of the 2016 election, one would expect these trends to continue in the United States. Indeed, there is daily evidence that they have intensified.

This disappointment with administrative governance may, of course, have many causes. Rounding up the usual suspects, we might include at least the following: the displacement of blame for sometimes frustrating bureaucratic encounters from congresses who over-promise and under-budget to the administrators who are the immediate cause of our disappointment.[1] The ascendance of pro-market ideology surely also plays a part in many countries, particularly the United States, although a look at our collective practices suggest that we are ideological conservatives and operational liberals. Many of our demands on government are precisely for public bureaucrats to protect us from the private ones that we encounter in product,

---

[1] The IRS is a sad paragon of this problem. *See 2013 Annual Report to Congress: Vol. I*, Nat'l Taxpayer Advocate 20–37 (Dec. 31, 2013), available at: https://taxpayeradvocate.irs.gov/2013-Annual-Report/downloads/Volume-1.pdf (Last accessed May 25, 2018).

labor, and financial markets. General postmodern skepticism of rationality itself conceivably plays a part. Yet again, our practices belie a strong commitment to a thorough-going postmodern sensibility. We recognize that our collective life must be managed, not merely interpreted.

There are, of course, also a substantial number of myths about bureaucracy. Conventional wisdom in the United States tells us that government bureaucracies are immensely wasteful and inefficient. That Medicare administrative costs are a small fraction of private health insurers' costs for performing essentially the same functions fails to penetrate public consciousness.[2] Many believe, counterfactually, that the number of federal government employees continually expands although the number of federal civilian employees in relation to the US population is now lower than it was in the 1950s.[3] The litany goes on and on. For the most part,[4] these claims are exaggerated, over-blown and often just plain wrong. But, as is the nature of myths, these beliefs are virtually impervious to factual disproof.

While not denying that these usual suspects have some explanatory power, I want to suggest two problems that present almost inseparable obstacles to the celebration that I believe warranted of our "deliberative polyarchy." One harks back to the discussion of administration and democracy in Chapter 7; the other lies at the heart of the project of rationality and reason-giving in administrative states. Reason-giving in the administrative state treats us as people for whom reasons matter, but it often fails to attend to the range of reasons that we care about.

DEMOCRACY AND DISTRUST

I label this section with the title of John Ely's famous book[5] because I view that book as a prime exhibit of the blinkered view of democracy that is widely held in the

[2] *See, e.g.,* Jacob S. Hacker, Healthy Competition – The Why and How of "Public-Plan Choice," 360 *New England J. of Med.* 2269, 2270 (2009) ("Public health insurance has much lower administrative expenses than private plans, it obtains larger volume discounts because of its broad reach, and it does not have to earn a profit, as many private plans do."); *see also* Drew Altman, Public vs. Private Health Insurance on Controlling Spending, Wall St. J.: Wash. Wire (Apr. 16, 2015, 7:05 AM), available at: http://blogs.wsj.com/washwire/2015/04/16/public-vs-private-health-insurance-on-controlling-spending/ (Last accessed May 25, 2018) (explaining that Medicare "control[s] per capita spending somewhat more effectively than private coverage does. That may be just the opposite of what many would presume in a country where the private market is generally expected to outperform the public sector.").

[3] Josh Zumbrun, The Federal Government Now Employs the Fewest People Since 1966, Wall St. J.: Real Time Econ. (Nov. 7, 2015), available at: http://blogs.wsj.com/economics/2014/11/07/the-federal-government-now-employs-the-fewest-people-since-1966/ (Last accessed May 25, 2018).

[4] But far from always. *See, e.g.,* Craig Whitlock and Bob Woodward, Pentagon Buries Evidence of $125 Billion in Bureaucratic Waste, Wash. Post (Dec. 5, 2016), available at: www.washingtonpost.com/investigations/pentagon-buries-evidence-of-125-billion-in-bureaucratic-waste/2016/12/05/e0668c76-9af6-11e6-a0ed-ab0774c1eaa5_story.html?utm_term=.c130ed09c3c4 (Last accessed May 25, 2018).

[5] John Hart Ely, *Democracy and Distrust: A Theory of Judicial Review* (1980).

American electorate. Ely's influential theory of judicial review for constitutionality argues that the principal job of the federal courts is to interpret the Constitution in ways that are democracy-reinforcing.[6] Although there is no full-blown theory of democracy in Ely's book, he seems to mean the reinforcement of the democratic functions of the political branches.[7] And for him, administration is not a part of the political conversation. He criticizes the federal courts for their unwillingness to force Congress to decide issues of public policy with specificity through the deployment of the nondelegation doctrine.[8] For Ely, vague delegations of authority to administrative agencies break the electoral connection between voters and representatives. Because Congress fails to decide policy issues with the requisite specificity, Ely argues that voters are unable to hold their representatives accountable.[9] Administrative policymaking thus is, for him, a deep flaw in American representative democracy.

I suggested earlier why the charge that Congress fails to make policy when it broadly delegates authority to administrators is unwarranted. A collective congressional decision that – given policy disagreements, limited information, and predictive uncertainties – a delegation of broad authority to administrators is superior to the status quo is a policy decision. These are the sorts of decisions that legislators are elected to make. If voters don't like the outcomes, they can vote for different representatives.

But there is a deeper problem with this vision of democracy. It imagines that democracy entails little more than voting, either in elections or in legislative assemblies. Or, to put the matter more generously, it imagines that democratic engagement with policy questions is represented institutionally only by elections and legislatures. On this view, if democracy means rule in accordance with the will of the people, that will is formed and expressed only through elections and the passage of legislation. For Ely, constitutional rights to free speech, freedom of assembly, freedom of the press, and so on, are to be understood primarily as means for reinforcing free and fair elections and the responsiveness of the people's representatives to voter preferences.[10]

Ely's model of representative democracy is both conventional and incomplete. As Chapter 7 argues, the development of public policies, and hence the will of the people, is a three-step process involving elections, legislation, and administrative implementation. These three institutional embodiments of democratic action have complex interrelations. But notwithstanding administration's importance to public policy development (and so to democracy itself), so long as administration

---

[6] Id., at 87 (arguing for a "participation-oriented, representation-reinforcing approach to judicial review").

[7] E.g., id., at 88–101.

[8] Id., at 131–4.

[9] Id., at 132.

[10] Id., at 100.

is understood as antidemocratic, or at best nondemocratic unless very tightly constrained through electoral processes, it will operate under a cloud. Administration becomes a regrettable feature of modern life, tolerated out of necessity rather than conviction.

The persistence of this Ely-type view of administration is pernicious, but it may be permanent. The micro-politics of administrative decision-making is virtually invisible in public discourse. The press reports on presidents and congresses notwithstanding the dominance of administrative action as the source of public law. It connects administration to democratic governance only by ascribing agency actions to the President or to the President's administration.[11] The underlying process of proposals, participation by interested parties, inter-agency negotiations, and elaborate explanations is not the stuff of a good news story. The press also often reports on conflict about administrative policy in connection with litigation, a context in which the administrative agency is accused of lawless behavior. Congressmen and Senators score political points by criticizing bureaucratic shortcomings, not by extolling the virtues of participatory and reasoned decision-making.

THE LIMITS OF ADMINISTRATIVE REASON

Administration's democratic deficit, I have argued, is more apparent than real. But appearances matter. Administration has an image problem that, given the standard practices of electoral politics and the attention span of the popular press, it is unlikely to shake. One might even argue that distrust of the government, often focused on administrators, is baked into American political culture and is a feature rather than a fault.[12] Distrust motivates a level of vigilance against bureaucratic abuses that may be salutatory, given our enormous dependence on administrative governance to do the public's business.

But, I believe that the public is frustrated and distrustful of administrative governance for an additional reason. Even if we were to recognize the liberty- and democracy-enhancing virtues of the reason-giving that American administrative agencies practice, we are likely to find those reasons incomplete. To structure this idea let me borrow, and misuse to some degree, categories about domains of reasons found in much of the work of Jürgen Habermas.

---

[11] This journalistic trope became particularly common during the interregnum between the Obama and Trump administrations. *E.g.,* Daniel Wiessner and Robert Iafolla, Judge Blocks Obama Rule Extending Overtime Pay to 4.2 Million U.S. Workers, Reuters (Nov. 23, 2016), available at: www .reuters.com/article/us-usa-employment-overtime-idUSKBN13H2JY (Last accessed May 25, 2018).

[12] *Beyond Distrust: How Americans View Their Government,* Pew Res. Ctr. (Nov. 2015), available at: www.people-press.org/files/2015/11/11-23-2015-Governance-release.pdf (Last accessed May 25, 2018). (While the Pew report finds high levels of government distrust, "most Americans have a lengthy to-do list for this object of their frustration: Majorities want the federal government to have a major role in addressing issues ranging from terrorism and disaster response to education and the environment." Id., at 4.).

Habermas suggests that everyone operates in three broad domains of rational action: the material, the social, and the personal. Rationality in these three domains functions quite differently. In the material world, the claim of rationality is to truth; in the social realm, the claim is about rightness or justice; and in the personal domain, rational validity sounds in authenticity.[13] The problem of state legitimacy, particularly administrative state legitimacy, may be its overcapacity to address truth claims combined with an under-capacity to address claims of justice and authenticity. While "truth" may somewhat overstate the matter given the necessity for decisions under uncertainty, our existing demands for reason-giving generally insist only that administrators demonstrate a purely instrumental rationality. They must explain, in short, why their actions satisfy the goals articulated by their governing statutes, given the existing state of the world and the likely effects of the policies that they have chosen. Administrative reason-giving takes the general form: "If you want X (the statutory goal), given the current state of the world Y (as demonstrated in the record of the administrative proceeding), then we must adopt policy Z (which for technocratic reasons promise to produce the desired results)."

The Problem of Authenticity

Administrators whose decisions routinely survive judicial and political oversight are quite adept at providing these sorts of reasons. Yet, we also routinely confront rules that, even if rational in Habermas' material sense, do not seem to fit our particular cases, that falsify our experience and challenge our conceptions of ourselves. In studying the processes for adjudicating social security disability claims in the United States,[14] I discovered that claimants for benefits tend to be disappointed whether they win or lose. Half of those who apply for benefits have their claims denied on the grounds that they can do some jobs available in the national economy.[15] Very often, these same persons have struggled for years to work, despite serious impairments and advice from family and physicians that they really should not work. Having finally decided to apply for disability benefits, they are told that they were wrong. They may be a "failed" worker, but according to the Social Security Administration's (SSA) rules, they are not disabled. Insult is often added to injury by a vocational rehabilitation service's further determination that the same claimant is too disabled to qualify for rehabilitations services designed to get them back into the labor market.[16]

---

[13] E.g., David Ingram, *Habermas and the Dialectic of Reason* 28 (1987) ("Validity claims refer beliefs to various domains of reality; claims to truth refer to the world of spatiotemporal objects, claims to rightness and justice to the world of social norms, and claims to sincerity and authenticity to the world of a person's own feelings and desires.").

[14] Jerry L. Mashaw, *Bureaucratic Justice: Managing Social Security Disability Claims* (1983).

[15] Jerry Mashaw, Public Reason and Administrative Legitimacy, in *Public Law Adjudication in Common Law Systems: Process and Substance* 20 (John Bell et al. eds., 2015).

[16] Id., at 21.

Moreover, many successful claimants are unhappy with their favorable result because of its connotations. To receive needed income support, they have been forced to accept a label – "disabled" – that they reject. The system demands an all-or-nothing result. Binary judgments can falsify a complex reality whether applicants experience a grant or a denial of their claims. While recipients value the income support that disability benefits provide, many would prefer assistance to make them more functional and competitive in the labor market.

But while this example perhaps helps to explain one basis for popular dissatisfaction with administration, it may also illustrate why it is impossible to address the underlying problem of authenticity in the context of administering complex administrative programs. The social security disability system must decide literally millions of claims each year.[17] If the SSA's thousands of adjudicators are to be reasonably consistent across these millions of claims, "rulishness" is the order of the day. Thus, the right balance between rule-bound administration and individualized discretionary judgment presents an almost intractable conundrum for institutional designers. And yet, that both winners and losers perceive that their situations have been somehow falsified, or more mildly, not adequately attended to, has serious consequences for the perceived legitimacy of administrative action. It easily yields a sense of being an object of social control, rather than an independent subject entitled to authentic respect and concern.

This example also illustrates another continual and serious problem with the perception of administrative governance: The displacement of disappointment with a program's structure onto the performance of program administrators. The American disability insurance program responds to political and policy imperatives that are generally opaque to most of those who deal with the system. Because of the statute's stringent criteria, many applicants with serious impairments are determined not to satisfy the statutory work disability requirements. Congress was determined not to make the disability program into a long-term unemployment program. To distinguish disability from unemployment, the program requires that applicants be unable to do any jobs supplying "substantial gainful employment" available anywhere in the national economy.[18] That denied applicants might stand so far back in the labor queue that they would not be hired, or that access to jobs that they might do requires relocation far from family and existing support networks, does not make them eligible for disability benefits. That many people with serious problems are thus denied benefits may be a regrettable feature of the statutory scheme, but it is not evidence of bad administration.

---

[17] In 2014 alone, the SSA handled over three million disability claims, including 2.8 million worker claims. *Annual Statistical Supplement to the Social Security Bulletin, 2015*, Soc. Security Admin. 2.78 tbl.2.F5 (Apr. 2016), available at: www.ssa.gov/policy/docs/statcomps/supplement/2015/supplement15.pdf (Last accessed May 25, 2018).

[18] 42 U.S.C. § 423(d)(2)(A) (2012).

Similarly, the seeming irony of being denied disability benefits and refused vocational rehabilitation services is again explicable in terms of the rehabilitation system's conscious design. To receive services under these state-administered programs,
applicants must have an impairment that limits their employability, but not one
so serious that they are unlikely to actually get a job after those services have been
provided.[19] States, whose programs are supported only in part by federal funds, do
not want to spend their resources on lost causes.[20] This is perfectly understandable,
but, once again, it is a program-design feature that looks irrational, even cruel, when
applied to a denied applicant for Social Security Disability benefits. The claimant who receives a double denial, both from the Social Security disability system
and state rehabilitation services, must surely think someone has made a mistake.
And, of course, administrative mistakes do occur. But, the apparent lack of coordination between these programs is a function of their statutory structures, not errant
administration.

Finally, the disappointment of successful disability claimants has a similar explanation. That disappointment derives, in many cases, from the fact that the claimants
do not really wish to be out of the workforce. Many would prefer to have services and
accommodations that allow them to continue to be gainfully employed. Being on
benefits and out of the workforce is a serious blow to self-esteem, as well as a serious
loss of important social contacts. To be labeled incapable of work and self-support –
when the beneficiary's self-perception is that he or she could continue to work with
appropriate support – is both humiliating and infuriating. But once again, the problem is not bureaucratic incompetence or maladministration; it is the paucity of support services that might make a critical difference in these beneficiaries' lives. That
it may be cheaper to pay them benefits than to provide the support necessary to
keep them working does little to quash their feeling that the government, meaning
the SSA and state vocational rehabilitation services, has treated them as cases rather
than as people – as different from the people that they believe they really are.

These problems of authenticity do not all result, of course, from program design
at the legislative level. Bureaucratic imperatives also push administration in the
direction of rulishness. To continue the Social Security disability example, the SSA
receives around three million applications a year.[21] These initial claims are determined by over 10,000 state employees who make eligibility determinations on the
basis of wholly documentary evidence while applying the SSA's guidelines in its

---

[19] E.g., Div. of Disability & Rehabilitative Servs., *Policy and Procedure Manual*, Ind. Family & Social
     Servs. Admin. § 421.07(2) (Nov. 1, 2006) (stating that an applicant for rehabilitative services is
     ineligible if "the applicant is incapable of achieving an employment outcome due to the significance
     (severity) of the disability"); R.I. Dep't of Human Servs., *Policy and Procedures Manual*, Off. of
     Rehabilitation Servs. § 115.2.IV.A.4 (Jan. 2015) (deeming ineligibility if "[t]he individual is incapable
     of benefiting from … services in terms of an employment outcome due to severity of the individual's
     functional limitations").
[20] *See* Mashaw, *supra* note [15], at 45.
[21] *See* Mashaw, *supra* note [15].

Disability Insurance State Manual. For denied applicants, truly faceless bureaucrats determine their claims on the basis of rules that the applicants have never seen. A face-to-face meeting and a fulsome explanation of both the applicable rules and how the claimant's facts fit or do not fit within the benefit criteria would be vastly preferable from the perspective of treating individuals as individuals, who are entitled to reasons for a disappointing decision. But, given the scale of the program, the initial levels of decision-making have been structured for mass production, not craft disposition. Congress is unwilling to bear the administrative costs of a more particularized and personal decision process.

However, disappointed claimants may appeal their denials to Administrative Law Judges (ALJs), and they are entitled to a full, face-to-face hearing concerning the facts of their case and the applicable rules and standard of the disability system.[22] This encounter is much more satisfying, but it is still frustratingly rule-bound. In one of the largest administrative adjudication systems in the world, over 1,500 administrative law judges spread across the country annually adjudicate hundreds of thousands of disability cases.[23] The variance in their award rates is a serious cause for concern.[24] The SSA is supposed to be running a standardized, national program in which benefit determinations do not turn on whether a "generous" or "stingy" ALJ happens to hear a case. Hence, the SSA has attempted to promote consistency by a set of rules known colloquially as its "grid regulations."[25] Those regulations track the statutory criteria for disability determinations. A claimant's eligibility is determined by comparing his or her physical capacities and vocational characteristics (that is, age, education level, and work experience) with the requirements of jobs available in the national economy. The regulations direct the ALJ to make findings of fact concerning the claimant's physical capacities (that is, capacity to do heavy, medium, light, or only sedentary work) and the claimant's vocational factors (age, education, and work experience). Once these facts are found, they can be plugged into the decisional "grid" specified by SSA regulations, which, for every combination of physical capacity and vocational factors, provides a conclusion – disabled or not disabled.

---

[22] 20 C.F.R. § 404.929 (as amended 2014) (describing the claimant's "right to appear" at the administrative hearing).

[23] *Information About SSA's Office of Disability Adjudication and Review*, Soc. Security Admin., available at: www.ssa.gov/appeals/about_odar.html (last visited Jan. 6, 2017) ("Each year, more than 1,500 ALJs render over 636,285 decisions at the hearing level.").

[24] *See, e.g., Nash v. Califano*, 613 F.2d 10, 13 (2nd Cir. 1980) (discussing a "Quality Assurance Program" for ALJs that allegedly aimed to standardize decision rates across ALJs); Richard J. Pierce, Jr., Political Control Versus Impermissible Bias in Agency Decisionmaking: Lessons from Chevron and Mistretta, 57 U. Chi. L. Rev. 481, 509 (1990) ("Given the large number of cases decided by each ALJ and the random assignment of cases to ALJs, the wide variation in reversal rates suggests that ALJs are using much different decisional standards.").

[25] 20 C.F.R. § 404, subpt. P, app. 2 (as amended 2008).

If claimants understand this grid system, it is hard for them to believe that they have been treated to an individual hearing that takes seriously their unique personal characteristics and other contextual factors, such as access to or absence of family supports, effective medical or rehabilitation services, and so on. Yet, this rulishness on the part of the SSA can hardly be faulted as just bureaucratic obtuseness. The Administration is caught on the horns of a dilemma. To determine claims on the basis of a given ALJ's idiosyncratic psychology or legal understanding is almost the definition of arbitrariness. Thus, an attempt to provide consistency across deciders by binding rules is virtually necessary to the rule of law. The SSA's rules cannot make that attempt and also provide a process that truly individualizes adjudication and treats claimants authentically as unique individuals.

Indeed, one might go further to suggest that the practice of reason-giving is, of necessity, one that sacrifices some degree of authenticity. As Frederick Schauer has argued, to give a reason is necessarily to generalize from the specific case to some more abstract premise or value.[26] This is as true in the adoption of rules or general policies as in the adjudication of particular cases. Reason-giving's appeal to general public values or standards necessarily retreats some distance from the particular, and therefore from the authentic situation of persons subject to administrative actions.

Rulishness that denies our authenticity is, of course, not the exclusive domain of government bureaucracies. It is a feature of bureaucratic decision-making more generally – as our daily experience with banks, insurance companies, airlines, and a host of other private organizations demonstrates. Their relentless advertising claims to be focused on "you" and to give you what "you deserve" should be perceived as little more than an admission that these claims are false. Organizations of any significant scale recognize that they must make decisions on the basis of institutional rules. The bank that gives its loan officers free reign to provide loans to whomever they judge to be credit-worthy is not long for the marketplace. In short, the authenticity problem is not government, it is the imperatives of bureaucratic organization – a problem that can be managed to some degree, but not solved.

The Problem of Justice

Deliberation about the rightness or justice of the rules themselves is often no more articulate than the administrative state's encounters with issues of authenticity. Administrators do not claim to make value judgments; indeed, they largely deny that they are doing so. Yet, the technocratic analyses that appear in explanations of agency rules often seem simply to sweep value questions under the rug. Cost–benefit

---

[26] *See* Frederick Schauer, Giving Reasons, 47 *Stan. L. Rev.* 633, 651 (1995) ("[I]f giving reasons is centrally explained by a reason's generality and the reason giver's commitment to that generality, then giving a reason is like setting forth a rule. Justifying reason-giving will thus track justifying rule-based decision-making and, conversely, justifying the avoidance of reason-giving will parallel justifying highly particularistic decision-making.").

analyses, for example, are done to determine whether, on some set of highly debatable assumptions, social welfare will go up because of the adoption of a rule. In the process, excruciatingly difficult questions concerning the value of human life – whether that value can be expressed in monetary terms, whether monetary valuations should be discounted if the life is to be saved at some future date, and so on – lie just below the surface of the analysis. To be sure, academic literature debates such questions endlessly, but administrators, perhaps for good reasons, believe that they must simply get on with their jobs. Participants in rulemaking processes may question the rationality of these exercises in social-cost accounting, but only within the confines of the professional norms that have been developed to make the analytic exercise possible in the first place. Ultimate issues are sidestepped.

To put this point another way, reasonable discourse is structured to minimize or even preclude certain sorts of judgments based on broad notions of public morality or public acceptability. Let me illustrate this point with a few examples from the operations of the National Highway Traffic Safety Administration (NHTSA), another area that I have studied extensively with my co-author David Harfst.[27] As it turns out, these examples are also examples of the previously-mentioned judicial aphorism that "no rule of administrative law applies to acts of Congress."[28]

First, consider the NHTSA's allocation of resources in its overall safety program. As previously mentioned, the agency has a broad mandate to adopt safety standards that "meet the need" for vehicle safety. It also has the responsibility to enforce a recall program that requires manufacturers to recall and repair vehicles that have a defect related to vehicle safety.[29] Both Congress and the general public are enthusiastic about the recall program. It provides extended warranty service to consumers, but leaves them free to decide whether or not to return their vehicles for repair. More importantly, the program responds to a standard morality tale. There is a villain, the negligent manufacturer, and a victim, the consumer driving a "defective" vehicle. The villain should, in justice, make the victim whole.

On the other hand, were the NHTSA left to its own devices – that is, were it not following a congressional mandate – it would have great difficulty justifying spending any of its resources on the recall program. No one believes that mechanical or electrical defects account for more than about 3 percent of vehicle accidents.[30] And, an unknown, but probably large, proportion of that 3 percent is attributable to

---

[27] *E.g.*, Jerry L. Mashaw and David L. Harfst, The Transformation of Auto Safety Regulation: Bureaucratic Adaptation to Legal Culture, 34 *Yale J. on Reg.* 167 (2017).

[28] *Cf. Nat'l Tire Dealers & Retreaders Ass'n, Inc. v. Brinegar*, 491 F.2d 31, 37 (D.C. Cir. 1974) ("No administrative procedure test applies to an act of Congress.").

[29] 49 U.S.C. §§ 30118-30120A (2012).

[30] A NHTSA study of car accidents found that vehicle issues caused *under 2.5 percent* of accidents in the data set. *National Motor Vehicle Crash Causation Survey*, DOT-HS-811-059, Nat'l Highway Traffic Safety Admin. 24–26, tbls.9(a)–(c) (July 2008), available at: https://crashstats.nhtsa.dot.gov/Api/Public/ViewPublication/811059 (Last accessed May 25, 2018).

maintenance issues rather than manufacturing defects.[31] Nor does the statute require that a defect be demonstrated to have caused any accidents, injuries, or deaths for it to be subject to recall. The result is that millions of cars are recalled each year for safety defects at an enormous cost, but without any significant contribution to overall vehicle safety. The economic costs almost certainly outweigh, to a massive degree, the economic benefits of the recall program. Had the NHTSA attempted to establish this program by rule, it could not have justified it. Demonstrating that the recall program, as currently structured, is a reasonable and appropriate way to meet the need for automobile safety would be impossible. Simply declaring that it would be "unjust" for manufacturers not to fix defective products, the judgment that seems to undergird Congress' recall mandate, would be to give an irrelevant reason under the NHTSA's authorizing statute. In the common utilitarian vernacular of administrative policymaking, focused as it is on "welfarist" criteria, doing "justice" is sometimes unreasonable.

This disjunction between legislative moral judgments and administrative instrumental rationality has produced a series of conflicts between the NHTSA and its legislative overseers. Perhaps the most notorious episode involves the so-called ignition interlock system. We need not here detail the peculiar context (see Chapter 4) within which the ignition interlock became a requirement for all vehicles manufactured in the model year 1974 or later. Suffice it to say that it was a highly cost-effective public health measure. The interlock simply made it impossible to start a vehicle without having the occupants engage their lap and shoulder belts. The estimate was that this requirement, when fully implemented, would save nearly 10,000 lives every year. And, the cost per vehicle was $40 or less.

Congress reacted to this instrumentally rational and economically reasonable requirement by legislation that both repealed the rule and prohibited the agency from adopting anything like it ever again.[32] Why? Because motorists hated it. It was too great an incursion on individual liberty. The idea that the government should force people to wear a safeguard they disliked to protect against a risk they were willing to run was morally repugnant. The NHTSA, of course, had no mandate to permit liberty to trump safety in setting vehicle performance standards. Indeed, it was precisely the belief that the unregulated market for motor vehicles would not provide adequate safety performance that undergirded the Motor Vehicle Safety Act of 1966. The NHTSA now recognizes the moral value of individual autonomy by translating it into the language of efficacy – i.e., "public acceptance."

Nor does Congress always think that liberty trumps safety. Where vulnerable populations are concerned, Congress has ordered the NHTSA to adopt regulations

---

[31]   Indeed, in that NHTSA study, over two-thirds of vehicle-caused accidents were due to degradation or failure of tires, wheels, or brakes. Id., at 26 tbl.9(b). As any car owner bitterly knows, tires and break systems commonly require maintenance and monitoring.

[32]   *See* 49 U.S.C. § 30124.

that override both cost–benefit considerations and individual choice. For example, a small number of deaths and injuries every year result from motorists backing over pedestrians, usually small children or people in wheelchairs who are invisible when looking through standard rear-view mirrors. The NHTSA was aware of the problem. But given the vanishingly small number of deaths and injuries involved and the substantial expense of rear-view cameras, it had declined to require that equipment in new vehicles. Congress, besieged in part by parents who had had the horrible experience of backing over their own children, mandated that the agency adopt a regulation that would avoid back-over accidents.[33] And as the agency had previously concluded, only rear-view cameras would do the job. The NHTSA's arguments concerning cost versus benefits, and that this technology was available as an option on virtually all new vehicles, fell on deaf congressional ears. For Congress, influenced surely to some degree by the heartbreaking stories of grieving parents, it was socially and morally unacceptable that federal regulatory policy ignore a preventable risk to these vulnerable populations.

Once again, we must ask what is to be done. Our democratic ideology suggests that administrators should be implementers, not Platonic guardians who decide questions of ultimate social value. It may simply be the case that these tensions among the domains of rational action – the conflict inherent in our attempts to choose just ends, effectively manipulate the material world, and live authentic lives – are inevitable and unresolvable at the level of administrative decision-making. Even at the individual level, as we decide how to live our lives and what decisions we should make, these tensions can at best be managed, not resolved. Perhaps we can do little better than to bracket these questions of social justice and individual authenticity when deciding how administrators should engage in implementing vague statutory directives.

Yet I fear that that path is dangerous. These disappointments with "bureaucratic rationality" may cause us to devalue the triumphs of administrative rationality that have been won in Habermas' material domain. And those gains are easily lost. As these words are being written, the Trump administration is engaged in multiple assaults on the basic foundations of reasoned administration. These range from undermining the basic scientific capacities of regulatory agencies,[34] to evading the

---

[33] K.T. Safety Act of 2007, Pub. L. No. 110-189, § 2(b), 122 Stat. 639, 639–40 (2008).

> A judge, like an executive advisor, may be surprised at the poverty of really useful and unambiguous authority applicable to concrete problems of executive power as they actually present themselves. Just what our forefathers did envision, or would have envisioned had they foreseen modern conditions, must be divined from materials almost as enigmatic as the dreams Joseph was called upon to interpret for the Pharaoh.

[34] For example, Administrator Pruitt at the EPA has, among other anti-science actions, removed a number of academic scientists from EPA advisory boards to be replaced with representatives from the

requirements of notice and comment rulemaking,[35] to decisions that transparently fly in the face of the factual predicate upon which they are purportedly based.[36] Those actions demonstrate simultaneously how important administrative governance has become and how politically fragile the values of reasoned administration may be in a polity that generally ignores or misunderstands the democratic pedigree of much administrative policy making. For, as Chapter 7 argues, administrative policymaking has moved some distance toward instantiating a working model of deliberative polyarchy that seems increasingly elusive in the presumptively democratic, but highly politicized, discourse of legislatures.

Hence, to fail to even try to address these disappointments with the modern administrative state would deny some of our deepest aspirations. If we want to continue to understand ourselves as *Homo sapiens*, not just as *Homo oeconomicus*, we must attempt to broaden the domains of administrative reason, not abandon it as a failed idea. Public reason must, in John Rawls' terms, address what is "reasonable" as well as what is "rational."

SOME MODEST PROPOSALS

Administrative agencies may have an image problem that is highly resistant to change. And the trade-off between particularized attention to context and general rules will almost always leave either a gap between legal rules and the fine-grained reality of individual circumstances, or a nagging concern that individualized judgment is producing inconsistent (and therefore arbitrary) decisions. Yet, not all of our concerns about the democratic pedigree of administrative decision-making are based in deeply ingrained cultural norms or pose conundrums like the appropriate generality of legal rules. If we think broadly about the various stages of administrative agency decision-making, there are modest, democracy-reinforcing changes that might make administrative governance more open to contestation and more transparent about the grounds for administrative action. I will not here develop these proposals in any detail, but merely suggest a laundry list of possible reforms, some of which merely generalize practices that are already routine at some agencies.

regulated industries. Available at: www.nytimes.com/2017/10/31/climate/pruitt-epa-science-advisory-boards.html?smid=nytcore-ipad-share&smprod=nytcore-ipad

[35] *See Clean Air Council* v. *Pruitt*, 862 F.3d 1 (D.C. Cir. 2017); Lisa Friedman, Court Blocks Effort To Suspend Obama-Era Methane Rule, N.Y. Times (July 3, 2017), available at: www.nytimes.com/2017/07/03/climate/court-blocks-epa-effort-to-suspend-obama-era-methane-rule.html (Last accessed May 25, 2018); Lisa Friedman, E.P.A. Reverses Course on Ozone Rule, N.Y. Times (Aug. 3, 2017), available at: www.nytimes.com/2017/08/03/climate/epa-reverses-course-on-ozone-rule.html (Last accessed May 25, 2018).

[36] For example, a district court blocked President Donald Trump's ban on transgender military service on the ground that it was contrary to every study of the effects of transgender service by multiple military authorities and therefore could not possibly serve the military effectiveness purposes offered to justify the President's action. Available at: www.slate.com/blogs/outward/2017/10/30/federal_judge_blocks_trans_troops_ban.html (Last accessed May 25, 2018).

Agenda Setting

Agenda control is one of the most important elements of policymaking, and, to some degree, administrative agency agendas are transparent and subject to public participation. All agencies are, by executive order, required to provide the Office of Management and Budget (OMB) with annual regulatory agendas. And, the Administrative Procedure Act (APA) requires that agencies accept petitions for the adoption, amendment, or rescission of rules, and that they provide responses to those petitions.[37] On the other hand, as we have seen, reviewing courts are reluctant to force agency rulemaking,[38] and they treat agency enforcement discretion as presumptively unreviewable. These limitations on judicial review are, I believe, both understandable and appropriate. But, this judicial stance does not prevent agencies from doing more.

We are not likely to think it sensible to have agency enforcement priorities held hostage to the preferences of private petitioners. But as Justice Thurgood Marshall suggested in his concurrence in *Heckler* v. *Chaney*,[39] agencies can be required to provide reasons for declining enforcement requests, and judicial review can be limited to determining – on a deferential basis – only whether they have done so. More importantly, agencies can structure internal appeal processes that give disappointed petitioners an opportunity to attempt to persuade the agency to act. The National Labor Relations Board (NLRB), for example, has had such an internal appeal process within the General Counsel's Office for many decades.

On the rulemaking side, there is a serious concern both: (i) that repeat industry players differentially influence agendas, and (ii) that proposals for new rules are so well-developed at the point that a Notice of Proposed Rulemaking is announced that the rulemaking process, with its requirements for fulsome participation and well-reasoned action, has only marginal effects on policy. Agencies might do a number of things to combat these tendencies. Annual regulatory agendas could be noticed for comment by interested parties. Petitions by outside parties could be given the same treatment. As soon as agencies begin in-house research and development to support a potential rulemaking, they could generalize the practice of seeking comments through an Advanced Notice of Proposed Rulemaking. As some agencies have done effectively, such notices need only give potential commenters a general sense of what is under study and suggest some issues about which the agency would welcome input. Such preliminary proceedings permit a much broader range of suggestions about how the agency might proceed than remains possible when the agency has a fully developed proposal. Equally importantly, at this stage deliberations are

---

[37] 5 U.S.C. § 553(e).

[38] Some courts seem to be moving toward a position that requires limited reason-giving, subject to substantive review for adequacy, where petitions for rules raise serious issues. *Flyers' Rights Education Fund, Inc.* v. *FAA*, 2017 WL 3203268 (D.C. Cir. 2017).

[39] 470 U.S. 821, 840 (1985) (Marshall, J., concurring).

not yet cast in a technocratic mode. Questions of policy priorities based on ideas of public morality and collective responsibility remain pertinent. Justice more easily enters the conversation.

The Problem of "Guidance" and Other "Informal" Agency Action

While agency-published rules and formal adjudicatory actions make much more law than congressional statutes, these administrative actions are in turn dwarfed by informal agency actions that, while they make no law, have significant consequences. One such "informal" activity is the issuance of "guidance". This term covers a substantial number of agency issuances that carry various headings – memoranda, opinion letters, manual issuances, and the like. This guidance provides important, often crucial, information concerning the agencies' understanding of their statutes and regulations, their enforcement posture with respect to matters within their jurisdictions, and their plans for future policymaking. Unless construed as making binding law, guidance documents are not subject to any procedural requirements under the APA. But, by the same token, nothing in the APA prevents agencies from employing processes for consultation and dialogue concerning guidance. And, in many cases, the democratic pedigree of agency policymaking would be enhanced by the adoption of procedures that provide some of the opportunities for comments and responsive agency reason-giving that inhabits legislative rulemaking and formal adjudicatory processes.

While I indicated earlier my disagreement with the holding in the Fifth Circuit's decision in *Texas* v. *United States*,[40] that court's belief that something as important and controversial as the Department of Homeland Security's Deferred Action for Parents of American Citizens (DAPA) enforcement policy should have been vetted in some forum broader than the internal deliberations of the Executive Branch seems understandable. To be fair, that policy was formulated with the participation not only of the Department of Homeland Security, but also the Executive Office of the President and the Office of Legal Counsel (OLC) in the Justice Department, and was supported by a closely reasoned legal analysis by the OLC. But that process was a far cry from a request for comments from outsiders that would have involved the state governments that challenged the DAPA policy as well as immigrant rights groups, individual members of Congress, and others who might have cared to participate.

That such vetting can be useful and supportive of the legitimacy of agency policymaking is evidenced by the fact that some agencies already engage in this process when issuing important or controversial guidance documents. The Food and Drug

---

[40]   787 F.3d 733 (5th Cir. 2015) aff'd by equally divided court sub nom. *United States* v. *Texas* 1136 S.Ct 2271 (2016).

Administration (FDA) has done so for many years[41] and has had its practice codified by statute.[42] To take another example, the NHTSA in 2016 issued guidance on its regulatory policy concerning highly automated vehicles (HAVs). Its request for comments produced extensive and sophisticated analyses by the automotive industry, developers of software for automated vehicles, consumer groups interested in vehicle safety, property and causality insurers, state motor vehicle regulators, and others. The agency then updated its guidance in response to this commentary.[43] Other agencies have requested commentary on their regulatory priorities, their research agendas, and their interpretations of relevant statutes and rules. These sorts of initiatives are all the more important in a rulemaking environment in which constrained resources and multiple analytic and procedural hurdles push agencies in the direction of using guidance, rather than rules, to accomplish their regulatory missions.

Informal action in the adjudicatory context may be no less important. Agencies receive multitudes of requests to engage in particular enforcement actions concerning alleged violations of the statutes and regulations within their jurisdictions. These decisions about individual enforcement actions are presumptively free from judicial review and are subject to no reason-giving requirements under the APA. But, again, nothing prevents agencies from doing more. As previously mentioned, the NLRB has an appeals process within the office of its General Counsel that is available to petitioning parties whose requests for an enforcement action have been denied. After hearing these appeals, the Office of the General Counsel either accedes to the request or provides reasons why it believes that the agency should decline enforcement.

The Federal Trade Commission (FTC) exercises a similar enforcement authority under the broad terms of the Federal Trade Commission Act (FTCA) – an authority that is formally subject to formal trial-type adjudicatory process and that requires a reasoned decision based on the trial-type hearing's evidentiary record. But, as a practical matter, most FTC enforcement actions are settled by a consent decree. Under the FTC's rules it provides an enforcement target a proposed complaint and enforcement order prior to actually issuing a complaint. The respondent may then engage the agency in negotiations concerning its charges. If those negotiations are successful, which in the vast majority of cases they are, a proposed consent decree is then noticed in the Federal Register for comment by other parties who might be affected by the judgment. The order is finalized only after the comment period has been closed.[44]

I'm not here suggesting that the APA be amended to mandate procedures like the ones described above in all cases of consequential agency informal action. It may

---

[41] FDA, Development Issuance and Use of Guidance Documents, 62 Fed. Reg. 8961 (1997).

[42] Food and Drug Administration Modernization Act of 1997, 21 U.S.C. 371(h).

[43] The revised guidance is available at: www.nhtsa.gov/press-releases/us-dot-releases-new-automated-driving-systems-guidance (May 25, 2018).

[44] The FTC "Rules of Practice" concerning consent decrees are at 16 C.F.R 325.

be possible and desirable to do so in discrete situations, but prescribing when these processes are sufficiently useful to mandate their deployment in an enormously heterogeneous administrative environment is a challenging task. As is often repeated, informal action is the life blood of the administrative process. Formality can easily lead to paralysis, or promote evasion. But, agencies can innovate to improve the perceived legitimacy, as well as the quality, of their policymaking in areas where a legislative or judicial mandate might well be counterproductive.

Final Decisions

The rulemaking process itself is remarkably open and transparent, and final rules must supply a reasoned response to the issues that participants raise. Kenneth Culp Davis once described this process as the greatest achievement of modern administrative governance.[45] Perhaps. But great achievements can always be improved. The current exemptions for rules relating to grants, contracts, and all military and foreign affairs functions are much too broad. Proposals have been made in Congress to cut these down to size,[46] but in the absence of congressional action, agencies can act to limit these exemptions themselves. Important grant agencies like the SSA, for example, have by rule bound themselves to use the notice and comment procedure for rules concerning its benefit programs. The Administrative Conference of the United States has urged all agencies to follow this practice,[47] and a number have done so. Similarly, the judicial doctrine that gives complete deference to agencies about whether to use rulemaking or adjudication for the formulation of general policies seems much too deferential. Where agencies adopt essentially per se or bright-line rules, adjudication is an inappropriate process. Agencies like the NLRB, which essentially never makes rules, sometimes invite amicus briefs in adjudicatory proceedings that hold out the prospect of developing new standards or requirements applicable to all regulated parties. But this is not the same open, participatory process that is contemplated by administrative rulemaking under the APA.

It may well be that agencies are poorly situated to take certain broad justice claims into account or to utilize those claims as a basis for rulemaking decisions. The NHTSA's rear-view visibility rule may be a case in point. But I am not entirely convinced. That costs and benefits must be considered does not force agencies into a narrow instrumentalist or technocratic process of decision-making and reason-giving.

---

[45] Kenneth C. Davis and Walter Gellhorn, Present at the Creation: Regulatory Reform Before 1946, 38 *Admin. L. Rev.* 511, 520 (1986).

[46] E.g., Regulatory Reform Act, S.1080, 97th Cong. (1981).

[47] *Recommendation 73–5: Elimination of the* "Military or Foreign Affairs Function" Exemption from APA Rulemaking Requirements, Admin. Conf. of the United States (Dec. 18, 1973), available at: www.acus.gov/sites/default/files/documents/73-5.pdf (Last accessed May 25, 2018).

For example, the Motor Vehicle Safety Act of 1966 charges the NHTSA with regulating unreasonable risks to motor vehicle safety. A petition to the agency concerning rear-view visibility raises precisely the issue of whether the often-poignant circumstances of back-over injuries and deaths justify a determination that this risk is unreasonable, notwithstanding its poor quantitative cost–benefit ratios. Similarly, the practice of quantitative risk–benefit analysis that many health and safety agencies utilize, and that the Supreme Court's *Benzene* decision seemingly demanded,[48] need not be narrowly confined to technocratic scientific and economic criteria. Agencies can ask for comments on the degree to which particular risks are viewed as worth limiting, whatever the quantified health and safety effects if the risks are realized.

Pursuing these sorts of questions puts agencies in uncomfortable positions. The analysis and reasoning that would have to be provided in response to comments on these matters would expose agencies as value-oriented, and as playing a creative role in giving meaning to the incompletely specified statutes in their charge. They would be seen as exercising judgment that goes beyond technocratic expertise in engineering, biological science, or some other relevant discipline. They would be seen as participating in a democratic dialogue about what we the people want from our government. But, of course, that is what administrative governance is really about. Reasoned administration contributes to the realization of democratic governance. Constraining the domain of reasons to guard against claims of "undemocratic" administrative value choice ill serves that high purpose.

---

[48] *Indus. Union Dep't v. Am. Petroleum Inst. (The Benzene Case)*, 448 U.S. 607 (1980).

Index